"It is rare to find a good book on the 'self,' much less any book on the self, that provides a crystal clear picture of what we mean by the self. *A Contextual Behavioral Guide to the Self* creates a marvelous balance between cutting-edge science and practical clinical applications to help the practicing clinician effectively intervene with a variety of self-related problems. The writing is exceptionally clear and the clinical examples make important points seem easy to grasp. Getting a handle on what exactly we mean by 'self' and how to work to improve self-related functioning has been a serious, long-term challenge in clinical psychology. This book moves us forward in a major way. Highly recommended!"

—**Kirk Strosahl, PhD**, cofounder of acceptance and commitment therapy (ACT), and coauthor of *Inside This Moment*

"*A Contextual Behavioral Guide to the Self* is a gold mine of information that can empower both your knowledge and your practice. The book is a masterful guide to some of our most advanced research on 'self' experience. I would recommend this to anyone seeking to deepen their ACT practice, or their understanding of what it is to be human and to have 'a self.'"

—**Dennis Tirch, PhD**, founder of The Center for Compassion Focused Therapy, associate clinical professor at Mount Sinai, and coauthor of *The ACT Practitioner's Guide to the Science of Compassion*

"This is a truly remarkable book. The authors use their thorough knowledge of the complex phenomenon of 'the self,' and work themselves all the way from basic science up to practical, clinical recommendations for psychological treatment. An important read for researchers and clinicians alike."

—**Niklas Törneke, MD**, author of *Learning RFT* and *Metaphor in Practice*

"Few books are able to bring theory to life as well as *A Contextual Behavioral Guide to the Self*. The authors take us on a fascinating journey to discovering the self—how it develops, how it can lead to psychological suffering, and how to turn it into a source of well-being and growth. Read this book to discover a number of innovative, practical tools and new ways to conceptualize the self with cutting-edge relational frame theory (RFT) research."

—**Matthieu Villatte, PhD**, assistant professor in the department of counseling and health psychology at Bastyr University, and coauthor of *Mastering the Clinical Conversation*

"This excellent book offers an insightful, cutting-edge look at the concept of 'self.' You'll learn about our different senses of self, how these 'selves' develop, what can go wrong with these processes, and what we can do about it therapeutically. There's a gold mine of clinically useful material in here, to help both you and your clients. If you've ever struggled to understand complex ACT concepts such as self-as-context and self-as-process (and let's face it, haven't we all?) this book will set you straight. An essential addition to the library of all contextual behavioral practitioners."

—**Russ Harris**, author of *The Happiness Trap* and *ACT Made Simple*

"All of us working with people know that psychological challenges are fundamentally issues of 'self.' Traditionally, behaviorism—unlike other branches of psychotherapy—has had no room for a 'self' concept. In contrast, this unique book—based in behavioral analysis and RFT—places the self up front and center stage. The authors show you clearly, in a scientific and practical framework, how and why the self matters. The underpinning is functional contextualism or contextual behavioral psychology. As you read this book you will understand how the self is created and maintained based on RFT. You will learn a new word, 'selfing,' which describes how we verbally respond to our own responding. The authors illustrate what is needed for healthy 'selfing,' and what types of problems and issues may occur. Readers will find generous portions of tips on how to measure, evaluate, and treat problems with 'selfing.' This book is solidly based in RFT research, but it offers a great, practical approach that I am certain all of us who serve people will find useful."

—**JoAnne Dahl, PhD**, professor in the department of psychology at Uppsala University in Uppsala, Sweden; licensed psychologist; psychotherapist; peer-reviewed ACT trainer; and Association for Contextual Behavioral Science fellow

A CONTEXTUAL BEHAVIORAL GUIDE *to* *the* SELF

THEORY & PRACTICE

LOUISE M^CHUGH, PHD
IAN STEWART, PHD
PRISCILLA ALMADA, PHD

CONTEXT PRESS
An Imprint of New Harbinger Publications, Inc.

Publisher's Note

This publication is designed to provide accurate and authoritative information in regard to the subject matter covered. It is sold with the understanding that the publisher is not engaged in rendering psychological, financial, legal, or other professional services. If expert assistance or counseling is needed, the services of a competent professional should be sought.

Distributed in Canada by Raincoast Books

Copyright © 2019 by Louise McHugh, Ian Stewart, and Priscilla Almada
        Context Press
        An imprint of New Harbinger Publications, Inc.
        5674 Shattuck Avenue
        Oakland, CA 94609
        www.newharbinger.com

Cover design by Amy Shoup

Acquired by Jennye Garibaldi

Edited by Xavier Callahan

Indexed by James Minkin

All Rights Reserved

Library of Congress Cataloging-in-Publication Data on file

21	20	19								
10	9	8	7	6	5	4	3	2	1	First Printing

Contents

Acknowledgments v

Foreword: Understanding the Role of Self in Practice:
Why the Science Road Matters. vii

Introduction: Self Matters 1

1 Functional Contextualism and Contextual Behavioral
   Psychology 7

2 Relational Frame Theory 31

3 Relational Frame Theory and the Self. 61

4 Acquiring Selfing 77

5 The Three Selfing Repertoires 105

6 Self Content Issues 121

7 Toward Healthy Selfing 135

8 Assessing for Selfing Problems 165

   Afterword 195

   References 197

   Index 209

Acknowledgments

The authors would like to warmly thank Robyn Walser, Niklas Törneke, Russ Harris, Matthieu Villatte, and Emily Sandoz for their feedback and comments on earlier versions of the manuscript. We would also like to thank the editorial and production teams from New Harbinger for all their work on bringing this book to fruition: Camille Hayes, Tesilya Hanauer, Jennye Garibaldi, Clancy Drake, Jesse Burson, Xavier Callahan, and Michele Waters.

FOREWORD

Understanding the Role of Self in Practice: Why the Science Road Matters

Take an odd question seriously, just for a moment: *Who are you?*

There are so many ways to respond to that question. And it is not as if you can avoid it. If you are interviewing for a job, it will be completely normal for you to be asked to tell the interviewer about yourself, and you will be unlikely to get the job if you cannot answer. If you are on a first date, the question may be tweaked just a bit—"Tell me what you like to do," perhaps—but the meta-message will be the same, namely, that you should have a well worked-out self-concept that you can readily share with others. A second date will be unlikely unless you can step up to this verbal challenge.

The human community is clear on this. Each of us should have a well-established way of speaking about our history, preferences, reasons for acting, experiences, goals, emotions, self-evaluations, personality, and any of a hundred similar topics and domains. We should know ourselves from top to bottom and be ready, willing, and able to share that information on demand.

Our stories, descriptions, and evaluations are not just used for social communication. They also have an impact on our behavior. People who believe they are worthless may act differently from people who believe they are the greatest. Either self-concept can be a problem—but that is not the point. The point is that our self-concept can make a difference.

The content of our self-descriptions may actually matter less than how we relate to them, and appearances can be deceptive. In some ways, for example, a person who firmly believes he is dumb may be more similar than expected to a person who firmly believes she is smart. "I'm dumb" looks like a description, but it is secretly a comparison: "I'm dumber *than others*." "I'm smart" presents itself as a fact, but it can even more powerfully mean, "I'm smarter *than others*." These comparisons, then, positive or negative, and our attachment to them, may *separate* us from others ("I'm better—or worse—than you") at the very same time that we use them to seek *inclusion* in the group ("You need me—I'm smart" or "You need to care for me—I'm dumb").

Self-awareness and consciousness itself extend issues of self into each moment of awareness. As we walk down the hall or open the refrigerator; as we take a shower or shake the hand of a friend, we treat these action patterns as expressions of self, and when we notice them, it seems as if a self knows them. Our ways of being at a party may be different from our ways of being at work, almost as if we had multiple selves competing for our moments.

Who are you?

It's a powerful question, and you cannot avoid it. Nor can mental and behavioral health practitioners avoid this question as it applies to their clients.

This book examines all the aforementioned expressions of self, and several more, exploring their cognitive and behavioral bases and their practical implications. It provides the range of conceptual tools—based in an extensive scientific research program—that you will need in order to tackle the multidimensional issues of self-description, personality, self-awareness, perspective taking, and consciousness and bring their related experiences to bear as expressions of understandable combinations of biopsychosocial processes.

When the multiple meanings of the term "self" are more fully understood, and when their underlying principles are revealed, it is easier to think through how issues of self might be dealt with in practice. For example, a rigid self-concept may be due to the ways in which the socioverbal community fosters simplistic, overgeneralized rules about roles and one's place in the community. These rules can be applied with extreme inaccuracy; they may be unfair expressions of stigma and bias. There is a temptation—one that many clinicians fall prey to—for practitioners to directly challenge and change their clients' self-concepts. Often, however, that is the more difficult course. Clinically, it may be far more difficult to lay out new sets of rules or new evaluations of roles than to help a client radically redefine what a self-concept is, and to change the place of the self-concept in the client's system of thinking and behaving.

Healthy selfing is a skill that can be learned, but it is not one that society does a good job of teaching. Part of the problem is that lay theories of self get in the way, but another part is that unhealthy selfing can often pay off for others. For example, if an advertiser manages to provide a product as the solution to a toxic way of addressing issues of self-concept, then toxicity can pay off for a commercial entity. That is one reason why it is important for practitioners to have thought deeply and scientifically about issues of self. The culture, unaided by scientific theory and data, simply cannot be trusted to provide good guidance.

The science road is not an easy one, precisely because a prescientific understanding of self is so pervasive. But the science road is important because the understanding one can glean from it has powerful, creative implications that can open new and useful domains for exploration by clinical work.

This book, written by experts in the areas of science it explores, will teach you how to walk the science road with yourself as well as with your clients. Comprehensive, coherent, and unafraid, the book brings current behavioral and cognitive science directly to the key question *Who are you?* and is unyielding in its pursuit of an adequate and useful set of answers. Your life and the lives of your clients will be influenced by the answers you find here.

—Steven C. Hayes
Foundation Professor of Psychology
University of Nevada, Reno

INTRODUCTION

Self Matters

Many of the key psychological challenges that people face in life—what career path to choose, how to interact successfully with other people, how to maintain a successful relationship, how to cope with negative life events—are fundamentally issues of self. In other words, they have to do with questions like these:

- Who am I?

- What do I want?

- What do I believe?

- What do I feel?

- What do I want to do with my life?

Consider table I.1, for example, which presents a number of self-relevant issues that are frequently found in psychotherapy but have probably affected all of us at least to some extent, at one time or another. Given the centrality and ubiquity of self issues such as these, understanding the psychological processes underlying our experience of self is critically important, both for the individual herself as well as for the practitioner who treats or advises her.

Table I.1. Some Relatively Common Self Issues

Issue	Typical statement expressing the issue
Lack of clarity about values	I don't really know what I care about.
Self-righteousness	I'm more honest than you—I'd never lie like that.
Operating on autopilot	Sorry, I missed that—I'm up to my neck in it.
Feeling of threat from internal experiences	I can't stand these feelings.
Lack of perspective	I don't care how he feels—he brought it on himself!
Hyperattentiveness to views of others	Have I offended you? Are you upset with me?
Lack of connectedness to others	I don't fit in—I'm different.
Personal rigidity	But this is just who I am.
Sense of emptiness	I feel empty—there is nothing to me.
Painful self-judgments	I should have said something—I'm so weak!

In this book, we present a unique way of understanding and dealing with self issues on the basis of two approaches:

1. *Contextual behavioral science*, or CBS (Hayes, Barnes-Holmes, & Wilson, 2012), a modern scientific approach to understanding human behavior

2. *Relational frame theory*, or RFT (O'Connor, Farrell, Munnelly, & McHugh, 2017), the CBS approach to human language and cognition

We aim to provide you with an understanding, in CBS/RFT terms, of how our sense of self develops from infancy to adulthood, an understanding that considers features of the healthy self as well as processes that can lead to problems of self. A key focus throughout is how CBS/RFT links with clinical work, and how you, as a practitioner, can use your knowledge of CBS/RFT to enhance your practice and design interventions that specifically target the unique self-related problems of your clients.

Of course, the CBS approach is far from the first in psychology to address issues of the self; there have been previous approaches, many of which provided particularly important insights into the self. For example, early psychologists, such as William James (1981), highlighted the importance of the distinction between *I* (subject) and *me* (object). Various thinkers from the psychodynamic tradition have discussed and debated the place of the ego in human psychology. The humanist tradition and the positive psychology tradition that succeeded it were and are deeply concerned with what constitutes psychological health; both see the promotion of a healthy self as a key component. More recently, cognitive developmental and neurocognitive approaches have produced a wealth of empirical data concerning processes of self and their development. Undoubtedly, each of these major approaches has contributed significantly to our knowledge base. As explained in chapter 1, however, the CBS approach has one critical feature that makes it unique among this diversity of approaches—its fundamental emphasis on behavioral intervention. From the CBS perspective, the possibility of practical interventions to help influence behavior is not simply an afterthought; rather, it is a fundamental theoretical requirement. We explain in detail what we mean by this in chapter 1, but for now the thing to understand is that this feature gives the CBS approach an intensely practical orientation.

You may respond that approaches other than CBS have also influenced clinicians and practitioners in terms of how they have approached self issues in practice. For example, a number of different clinical paradigms, such as psychoanalysis and cognitive behavioral therapy, are based on or influenced by some of the theoretical approaches just named, and these of course invoke psychological processes relevant to the self in the course of therapy. As chapter 1 explains in more detail, however, the fundamental philosophical assumptions underlying these approaches (as well as others in psychology) do not entail a requirement for behavioral intervention, and so they do not require the specification of directly manipulable (that is, environmental) variables relevant to intervention. This in turn means that there is no consistent and mutually productive connection between theory and practice in those approaches. CBS, by contrast, is the only approach whose philosophy *requires* practical influence, and so, as we hope will become more apparent in the chapters to come, the theory is closely connected with practice. As a result, the theory is relevant in that it facilitates practical outcomes, whereas the practice can evolve and be updated on the basis of science. As already mentioned, we will more fully explain this critical feature of the CBS approach in chapter 1. For now, we will simply note that the unique advantage of CBS is its fundamental focus on behavioral change.

In this book, as we introduce and discuss the CBS/RFT approach to the self, our aim is to help you understand what the self is from the perspective of CBS/RFT. We focus on how problems with the self manifest, and on how to go about intervening when self issues arise in the lives of the individuals and groups with whom you work. To understand the CBS/RFT approach, it is important for you to understand some of the basic concepts behind CBS. We put this approach in context by exploring functional contextualism and behavior analysis in chapter 1, laying out the philosophical and theoretical assumptions that underlie the CBS approach, and introducing behavior analysis as a basic scientific approach to behavior.

Behavior analysis in turn provides the bedrock for our introduction of RFT in chapter 2. RFT is the functional contextual and behavior analytic account of human language and cognition, and it specifically provides the core theoretical explanations of self processes on which we draw in this book. The chapter includes both an explanation of the basic process implicated by RFT in language and cognition (i.e., relational framing) and an explanation of how that process gives rise to key aspects of human language and thought. These key aspects include linguistic reference, rule following, and coherence, each of which plays an important role in understanding the construction of self as well as other psychologically relevant concepts.

Chapter 3 discusses the specific application of RFT to the self. The chapter begins with an earlier basic behavior analytic definition of self (or, more appropriately from a behavioral point of view, of *selfing*) as responding to one's own responding. The chapter then explains that even though responding to one's own responding is indeed a key aspect of self, this explanation by itself is not enough to account for the phenomenon of self. The critical missing ingredient is relational framing. When relational framing is combined with responding to one's own responding, a verbal or symbolic self-concept becomes possible, and this more intricate pattern of behavior is what facilitates the kind of complexity that we associate with the concept of self.

Chapter 4 delves into the early developmental origins of self and examines not only deficits in early emergent repertoires but also possible remediation.

That is, the chapter explores how some children don't receive adequate training to develop the sophisticated sense of self with which most of us are familiar, and thus, how they do not acquire a fully developed sense of self. The chapter explains the conditions (developmental delays, an impoverished social environment, or some combination of the two) in which certain selfing repertoires can fail to emerge, and it explores how appropriate training can remediate these problems.

If adequate training is received, however, then the result is the emergence of a fully developed verbal self. As explained in chapter 5, three separate repertoires of selfing typically emerge once we can relationally frame about the world, including ourselves and our environment. Thereafter, these repertoires of selfing play a psychologically central role in our lives. The chapter describes each of the three repertoires in detail, and it considers how the CBS approach compares with other psychological approaches to the self.

At the same time, the fact that these three repertoires of selfing have been acquired does not guarantee psychological health. Things can still go wrong; indeed, the breadth and complexity of these repertoires mean that there is actually *more* scope for things to go wrong. This is principally so with respect to our repertoire of self content, which comprises the things we believe about ourselves, including the kind of person we think we are. Chapter 6 considers issues of self content in detail, examining how aspects of our learning with respect to self content can trap us in rigid, self-limiting patterns of behavior.

This brings us to chapter 7, which aims to show how theory and concepts from earlier chapters guide the promotion of a flexible (that is, healthy) self. The chapter presents and explains the key areas that you can target to promote a healthy self in the work you do with your clients.

In order to do so, you must also have a good, functionally based idea of how a client's selfing repertoire is doing in the current context. Chapter 8, the final chapter, looks at how you can conduct a functional assessment of selfing.

Two of us (Louise McHugh and Ian Stewart), after coediting a book in which various authors from the CBS community and beyond shared their knowledge and expertise in the areas of self and perspective taking, became interested in coauthoring the present book with Priscilla Almada, whose research and expertise are in the area of the self and relationships with others. The journey has been interesting and rewarding for all of us. We hope that the book will be an effective guide for you as you develop therapeutic techniques that can foster a vital life and a healthy pattern of selfing in your clients.

CHAPTER 1

Functional Contextualism and Contextual Behavioral Psychology

In the well-known parable of the five (or six, or seven…) blind men who encounter an elephant, each of the men touches a single part of the animal, and they individually declare the elephant to be a tree, a snake, a wall, a rope, and so forth. This parable, in its many versions, is a metaphor for how our basic assumptions in our search for scientific truth influence our scientific approach to the world.

One of our core aims in this book is to explain the human self from the standpoint of contextual behavioral science (CBS) in such a way as to help inform your work with your clients. In order for us to do so, however, it is important that we explain not only the fundamental philosophical assumptions underlying the CBS approach but also the science that is based on those assumptions; that is, we want you to know that we are starting from a particular place in this work regarding the self. Table 1.1 provides definitions of some of the key terms we will be using in this chapter.

Table 1.1. Key Technical Terms in Behavior Analysis

Term	Meaning
antecedent	A preceding event, condition, cause, phrase, or word; the antecedent is an event that occurs immediately before behavior
appetitive	An adjective describing a stimulus likely to reinforce behavior
aversive	An adjective describing a stimulus likely to punish behavior
behavior	Anything that an organism does (walk, talk, think, feel, see, dance, remember, and so forth)
consequence	The reinforcing or punishing outcome of the behavior of interest
context	The environmental setting or situation in which behavior occurs
discriminative stimulus	Any event in the presence of which a target behavior is likely to have consequences that affect the behavior's frequency
extinction	A process whereby the contingency that has produced conditioning (whether respondent conditioning or operant conditioning) is no longer in operation, with the typical result that the conditioning effect is reversed
function	A term whose meaning varies across different contexts, although in all contexts it means roughly what the word "function" means as defined in a dictionary (i.e., the function of a thing is how that thing works), with the term "stimulus function" denoting the effect that the stimulus has on responding, and with the term "response function" denoting the environmental consequences that the particular response produces

generalization	An effect whereby an individual's abilities or skills extend beyond the scope that has been specifically taught (strictly speaking, the term denotes only such extension as is based on physical similarity between either stimuli or responses)
motivating operation	In operant conditioning, something that is done to change (increase or decrease) the momentary effectiveness of consequences
operant learning	A form of learning in which an individual's behavior is modified (changed in form, frequency, or strength) by its consequences
punishment	The addition of something that is contingent on a particular response, and that results, over time, in a decrease in that response (chastising a child who argues with her brother may decrease the frequency of her arguing)
reinforcement	The addition of something that is contingent on a particular response, and that results, over time, in an increase in that response (providing certain foods if a child sits down may increase the frequency of her sitting down, or providing praise to a child who cleans his room may increase the chances that he will continue to clean his room)
respondent learning/ respondent conditioning	A form of learning in which one stimulus (the conditioned stimulus, or CS) comes to signal the occurrence of a second stimulus (the unconditioned stimulus, or US) through pairing or association of the two stimuli (the CS, as a result of coming to predict the US, eventually produces some of the same responses as the US)
shaping	The process of changing behavior through the differential reinforcement of successive approximations of the final desired form of responding

We begin the chapter by introducing *functional contextualism* (Hayes, Barnes-Holmes, & Roche, 2001), our set of fundamental assumptions, or *worldview*. We then introduce the core scientific approach to psychology that functional contextualism supports, namely, *contextual behavioral psychology*. In describing the *operant* (the conceptualization of behavior as "operating" on the environment), which is the key scientific concept associated with contextual behavioral psychology, we hope to convey the core of our approach to explaining human behavior. This description also prepares the ground for our description of *relational frame theory* (RFT), the contextual behavioral approach to language at the heart of our explanation of self.

The Worldview of Functional Contextualism

A scientific worldview is a set of philosophical assumptions constituting a basic understanding of the nature and purpose of the scientific endeavor itself (see Biglan & Hayes, 1996). You may be surprised to learn that there are differences among scientists with regard to the nature and purposes of science. Maybe you've always thought that scientists at least agree on what science is, and on what scientists should be doing. This is not the case, however. There are fundamental philosophical differences among scientists, and these differences are reflected in their scientific contributions. Not all scientists emphasize their basic philosophical worldviews, but proponents of CBS do, for two main reasons:

1. The assumptions that we make in CBS are atypical in the realm of science.

2. The practice of being explicit about the aims of our scientific activity is embedded in the philosophical assumptions themselves.

For clarity, then, we will explain the core assumptions of functional contextualism, beginning with a brief description of scientific philosophical worldviews in general and going on to describe the most predominant current worldview as well as an important alternative.

Worldviews differ in terms of their *root metaphors* and *truth criteria* (Hayes, Hayes, & Reese, 1988; Pepper, 1942; Zettle, Hayes, Barnes-Holmes, & Biglan, 2016). A root metaphor represents a commonsense way of thinking about and interacting with the scientific domain in which we are interested. The truth criterion is the means by which we decide whether something we say about that domain is or is not true. For a concrete example of a worldview, consider *mechanism*, the most popular and widespread worldview in science, including psychological science. The root metaphor of this worldview is the machine. In other words, the core assumption of mechanism is that the universe and everything in it can be thought of as a giant machine—an object composed of interacting parts that work together to produce a particular effect. In mechanism, moreover, the aim of science is to discover the parts of what is examined and then to describe, as fully as possible, the parts themselves as well as how they interact. The truth criterion of this worldview is correspondence between the world (for our purposes, the world of human behavior) as it is described by a theory and the world as it is discovered to be in reality. As for reality, it is confirmed through *predictive verification*, which is to say that what the scientist has predicted is verified. This means that scientists who take mechanism as their approach form a theory about the way a particular part of the world works, and if the results of their experiments cohere (fit together) with their prediction, then the accuracy of their theory is supported.

The mechanistic worldview is a popular one. We need to become aware of ingrained assumptions such as those that underlie mechanism, and we need to realize how pervasive and influential they can be. In psychology, a substantial amount of research is based on or at least strongly influenced by mechanistic assumptions. From the mechanistic perspective, researchers working to understand human behavior see behavior as an outcome of the operation of an underlying machinelike mental system, and they test their particular theories by assessing whether people behave as they might be predicted to behave if those theories were correct. This approach to discovering scientific truth is widely accepted in psychology. An obvious example of the mechanistic approach is cognitive psychology, which has been dominant for many years. Cognitive psychology compares the human mind/brain to a computer that processes sensory information from the environment and then produces behavior as the output of this processing. This subdiscipline of psychology has influenced other subdisciplines, too, such as social cognitive psychology and cognitive developmental psychology. Mechanistic assumptions are also found in other well-known psychology paradigms that would be seen as antithetical to cognitive psychology. In behavioral psychology, for example, John Watson and other theorists reduced behavior to machinelike interactions (such as contiguous stimulus-response interactions). Mechanism, then, has been profoundly influential in psychology. Despite its predominance, however, mechanism is not the only practicable scientific worldview. An increasingly popular alternative is *contextualism* (or, as it is also called, *pragmatism*).

The root metaphor of contextualism is the *event-in-context*, reflecting the idea that the investigation of any phenomenon requires the investigator to see how it relates to or is situated in a particular context—to see, for example, how a species participates in its ecosystem. In psychology, we are interested in behavior, and so the contextualist root metaphor is more specifically the *act-in-context* (that is, the particular behavior in context). Examples are a child turning his head (act/event/behavior) when he hears a novel sound (context), or an adult making a joke (act) in the middle of a conversation with a friend (context). The key point of this metaphor is that knowing a behavior's context is critical to determining that behavior's meaning or function. The same behavior can have completely different functions in different contexts. For example, imagine a woman who is sweating, out of breath, and running as fast as she can. She may be trying to avoid something bad, or aversive (for example, escaping from a ferocious dog), or she may be trying to obtain something good, or appetitive (for example, racing toward the finish line in a marathon). Or consider someone who spends the night drinking in a bar. Engaging in this behavior in the company of his friends in order to relax or lower his social inhibitions is different from drinking alone to reduce his feelings of loneliness or to escape depression. In both examples, the *topography* of the behavior (that is, what the behavior looks like) is similar, but the context is different, and the function or meaning of the behavior is drastically changed by its context.

The idea that behavior has meaning only in a context is a critical aspect of contextualism, and one that is directly linked to contextualism's truth criterion. The truth criteria of each of the other worldviews—apart from mechanism, with its criterion of predictive verification, which includes formism and organicism; see Pepper (1942) and Hayes et al. (1988)—are grounded in the idea that science ultimately will provide an accurate description of objective reality. In contextualism, however, it is assumed that because scientific analysis is a contextually determined activity, it cannot, even in principle, yield such a description. In contextualism, rather, the truth criterion is the accomplishment of some predetermined goal: if one's analysis facilitates achieving that goal, then one's analysis is true; otherwise, it is not true. In principle, the goal itself can be anything—to look clever, get rich, impress people, make friends, and so forth. In practice, however, most contextualists fall into one of a limited number of groups whose members all share a prestated goal and therefore also share a yardstick for what kind of analysis counts as true (meets the truth criterion; see Hayes, 1993).

The form of contextualism known as functional contextualism is the philosophy that underlies our approach to self inside an understanding of human behavior (Hayes, 1993). The shared goals of functional contextualists are *prediction* and *influence over behavior* (with precision, scope, and depth, as we'll see later). Therefore, from the perspective of functional contextualism, an analysis is true if it allows, at least in principle, both prediction and influence over behavior.

Imagine, for example, that a practitioner is interested in how children learn to label their own behavior and distinguish it from others' behavior. A mechanistic theorist (such as a cognitive psychological theorist) may postulate the development, occurring at a certain age, of particular types of neural or mental structures (schemas) that process information in a specific way. The theorist may then test, on the basis of this theoretical conception, whether patterns of behavior that might be predicted to occur actually do occur. If the theory accurately predicts the relevant behavior, then the truth of the theory is supported. By contrast, a functional contextualist will not be satisfied unless her theoretical description of how children learn to label their own behavior, as distinct from others' behavior, not only allows her to predict such labeling on the basis of what she knows about a child's past and present performance but also indicates what is needed, at least in principle, in order for this labeling to be influenced in a clearly specifiable way (as when an acceleration is produced in the child's learning of the relevant selfing repertoire).

The fact that influence is a key goal of functional contextualist analysis means that such analysis *requires* specification of variables that allow influence. In the case of a child learning accurate labeling of his own and others' behavior, we need to know, as scientists and practitioners, what variables we can manipulate that will clearly and effectively influence the child's behavior. This in turn means that we must be able to specify those environmental variables that have been shown, through experimental observation and analysis, to consistently affect the child's act of distinguishing his own behavior from that of others. These environmental variables include *antecedent* variables (which precede the behavior) and *consequential* variables (which follow the behavior). For example, as you will see in later chapters, evidence from research involving RFT suggests that a key part of learning to label one's own behavior, as opposed to that of others, involves learning to respond appropriately in the presence of cues like the spoken words "I" and "you" or their equivalents—that is, learning how to respond appropriately to questions like "What am I doing now?" or "What were you doing then?" Such cues can be considered antecedents, whereas consequences might be praise or smiles from other people when the child, given such antecedents, responds appropriately. What is of key importance is that these variables be manipulable (susceptible to direct influence). A scientist or practitioner interested in children's learning about self and others could manipulate properties of the antecedents (such as the frequency or consistency with which cues such as "I" and "you" are presented), or she could manipulate properties of the consequences (such as the frequency or consistency of contingent praise) of responding in different situations. In later sections of this chapter, and in later chapters of the book, we will delve in greater detail into the types of analysis that allow such influence.

The fact that a functional contextual approach requires specification of manipulable variables so as to allow influence over behavior makes this an intensely pragmatic worldview, and thus one particularly amenable to practitioners. For practitioners, the goal is not simply theoretical or abstract understanding but successful intervention. A theoretical approach founded on functional contextualism necessarily specifies environmental variables (such as the cues "I" and "you" in questions presented to a child in the example just seen) that can be manipulated by practitioners so as to facilitate beneficial behavioral change. This means that scientific and practical progress go hand in hand, and that scientific insight is of direct practical relevance.

Earlier, when we introduced the goals of functional contextualism, we said that prediction and influence are joined with precision, scope, and depth. All things being equal, the relative goodness of different theories is further supported by these three additional criteria:

- The criterion of *precision* sets the greatest possible limitation on the number of different ways in which a phenomenon can be explained.

- The criterion of *scope* aims to produce an explanation that applies to as wide a range of phenomena as possible.

- The criterion of *depth* aims to ensure maximum coherence of an explanation across levels of analysis (to ensure, for example, that an explanation at the level of psychology coheres with explanations at the levels of neurophysiology, sociology, and so forth).

The practitioner who strives to meet these three additional criteria orients the analysis in a more scientifically efficacious direction, beyond the core criteria of prediction and influence per se.

A key aspect of functional contextualism, and one that distinguishes functional contextualism from other worldviews, is that it holds behavioral influence as part of its truth criterion (Hayes, 1993). The other major form of contextualism—descriptive contextualism—posits personal understanding as its goal, rather than either prediction or influence. Meanwhile, for noncontextualist worldviews (such as mechanism), providing an accurate description of reality is seen as the ultimate aim, and analytic goals are seen as the means to achieving this aim. Achieving prediction of events alone is seen as an adequate outcome of scientific analysis because prediction of events is seen as a sufficiently robust test of a description's accuracy. For this reason, correlational analysis involving the prediction of one type of behavior on the basis of another type (that is, for example, predicting levels of alcohol use on the basis of depressive-type behavior) is an appropriate analytic strategy for the majority of the subdisciplines in psychology. For functional contextualism, although such analysis may be facilitative, it is not sufficient in and of itself, because it does not specify manipulable variables that can influence behavior, as opposed to simply specifying examples of behavior itself.

Again, to summarize what we have said so far, scientific activity is always embedded in a worldview, which entails a root metaphor (a set of philosophical assumptions concerning the nature of the scientific enterprise) and a truth criterion. Contextual behavioral science—the scientific approach that we assume—is derived from functional contextualism, whose root metaphor is the act-in-context, and whose truth criterion is the achievement of both prediction and influence over behavior. The requirement of behavioral influence, a requirement unique to functional contextualism as a worldview, makes CBS a pragmatically oriented approach (Hayes, Barnes-Holmes, & Wilson, 2012). It is important for us to explicate these basic philosophical assumptions because they determine the nature not only of the psychological science that they support but also of the practical interventions supported by that science. The psychological science in this case is contextual behavioral psychology (that is, contextual behavioral analysis). The core concept involved in this approach is the operant, described later in this chapter.

What Is Contextual Behavioral Psychology?

This section formally introduces contextual behavioral psychology, or the application of contextual behavioral science in the domain of psychology. The core of contextual behavioral psychology is behavior analysis, or operant psychology. We describe the behavior analytic concept of the operant as a foundation of our approach. Although the work presented here is based on B. F. Skinner's operant psychology, we also point to subtle differences between the underlying philosophical assumptions of contextual behavioral psychology and those of traditional behavior analysis. It is important to clarify these differences because they have implications for the ultimate approach and scope of each approach.

Radical Behaviorism and Functional Contextualism

As explained earlier, the philosophy of science underlying contextual behavioral psychology, as one branch of CBS, is functional contextualism. Meanwhile, the philosophy of science underlying behavior analysis is radical behaviorism, another slightly different variant of contextualism. These two philosophies are very closely related because functional contextualism has its intellectual roots in radical behaviorism. Skinner, who developed radical behaviorism as the underpinning of behavior analysis (see Skinner, 1974), argued that the goal of psychological science should be to obtain prediction and control over behavior. Given the need to achieve control over behavior in particular, he argued that psychology must focus on identifying environmental determinants of behavior because these can be manipulated by scientists and practitioners, who can thus allow them to affect people's behavior. For Skinner, the only adequate explanations were psychological theories that explicitly specify environmental variables as causes of behavior.

The two main classes of environmental determinants that Skinner identified are antecedents (which precede behavior) and consequences (which follow behavior). An example of an antecedent might be a pause on the part of the person with whom I'm having a conversation, as a signal that I can speak. An example of a consequence might be my receiving an answer after asking a question. (These, of course, are core concepts in the famous three-term contingency of antecedent, behavior, and consequence—ABC—that defines the behavior analytic operant; we'll return to this contingency shortly.) Skinner (1974) and other behavior analysts used the operant concept to study the effects of antecedents and consequences on behavior by systematically manipulating these variables in the laboratory and observing the resulting behavioral changes. For ethical and logistical reasons, they worked largely with laboratory animals, but they saw this work with nonhumans as a step toward the effective functional analysis of human behavior—for Skinner, the ultimate goal.

Skinner contrasted accounts of behavior that specified environmental determinants of to-be-explained behavior with mainstream explanations, which, he argued, accepted other behavior as causes of behavior. For example, some sociocognitive theorists may explain failure on a task as resulting from low task self-efficacy. This type of explanation would be legitimate in mainstream psychology, but it contains two implicit assumptions, among others:

1. It assumes that patterns of thinking or cognition, which would be presumed to include self-efficacy, are different from such overt action as failure on a task.

2. It assumes that cognition can legitimately be said to cause overt action.

Skinner rejected these two assumptions.

As for his rejection of the first assumption, Skinner saw everything the organism does as a type of behavior, including both overt observable action verifiable by the community and covert activity or private behavior (such as thinking and feeling) that only individuals themselves experience. In this respect, behavior analysis is different from other forms of behaviorism; for instance, it is different from methodological behaviorism, in which the phenomena of scientific analysis must be publicly observable. For behavior analysis, the pragmatic goal of achieving prediction and control over behavior is what determines the scientific value of an observation, and so in a behavior analysis it is acceptable to refer to private experience (one's own or someone else's) if doing so helps achieve that goal. To cite the example given earlier, failure on a task *and* low task self-efficacy would both be considered types of behavior. And this brings us to Skinner's rejection of the second assumption—that cognition causes behavior. As we have just seen, Skinner viewed cognition *as* behavior. For him, then, a "cognition-behavior explanation" (or what he also referred to as a "mentalistic explanation") is what he would have seen as a "behavior-behavior explanation." He rejected such explanations because they specify no potentially manipulable environmental variables that might be used to control rather than simply predict behavior. With respect to our example, task self-efficacy does correlate with task performance, and so task self-efficacy can be used to predict task performance. Task self-efficacy is not directly manipulable, however, and so the scientist has no way to influence the target behavior (that is, task performance). A better explanation for Skinner, and one in line with his declared scientific goals of prediction and control over behavior, would be one that, for example, identified both task self-efficacy and task performance as functionally related to (affected or controlled by) the subject's level of exposure to the particular task (level of exposure being an environmentally manipulable variable).

Apart from Skinner's having made a distinction between behavior analytic explanations and mentalistic explanations, another important aspect of his radical behavioral philosophy was *analytic reflexivity*, or the analyst's awareness that the same type of analysis she applies to her subjects' behavior can also be applied to her own. In other words, the behavior of the scientist is yet more behavior to be explained in operant terms—explained, that is, as behavior emitted (exhibited) in a particular context in order to achieve a particular objective or consequence. An important implication of analytic reflexivity is that psychological explanations and theories are context-dependent and thus can never offer a completely objective account (a so-called God's-eye view) of reality.

It should be obvious from this description that radical behaviorism is contextualistic in character and very similar to functional contextualism. Several features—including an emphasis on the importance of context, a pragmatic truth criterion, and acknowledgment of the reflexivity of analysis—exemplify this strong similarity. This level of similarity should be expected, moreover, given that radical behaviorism is the intellectual forebear of functional contextualism. Despite these similarities, however, there are subtle differences between the two approaches. For one thing, radical behaviorism sees prediction and *control* over behavior as the goals of scientific analysis, whereas functional contextualism has prediction and *influence* over behavior as its goals. The CBS founders' preference for the term "influence" over the term "control" is both philosophical and political. Where the philosophical aspect is concerned, the term "control" suggests *exclusive* influence over behavior along with lack of behavioral variability, whereas behavior in the CBS model is multiply determined, and variability is both expected and desirable. As for the political aspect, a desire for control sounds overbearing and intrusive, and it is marked by a likelihood of rejection not associated with the term "influence." In addition, and apart from these differences, functional contextualism specifies particular dimensions—namely, precision, scope, and depth—along which prediction and influence are desired. These are important guides for the type of theoretical analysis that is required and that might be expected to facilitate scientific progress. Functional contextualism also acknowledges the fact that the selection of a particular goal as the truth criterion for scientific analysis is a *choice*, whereas radical behaviorism does not acknowledge this but simply claims its particular goal as its truth criterion. As such, then, the approach of radical behaviorism, by comparison with that of functional contextualism, can be viewed as dogmatic with respect to its goal.

This final difference between radical behaviorism and functional contextualism helps us make sense of the other differences. Radical behaviorism and functional contextualism are both contextualistic, but functional contextualism is more self-consciously and more deliberately so. Functional contextualism, then, acknowledges itself as a form of contextualism, owns the decision to select its pragmatic goal, and is explicit about its particular reasons for choosing that goal. This approach is in contrast with Skinner's radical behaviorism, whose contextualistic character was not explicitly acknowledged. Skinner's ambivalence about his philosophical assumptions also characterizes behavior analysis—the science of behavior—for which radical behaviorism serves as the foundation. For example, Skinner's writings on behavior analysis were somewhat ambiguous, reflecting aspects of both mechanism and contextualism, and consequently there has been some debate within the field of behavior analysis regarding whether behavior analysis should be seen as a contextualist approach. It has been strongly argued, however, and we agree, that the contextualistic features of behavior analysis are what mark it as distinctive and have enabled its efficacy in applied domains (see Zettle et al., 2016). Accordingly, CBS researchers traditionally use behavior analytic concepts and methods as the core of their basic scientific work, and these concepts and methods are what we will describe in the pages ahead. We should be clear, however, that we interpret and emphasize behavior analysis *as a contextualist approach*. If behavior analysis is interpreted contextualistically, then, arguably, an array of concepts and methods that is wider than those considered legitimate in traditional behavior analysis becomes legitimate in psychological research—and, indeed, this is what has happened in CBS. One example of this expanded array is seen in RFT, which depends on a contextualist interpretation of behavior analysis, as we will see in chapter 2. This expansion also has implications for explorations of the complex phenomenon of self, in particular as a result of the theoretical expansion allowed by RFT. Hence, in order to emphasize that what interests us is a contextualistic interpretation of behavior analysis, as opposed to traditional behavior analysis, we use the term "contextual behavioral psychology" (although, of course, "contextual behavioral psychology" is a logical name for the scientific application of CBS). In any event, at the core of contextual behavioral psychology are the concepts and methods of behavior analysis, and it is to these that we now turn.

Behavior Analysis: Operant Learning

The core concept in behavior analysis and contextual behavioral psychology alike is the operant. The word "operant" has the same origins as the word "operate," which denotes producing an effect or exerting force or influence. Through operant behavior, we operate on our world to produce consequences, and these consequences influence the likelihood that we will repeat the particular behavior in the future. As mentioned earlier, the operant is also known as the three-term (or ABC) contingency. Again, the three terms in question are the antecedent (A), the prior setting or situation; the behavior (B), also referred to as "responding" or "the response" produced in the setting or situation; and the consequence (C), contingent on the behavior and affecting the likelihood of future occurrences of that particular behavior (response). As an example of operant learning, imagine a young child learning to *put a coin* (B) in *the slot of a vending machine* (A) to *receive a snack* (C). Given this consequence, the child may be more likely to engage in the same behavior in a similar situation in the future. This example illustrates the concept of reinforcement, whereby a behavior becomes *more* likely on the basis of its consequences. As a second example, imagine that a child *puts her hand* (B) on *a hot stove* (A) and *gets burned* (C). In this case, the child may hesitate to repeat the same behavior in a similar situation—and, if that turns out to be the case, then this example illustrates punishment, whereby a behavior becomes *less* likely on the basis of its consequences.

Before we examine the concept of the operant in greater detail, let us briefly note the way in which this concept coheres with the philosophical foundations of contextualism and, more specifically, with those of functional contextualism. The root metaphor of contextualism is the act-in-context. The operant exemplifies the act-in-context: in the operant, the act or behavior (B) occurs in a context that includes the antecedent (A) and the consequence (C). Meanwhile, the concept of the operant facilitates the truth criterion of functional contextualism—namely, prediction and influence over behavior—in that, by allowing analysis of environment-behavior relations, it facilitates manipulation of those environmental variables that can influence responding. Finally, the concept of the operant is also effective as regards achieving the criteria of precision, scope, and depth. Reinforcement, for example, is precise to the extent that the only events classified as reinforcers are those that increase responding after the contingent presentation of particular stimuli. The concept of the operant has significant scope in that it can be used to study an infinite variety of actions in different contexts, ranging from very brief actions (blinking an eye) to extremely prolonged actions (writing a book), and including simple phenomena (snapping one's fingers) as well as complex phenomena (conducting an orchestra). Finally, as regards depth, the concept of the operant has been shown to cohere with other levels of analysis, including the neural level, for example, where the biological basis for reinforcement learning is visible.

Now that we've described how the concept of the operant exemplifies contextualism in general, and functional contextualism in particular, let us return to considering the features of the operant itself, first by looking in more detail at the A, B, and C terms involved in the three-term contingency and then by considering the idea of the operant as a class concept. Some of this background information may seem relatively abstract or theoretical, but we are providing it because we view it as essential to understanding and working with self processes from a functional contextual perspective. We hope that by laying this information out in relative detail here, we will facilitate your understanding of the more obviously self-relevant material that we cover later on.

BEHAVIOR

The core of the operant is the particular response involved—what the behaving organism does. As noted earlier, this response can range from one that is very brief and/or simple (pressing a button) to one that is very prolonged and/or complex (designing a car). From the current perspective, activities such as these occur in a context (for example, I may be pressing a button to phone someone or to ask for service in a hotel or to play music on a digital device). This context includes consequences, which can change the likelihood that a particular action will be emitted again in the future, and it also includes antecedent (discriminative) stimuli, which signal what the consequences of a particular action may be. The operant comprises all three elements—antecedent, behavior, and consequence—not just the behavior itself. As we will see in chapter 2, verbal humans come to learn a particular variety of operant that allows their learning (which includes the acquisition of a complex repertoire of self) to become extremely rapid and generative, and thus to go far beyond that of other species. Nevertheless, especially very early in our development, basic operant responding is an important part of our learning history, not to mention the fact that it underlies and includes the learning of the special variety of operant just referred to. At this point, therefore, it is critically important that we explain the characteristics of basic operant learning.

CONSEQUENCES

Consequences, which occur after a response, constitute one of two key categories of environmental influence on behavior (antecedents constitute the other category, as we'll see shortly). As mentioned earlier, an increase in the frequency of responding—an increase that is based on the contingent presentation of particular stimuli—is referred to as *reinforcement*. The consequences themselves are called *reinforcers*, and they include primary or biological reinforcers as well as secondary (or conditioned) reinforcers. To cite a stereotypical example of reinforcement in the animal laboratory, when a pellet of food is provided to a rat every time the rat presses a lever, the rat's pressing of the lever is observed to increase in frequency. With regard to human behavior, an example of reinforcement might involve a little girl who smiles at her infant brother every time he produces the sound "coo" (maybe she thinks this sound is funny), with the baby producing this sound more often as a result of his sister's reaction.

Primary reinforcers (such as water, food, sex, moderate temperatures, and sleep) include stimuli that we are evolutionarily adapted to find reinforcing, since working to obtain them improves organismic chances of survival and reproduction. *Secondary* or *conditioned* reinforcers are stimuli that become reinforcing through their association with primary reinforcers. Learning through stimulus association, referred to as *respondent conditioning* (also known as *classical* or *Pavlovian conditioning*), is a very basic and powerful form of learning in which a previously present reflexive reaction (the unconditioned response) produced by one stimulus (the *unconditioned stimulus*, or US) is acquired by a novel, previously neutral stimulus through association of the neutral stimulus with the US. The classic example is Pavlov's experiment in which a neutral bell tone first predicted the arrival of food for a dog (the food being a US that produced an unconditioned response of salivation in the dog) and eventually came to produce salivation in the dog, without the need for food to be present. When a neutral stimulus (such as a bell tone) becomes conditioned, we refer to it as a *conditioned stimulus* (CS), and we refer to the response it evokes as a *conditioned response*. In the case of Pavlov's dog, the bell tone became a CS for a conditioned response of salivation.

In the case of conditioned reinforcement, a previously neutral stimulus that predicts a primary reinforcer—or that perhaps predicts a previously established secondary reinforcer—can itself become reinforcing. For example, the appearance and attention of a caregiver (previously a neutral stimulus) can become strongly reinforcing (evoking a conditioned response) for an infant because of the infant's association of this individual with such an important primary reinforcer (US) as food or warmth. Likewise, someone else's physical characteristics (such as the previously neutral stimuli of his or her appearance, sound, or scent) can become strongly reinforcing after that person becomes one's sexual partner, a change that is due to the association of those stimuli with the primary reinforcer of sex. Other examples of secondary reinforcers are money, educational attainment, and problem solving, each of which comes to be strongly reinforcing by way of direct or indirect association with other reinforcers. Again, as we will see in chapter 2, verbal humans can learn to associate stimuli in ways that not only go far beyond this kind of simple respondent conditioning but can also fundamentally alter the effects of such respondent conditioning. Nevertheless, respondent conditioning is still a very important aspect of our learning history.

As mentioned earlier, a decrease in responding, when that decrease is due to the contingent presentation of particular stimuli, is referred to as *punishment*. The consequences themselves are called *punishers*. Analogous to reinforcers, punishers may be *primary* (biological) or *secondary* (conditioned). A stereotypical example of punishment in the animal laboratory would be the delivery of an electric shock to a rat every time the rat presses a lever, with a subsequently observed decrease in the frequency with which the rat presses the lever. With regard to human behavior, an example of punishment might be a teacher's chastising a young child when the child talks during class time, with a subsequently observed decrease in the frequency with which the child talks during class time.

Primary punishers are stimuli that produce pain or discomfort. They include electric shocks, poisonous or adulterated food, and extremes of temperature. Secondary punishers become secondary because of their association with previously established punishers, or with the loss of reinforcers. For example, if we eat something rotten or poisonous (US), we will probably become sick (unconditioned response). In addition, however, just the sight of the food that made us sick—a sight that previously was a neutral stimulus—can become enough to make us feel sick once again (a conditioned response to the new CS, the sight of the food). Another example of conditioned punishment might be social disapproval, which can come to predict the loss of such reinforcers as affection or sex.

Note, however, that the concept of punishment should not be confused with the concept of *extinction*. The latter is a process by which contingencies that were previously in effect, and that had brought about conditioning of some kind, cease to become operative, with the typical result that the effects of the conditioning are reversed. This process can take place with respect to any form of conditioning, including both operant and respondent conditioning and, where operant conditioning is concerned, encompassing both punishment and reinforcement. Recall the baby boy who produces the sound "coo" more often as his sister continues to smile at him when he produces this sound. Extinction of the baby's reinforced response might involve his sister's ceasing to smile when he produces the sound (maybe she has become bored with the game), and the baby therefore produces the sound less often.

Consequences of responding can involve either the addition (gain) of a stimulus or the removal (loss) of a stimulus, and the effect can be either an increase or a decrease in response frequency:

- An *increase* in response frequency that is due to the *addition* of a stimulus is called *positive reinforcement*: if Johnny's teacher were to issue tokens (that is, *reinforcing* or *appetitive* stimuli) for attentive behavior, and if Johnny became more attentive as a result, then this outcome would be an example of positive reinforcement.

- An *increase* in response frequency that is due to the *removal* of a stimulus is called *negative reinforcement*, and it occurs in two forms: *escape* and *avoidance*. In escape, a response is performed to remove an aversive stimulus that is already present: if Mary were to find that a particular pattern of gentle rocking stopped her baby from crying, and if her baby's reaction made Mary more likely to use this technique again in the future, then this outcome would be an example of the "escape" form of negative reinforcement. In avoidance, a response is performed in order to put off or avoid an aversive stimulus that is not yet present: if Mary were to rock her quiet baby to ensure that the baby didn't start crying, and if the baby stayed quiet, then Mary's response would be an example of the "avoidance" form of negative reinforcement.

- Punishment, as we've already seen, is a *decrease* in response frequency, and the decrease may be due either to the *addition* of an *aversive* stimulus or to the *removal* of an *appetitive* stimulus. If Joanne were to start giving her opinion less often in meetings because of her boss's continuous criticism (aversive stimulus), then we could say that Joanne's giving her opinion had been punished. If Sean's parents were to start docking his allowance (appetitive stimulus) whenever they saw an argument developing between Sean and his younger brother, and if Sean then became less argumentative with his brother, then we could say that Sean's argumentative behavior had been punished.

ANTECEDENTS

Antecedents, which occur before a response, also constitute one of two key categories of environmental influence on behavior (consequences, as we've seen, constitute the other category). The best-studied type of antecedent is the *discriminative stimulus*, which is a stimulus that signals the availability of particular consequences of responding. Recall the three-term contingency of antecedent, behavior, and consequence (ABC) and the earlier example of a pause on the part of the person with whom I'm having a conversation. My conversation partner's pause (A) is an antecedent stimulus, a signal that if I now begin to speak (B), my response will probably be reinforced (C) by my conversation partner's attention and positive feedback. But what if I attempt to speak while my partner is still speaking (A)? My response (B) may be punished by my partner's anger and complaints about the interruption (C). Either way, my conversation partner's action functions as an antecedent (discriminative) stimulus.

Another type of antecedent variable is the *motivating operation* (see Michael, 2007). Motivation, of course, is a fundamentally important concept for the self because it pertains to things like satisfaction and values. The term "motivating operation" refers not to stimuli (such as discriminative stimuli) that signal the availability of particular types of consequences but rather to processes or procedures that temporarily increase or decrease the effectiveness of particular consequences to act as reinforcers (to act, that is, as *establishing* operations) or as punishers (to act, that is, as *abolishing* operations). In other words, motivating operations change how much a person wants something or values something. For example, if someone has been deprived of food or sex, then food or sex can become even more reinforcing (an establishing operation); by contrast, if someone is satiated with respect to food or sex, then food or sex can become aversive (an abolishing operation). Here, as with other core behavioral phenomena, things become more complex when we are dealing with verbal human beings, and so we will return to the topic of motivation later in the book, when we consider values as a special type of (verbal) motivating operation. For now, however, the important thing is to be well grounded in basic concepts.

THE OPERANT AS A CLASS-BASED CONCEPT

Let us return now to exploring aspects of the basic assumptions that underlie behavior analysis so we can better appreciate the nuances of a functional approach and thus facilitate understanding of the concepts involved in relational frame theory, which is at the core of the CBS approach to human language. The key point to be grasped here is that such operant-related concepts as reinforcement, punishment, and discrimination are functional *class* concepts, which means that they are defined in terms of *patterns* of environment-behavior relations rather than in terms of the topography of particular or singular events.

Consider a simple environment–behavior interaction like a young child smiling (B) in the presence of her caregiver (A) and receiving a smile in return (C). Obviously, if we see the child smile once and then be smiled at in return by her caregiver, our recording of this single interaction does not allow us to categorize it as an instance of the reinforcement of smiling, since we have not seen the defining characteristic of reinforcement, namely, an increase in responding that is based on the presentation of a particular type of consequence. Before we can classify this interaction as an instance of reinforcement, we will need to record a higher rate of smiling (an increase in B) when the caregiver smiles back (C) than when the caregiver does *not* smile back. In other words, reinforcement is marked by a pattern of environment–behavior relations *over time*. Accordingly, each of the three events—A, B, and C—involved in a pattern of reinforcement (or in a pattern of punishment, for that matter) should be thought of as a class of events rather than as a single event. The response (B) in the example of the child and her caregiver is not a single response on the part of the child but rather a class of smiling responses on the part of the child in similar situations; likewise, the consequence (C) is not a single instance of the caregiver smiling back but rather a class of "caregiver smiling back" stimuli. The same goes for the antecedent (A) of the caregiver's presence—it is not one instance of being present but rather a class of "caregiver's presence" events.

Thus, the operant is defined in terms of classes of events, not in terms of singular events, and one feature of this definition is that variation (in terms of both responding and stimulation) is a basic assumption. The fact that responding can vary across instances allows *response induction*, whereby what is produced is not only the originally reinforced response but also other responses that are physically similar to the original response. For example, when a child learns to speak, he produces not only sounds similar to those he hears from adults (and for which social reinforcement is provided) but also sounds for which reinforcement is less likely. The opposite of response induction is *response differentiation*, whereby the range of the responses produced is narrowed down on the basis of reinforcement. A child learning to speak produces increasingly accurate pronunciation over time, as a result of the fact that reinforcement is more likely for typical than for atypical pronunciation.

As an example of the practical utility of behavior analysis, these processes of response induction and response differentiation can be harnessed in the service of an important form of behavior modification called *shaping*, whereby behavior is gradually changed into behavior of a more desirable or beneficial kind as the relevant contingencies are systematically changed over time. This type of behavior modification is typically associated with the training of animals to engage in complex forms of behavior, but the same kind of process also occurs with respect to human behavior, on the basis of deliberate as well as natural contingencies. As an example of deliberate contingencies, consider a football coach or a music teacher providing feedback on performance over time so as to shape increasingly effective play or musical performance. As an example of more natural contingencies, consider how the young athlete's or musician's performance might improve over time on the basis of nondeliberate social feedback.

The effects of variation apply not just to classes of responses but also to classes of stimuli. Here, the effects analogous to response induction and response differentiation are *generalization* and *discrimination*, respectively. As an example of generalization, a very young child might be taught to say "Daddy" in the presence of her father, but for a while she may say "Daddy" in reference not just to her father but also to other adult males. Eventually, as a result of receiving reinforcement for saying "Daddy" only in the presence of her father, and not in response to the presence of other men, the child will learn the correct discrimination of her father from other men.

The fact that operant events are event classes rather than singular events also means that the topography of individual responses and stimuli is less important. To return to the example of the child and her caregiver, the exact physical dimensions of the child's smile (B) don't matter as much as the *function* of the child's smiling, which is to bring about a particular class of consequence (that is, a smile from the caregiver). The same goes for the caregiver's presence (from the child's perspective, the antecedent stimulus) and smile (the consequential stimulus). Again, where the caregiver's presence (A) is concerned, things like the particular time or place of the caregiver's presence, or what the caregiver is wearing, matter less than the function of the caregiver's presence as part of a pattern of antecedent stimulation. As for the caregiver's returning the child's smile (C), the exact dimensions of the caregiver's smile matter less than the function of the caregiver's smile as part of a pattern of consequences for a particular type of response (B).

The emphasis on function as opposed to topography is a key feature of functional contextualism. Functional analysis is employed to determine the function of stimuli and responses in whatever domain of environment–behavior interaction (developmental, educational, organizational, therapeutic, and so forth) is of interest to a scientist or practitioner. Such analysis is usually undertaken to indicate what classes of behavior are being emitted in particular situations, and what environmental stimulation (in terms of both antecedents and consequences) seems to be affecting them. In a functional analysis, the form or topography of an individual response or stimulus is never sufficient in and of itself to determine its role; rather, what matters is its function as part of a current and historical pattern.

The fact that topography matters less than the functional pattern means that the operant is an extremely flexible unit of analysis. For example, we have just been considering a very simple environment–behavior event—the consequation of a child's smile—but there is no restriction on the size or complexity of an operant, for "even a large unit of behavior with widely varying topographies, such as writing a novel or driving to the beach, might be usefully analyzed as an operant" (Hayes, Fox, et al., 2001, p. 22). In addition, although topography often does contribute in relatively explicit ways to the definition of an operant—for example, the response (B) of the child's smiling and the consequence (C) of the adult's smiling back are defined to at least some extent by the topography of smiling itself as a physical activity—there are also operants that have relatively few defining topographical features. These are sometimes referred to as *generalized*, *overarching*, or *higher-order operants* (see Barnes-Holmes & Barnes-Holmes, 2000). Examples of such purely functional operants include novel responding in nonhumans (Pryor, Haag, & O'Reilly, 1969) and production of random number sequences in human participants (see Page & Neuringer, 1985). In these two cases, a defining feature of the operant being shaped is lack of topographical similarity or consistency across responding. But the best-known example of a generalized operant is generalized imitation (see Baer, Peterson, & Sherman, 1967), in which one person copies the actions of another. A good example of this pattern is the children's game Simon Says, in which the players copy the actions of another player who assumes the role of leader; if the leader touches his head or claps, then the other players touch their heads or clap. In the case of this game, lack of topographical similarity from one response to another is not a defining feature; topographical similarity of the emitted responses is irrelevant, and instead the relevant factor is similarity between the response of the individual player and the action of the leader. The concept of the generalized operant is particularly important for relational frame theory because, as we will see in chapter 2, RFT postulates a particular class of generalized operant, called *generalized relational responding,* as the key to language.

CHAPTER 2

Relational Frame Theory

In the eighteenth and early nineteenth centuries, scientists were aware of a variety of chemical substances with varying characteristics, but there was no systematic organization of these substances on the basis of their underlying chemical properties. Then, in 1869, Dmitry Mendeleyev published his famous periodic table, in which chemical elements were arranged in rows and columns on the basis of their atomic weight. This systematic organization, in accordance with a fundamentally important and empirically measurable property, allowed rapid progress in the world of chemistry and is an example of how such a breakthrough can transform a scientific field.

We would argue that historically, and right up to the current era, human psychology has been in a position somewhat similar to that of pre-Mendeleyevian chemistry, with increasing data about various important phenomena, and an increasing plethora of theories attempting to order those data, but with no fundamental paradigm allowing widespread systematic organization of these data and theories. We believe that with the advent of relational frame theory (RFT)—the contextual behavioral account of human language and cognition—a key conceptual and empirical breakthrough has been achieved. Rapid progress with regard to our understanding of important psychological phenomena, including the self, has now become possible. The purpose of this chapter is to explain and describe this breakthrough and some of the key ways in which it is beginning to be applied. We start with a discussion of the importance of human language and cognition, already widely recognized as transformational aspects of human psychology that separate us from other species and that have enabled rapid cultural and technological progress. The RFT breakthrough is to have conceptualized these repertoires in terms of a particular *operant* repertoire, which, once established, profoundly affects all other forms of learning. This functional analytic approach to complex human behavior has already facilitated an expanding, internationally diverse research program that has been making progress on several important applied fronts (see O'Connor et al., 2017). In this chapter, we explain the nature of the special operant at the heart of this program and consider how it underpins complex human behavior in general.

The Importance of Human Language

Symbolic language is critically important to every aspect of our lives as human beings. Because humans are a cooperative species, communication is vitally important, and our ability to use language has been a key facilitator in this regard (Wilson, Hayes, Biglan, & Embry, 2014). For example, through language we can convey precise information about ourselves (such as how we're currently feeling) or tell others important things about the environment ("Don't eat that—it's gone bad"), guiding behavior in useful ways. Language is also the basis of thinking, or cognition, and thus it has allowed us to gain insight into our world, facilitating the development of culture (such as Shakespearean literature) and technology (such as quantum computing) in a way that goes far beyond the culture of any other species. Language has allowed us to develop a complex concept of ourselves in relation to other people and the world, a concept that includes how we make choices regarding our lives and values. But even though language is hugely beneficial to us as individuals and as a species, it can also work against us. Clinical psychologists and other mental health professionals deal every day with the psychological suffering of humans, and how we think about ourselves is typically implicated at the heart of such suffering. Our capacity to use language is what enables us to experience this suffering. Without language, for example, we could not compare ourselves negatively to other people, view ourselves as failing, stigmatize others, ruminate on what we might have done better in the past, worry about what might happen to us in the future, and so forth.

Language is a pervasive and important aspect of our human situation. Accordingly, we need to understand language in order to be able to predict and influence behavior with sufficient precision, scope, and depth for the purposes of useful psychological intervention. An understanding of language from the contextual behavioral perspective sheds light on how this endeavor can be approached. Let's begin by examining the basic concepts of RFT.

RFT: Basic Concepts

The core of the RFT approach, as just suggested, is that language is a type of operant behavior. But it is a special operant, one that humans seem to have evolved uniquely to learn, and one that, once acquired, can change our situation dramatically (Monestès, 2016). The technical name of this operant is *arbitrarily applicable relational responding*, but it is better known by its more easily stated shorthand name, *relational framing* (Stewart, 2016). This type of operant behavior (relational framing) comes in a variety of patterns (called *relational frames*) and facilitates human language and cognition, including such complex human behavior as the development and maintenance of the self. We (typically) start engaging in relational framing before the age of two, and as we become proficient in this repertoire, it rapidly and profoundly changes the psychological functions of our environment; in other words, it changes the way in which we understand and respond to our surroundings and thus allows us to experience and interact with the world in greatly different ways from the ways in which other species do. But what, exactly, *is* relational framing? Let's take a look.

Relational Framing

We'll start by saying what we mean by the term "relating." This term can be defined as the act of responding to one thing in terms of its relationship with another, as, for example, when a person picks the biggest object from an array of objects of different sizes. Many nonhuman animals, too, can learn to relate things to one another on the basis of their physical properties in this way. For example, they can learn to discern that an object is physically the same as or different from a second object, or that it is physically bigger or smaller than another object (see, for example, Giurfa, Zhang, Jenett, Menzel, & Srinivasan, 2001). Thus, chimpanzees have been taught to choose the physically biggest object among a set of objects arrayed for comparison (say, by picking the largest stick from among a number of sticks of different sizes). This is a type of relational responding called *nonarbitrary relational responding*. The relations among the objects are nonarbitrary in the sense that they are not subject to change on the basis of human whim or convention.

Although humans learn nonarbitrary relational responding, we also learn (apparently uniquely) another, more abstract form of relating, which has already been briefly referred to—namely, *arbitrarily applicable relational responding*. This type of relational responding involves relating objects to one another not on the basis of their physical properties but instead on the basis of *contextual cues* that specify the relation among the objects, irrespective of their physical properties (Hayes et al., 2001). Such responding is called "arbitrarily applicable" relational responding because it involves relating objects or events in particular ways that do not depend on their physical properties. This is a critical concept in relational frame theory, and so we'll use an example or two to try to explain it as clearly as possible. Figure 2.1 illustrates the difference between nonarbitrary relational responding, on the one hand, and arbitrarily applicable relational responding, on the other.

Look at the task represented in the part of the figure labeled with the number 1. This task is a simple match-to-sample task that requires a nonarbitrary relational response. That is, in the upper part of the box labeled with the number 1 there is a sample circle of solid black, and there are three comparison circles in the lower part of the box. The task is to pick the comparison circle that goes with the sample circle, in accordance with a relation of physical sameness. It is easy to choose the correct comparison circle on the basis of the properties of the sample circle and the three comparison circles. The solid black (comparison) circle in the bottom right portion of the box is physically the same as the solid black (sample) circle at the top of the box, and so the correct choice is the solid black circle at the bottom of the box. Now, however, look at the task represented in the part of the figure labeled with the number 2. Here, the instruction might again be to pick the comparison circle that goes with the sample circle, but in this case the correct choice will not be based on the physical properties of the circles, and so it is not immediately clear which of the comparison circles matches the sample circle. But if the person trying to perform this task is shown a contextual cue—in the form, say, of a separate box containing the solid black circle and the white circle, with an equal sign (=) between them (see the portion of the figure labeled with the number 3)—then the task immediately becomes relatively straightforward (see the portion of the figure labeled with the number 4), at least for someone who is familiar with the equal sign. If the person performing the task gets the correct answer here, then his or her performance is an example of arbitrarily applicable relational responding, or relational framing. In this case, the correct response is not based on the physical properties of the circles, since the solid black circle and the white circle are no more physically similar to each other than they are to the other comparison circles. Instead, whoever created the task decided beforehand (on an arbitrary basis) which two circles, for the purposes of the task, would be a match, and then the creator of the task used the equal sign to cue that relation. As for

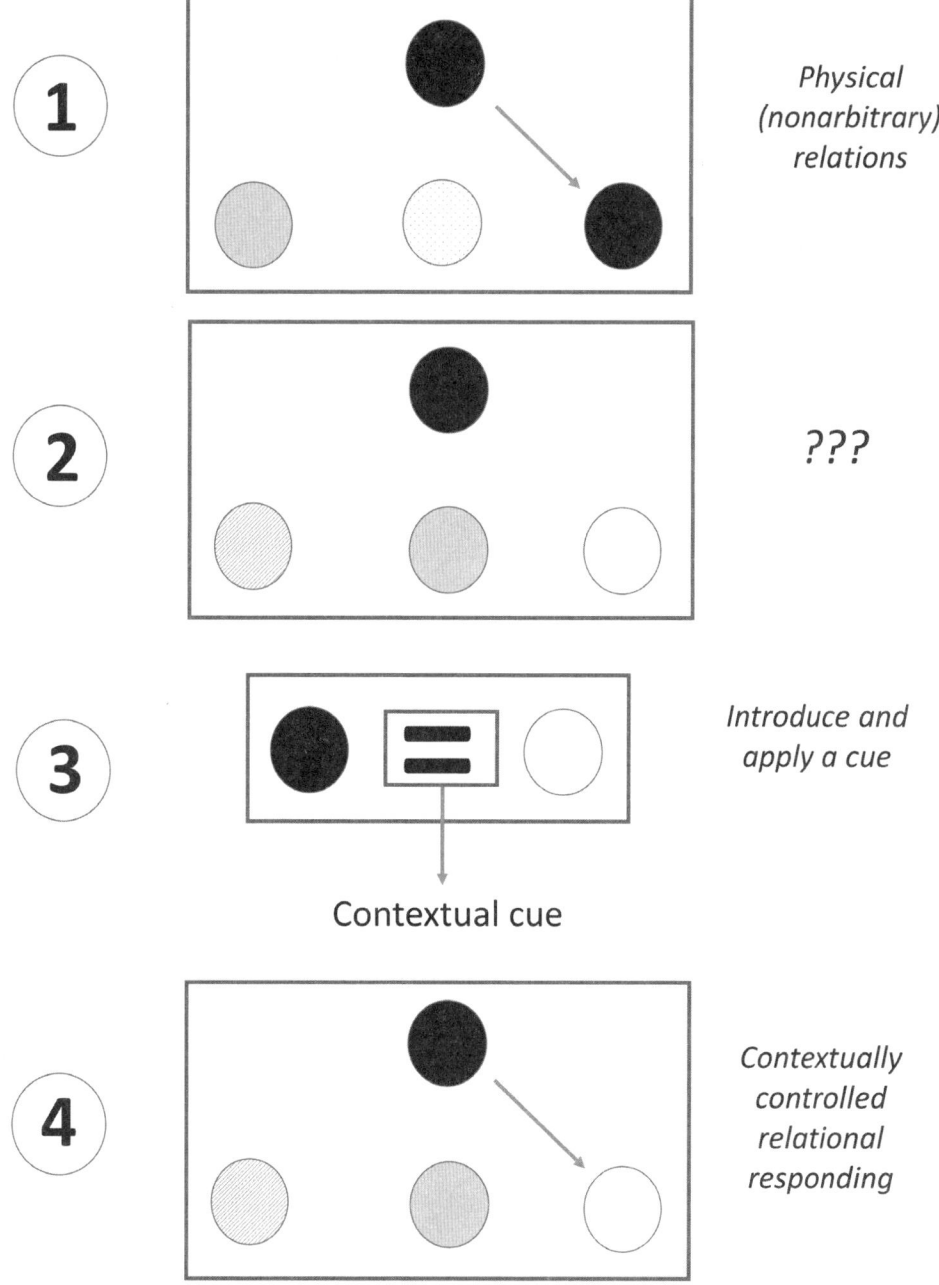

Figure 2.1. Nonarbitrary Relational Responding Versus Arbitrarily Applicable Relational Responding

the person performing the task, if she has learned to respond to the equal sign as a cue for the relation of sameness, then she may, in this context, equate the solid black sample circle with the white comparison circle and thus pick the white comparison circle as a match for the solid black sample circle. If so, her performance of this task will be an example of *arbitrarily applicable sameness* (or *coordinate*) *relational responding*, or—to emphasize the source of the control over the relational response—*sameness* (*coordinate*) *contextually controlled relational responding* or *sameness* (*coordinate*) *relational framing*.

Hopefully, figure 2.1. has given you some idea of the difference between nonarbitrary relational responding, or relating on the basis of the physical properties of related stimuli, and arbitrarily applicable relational responding, or relating on the basis of cues that determine the relation(s) involved. We used the match-to-sample task because it's simple and discrete. It allows us, with relative directness, to compare nonarbitrary and arbitrarily applicable relational responding.

Now let's take a look at a more common and ecologically valid example of arbitrarily applicable relational responding. Suppose we describe, as follows, three hypothetical characters to a verbally able child: "Jim is taller than Jon, and Jon is taller than Sam." If the child is developing as expected, is old enough, and has had a typical history of social interactions, then the child will probably derive a number of new relations from this description, such as "Jim is taller than Sam" and "Sam is shorter than Jim." The child will be able to do this even without having been explicitly taught these responses, and even though the physical or nonarbitrary properties of the stimuli involved don't support these responses. For instance, it isn't obvious just from the characters' names who is taller than whom. From an RFT perspective, we're presenting the child with a contextual cue ("is taller than") that was previously established in the child's learning history as controlling a particular pattern of generalized relational responding. When that cue is presented, that response pattern can be brought to bear on any arbitrarily chosen set of stimuli (such as "Jim," "Jon," and "Sam," or any other set of stimuli), no matter what their nonarbitrary properties may be, and regardless of the nonarbitrary relations between them, such that all the stimuli are brought into a coherent set of relations with each other.

As mentioned earlier, arbitrarily applicable relational responding is also referred to as relational framing, which itself is a metaphor that cues us to the functional relations involved. Just as a picture frame can hold any picture, no matter what the content of the picture may be, a relational frame can be applied to any stimuli, regardless of their physical properties. Furthermore, just as picture frames can come in different shapes and sizes, there are also multiple varieties of relational frames. And RFT research does suggest a variety of frames, including sameness (or coordination, as in "The French word *chien* means 'dog' "), distinction ("California is different from Kansas"), opposition ("Hot is the opposite of cold"), comparison ("A dime is worth more than a nickel"), hierarchy ("A whale is a type of mammal"), deixis ("I am here and you are there"), temporality ("Spring comes before summer"), and analogy ("Feet are to socks as hands are to gloves"), among others; see table 2.1 for further examples of these relations as well as of the cues and patterns of derivation involved in each.

Table 2.1. Relation Types, Examples, and Contextual Cues

Relation type	Example	Contextual cues
Coordination	TV is the same as television.	is; same as; like
Distinction	This song is not familiar.	different from; not; distinctive
Opposition	Sad is the opposite of happy.	unlike; opposite to
Comparison	Cookies are better than cabbage.	more than; less than; better than; worse than
Hierarchy	Siamese is a type of cat.	contains; includes; type of
Deixis	I am at the gym, and you are at the park.	I, you; here, there; now, then
Temporality	Yesterday came before today.	before, after
Analogy	Bees are to hives as dogs are to kennels.	A is to B as C is to D

Origins of Relational Framing

Relational frame theory holds that relational framing is an operant response learned through exposure to multiple natural-language interactions with caregivers and other members of one's community. The earliest pattern of arbitrarily applicable relating that children learn is the bidirectional relation between words and objects. Consider the kind of informal training that might occur between a child and a caregiver with respect to this foundational pattern of relational responding. The caregiver might ask the child where an object ("ball") is and then reinforce any orientation on the part of the child (looking or pointing) toward the correct object. In so doing, the caregiver would be directly training an exemplar of the relation "name A [the spoken word 'ball'] goes with object B [an actual physical ball]." The caregiver might also present the object and reinforce the response of producing the correct name. In this case, the caregiver would be directly training an exemplar of the relation "object B goes with name A." This kind of interaction, in which both directions of the relational pattern are explicitly taught (often but not necessarily in the same episode of teaching), probably takes place hundreds if not thousands of times across a huge variety of different objects (Dad, Mom, doll, biscuit, car, dog, cat, and so forth), until eventually the child has robustly learned the operant pattern of bidirectional name–object relations. At that stage, training in one direction with a completely novel object–name pair—being told, for example, "This [novel object A, such as a picture of a monkey] is a [novel name B, the spoken word 'monkey']—allows derivation in the other direction; that is, the child, after being asked, "Where is [novel name B, the spoken word 'monkey']," can readily point to [novel object A, a picture of a monkey].

Before this pattern of bidirectional relating can be learned, many precursor repertoires that support it need to be in place, including those listed here:

- Generalized conditional discrimination learning (the child, given an object, is able to learn to say a particular name, and/or the child, given a particular name, is able to learn to orient toward or point to an object)

- Echoic responding (the child is able to repeat, with some degree of approximation, what the caregiver says)

- Joint attention (the child is able to follow the focus of the caregiver's gaze toward a novel object)

All three of these repertoires are important as supports for learning the operant of bidirectional relational responding. Deficits in any of them could seriously delay the child's learning of the pattern. But if these repertoires are in place, then the bidirectional pattern will emerge in time, as long as there is sufficient exposure to the socioverbal environment and in particular to appropriate interactions with the caregiver.

The bidirectional name–object pattern is particularly important because it constitutes the key linguistic phenomenon of reference and provides the foundation for the relational frame of coordination (sameness), which appears to be one of the most common frames, and one of the most important. After we learn to respond to a relation of sameness between two stimuli (name and object) and learn to derive a new relation in the opposite direction of the taught relation, we learn, through continued exposure to natural language as well as through formal education, to also derive novel relations by combining two taught relations. For example, consider the following derivation:

> If [picture of an apple] is called "apple" [A = B], and if the English word "apple" is the same as the French word *pomme* [B = C], then the name of [picture of an apple] is *pomme* [A = C], and *pomme* is a name of [picture of an apple] [C = A].

Once again, this pattern of deriving novel relations by combining taught relations is something that a child learns through exposure to multiple exemplars of the pattern, exemplars that are presented through informal interactions with the child's language community.

So far, we have considered only how a child learns framing in terms of coordination or sameness. As already noted, this is a critically important type of framing because it allows linguistic reference (name = object, and object = name), and because it plays a key role in such important abilities as categorization or classification, whereby we group otherwise different concepts together and treat them as the same (dogs, cats, mice, and cows are all animals). The relational frame of coordination enables us to learn about and respond much more efficiently to our environment. Important though this frame is, however, it is only the first of many patterns of relational framing that we learn. Through continued exposure to our language community, we will also acquire other (noncoordinate) relational frames, such as those listed in table 2.1.

Consider, for example, how relational framing in accordance with comparison might emerge. In this case, a child probably first learns to choose the physically larger of two objects in the presence of an auditory stimulus like "bigger," and to choose the physically smaller of two objects in the presence of a stimulus like "smaller." Then, through exposure to multiple exemplars of this type of pattern in the presence of these stimuli (which thus become established as contextual cues for comparison relations), the relational response becomes abstracted in such a way that it can be applied in conditions in which there may be no obvious formal relation (thus the child, after being told, "Dragons are bigger than unicorns," need not come in contact with either "animal" or even see pictures of them to be able to derive the idea that unicorns are smaller than dragons).

Properties of Relational Framing

As we've suggested, we gradually acquire a variety of relational frames through exposure to the socioverbal (that is, language) environment (Hayes et al., 2001). From an RFT perspective, all frames have three characteristics, or properties:

1. Mutual entailment
2. Combinatorial entailment
3. Transformation of functions (TOF)

MUTUAL ENTAILMENT

Mutual entailment is the property whereby a given relation in one direction entails a derived relation in the other. We saw one obvious example of this property in the name–object relation, whereby learning in one direction (name–object) allows derivation in the other (object–name). As another example involving a comparison relation, imagine that a child, Susie, is shown two previously unseen foreign coins of the same size and is told that coin A is worth more than coin B. If Susie thereupon derives that coin B is worth less than coin A, then this also is mutual entailment.

COMBINATORIAL ENTAILMENT

Combinatorial entailment is the property whereby two taught relations can be combined to entail additional relations. Consider an example discussed earlier:

If [picture A] = [English name B], and if [English name B] = [French name C], then [picture A] = [French name C], and [French name C] = [picture A].

This is an example of combinatorial entailment in coordination relations. For another example, this time in comparison relations, let's return to Susie and the foreign coins. If I show Susie three foreign coins of the same size and tell her that coin A is worth more than coin B, and that coin B is worth more than coin C, and if Susie subsequently derives the relation that coin A is worth more than coin C, and that coin C is worth less than coin A, then this is combinatorial entailment (see figure 2.2).

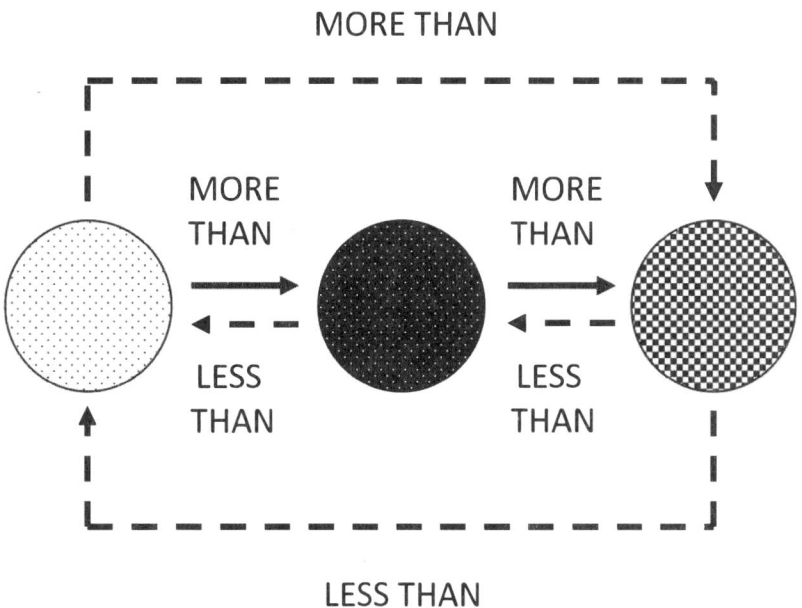

Figure 2.2. Derivation of Mutually Entailed and Combinatorially Entailed Relations in the Case of Comparison. *Solid line* = directly trained relation (between the leftmost coin and the middle coin, and between the middle coin and the rightmost coin). *Dashed line* = subsequently derived relation (two mutually entailed relations of "less than" can be derived between the middle coin and the leftmost coin, and between the rightmost coin and the middle coin, whereas two combinatorially entailed relations—one of "more than" and one of "less than"—can be derived between the leftmost coin and the rightmost coin).

TRANSFORMATION OF FUNCTIONS

The third property of relational framing is *transformation of functions*. This is extremely important in terms of the psychological relevance of relational framing because, from an RFT perspective, it is the process by which language can influence our behavior (see Dymond & Rehfeldt, 2000). TOF, as indicated earlier, is the property of relational framing whereby the psychological functions of stimuli in the environment can be changed or transformed. If two arbitrary stimuli, A and B, are in a relational frame, and if stimulus A has a psychological function, then under certain conditions the stimulus functions of B may be transformed in accordance with the relation involved. For instance, imagine that our friend Susie is in a foreign country where coins that she has never seen before can be used to buy things (in other words, the coins now have an appetitive function). Susie may have already used an instance of coin A to buy things in a shop. If so, then coin A probably has a directly conditioned appetitive function (in other words, coin A has probably become a conditioned positive reinforcer). One way to test for this possibility might be to offer Susie a choice between coin A and coin B, the latter being a second coin that she has never encountered before, one that might therefore be expected to have a neutral function. In that situation, it might be predicted that Susie would choose coin A. Imagine now, however, that she is offered the same choice again, but this time she is first told that coin B is worth more than coin A. Now, even though Susie has no previous experience with coin B and what it can or cannot buy, she chooses it over coin A, the conditioned reinforcer. Susie's choice illustrates how relational framing with respect to stimuli in the environment can transform the psychological functions of those stimuli.

The phenomenon of transformation of functions through arbitrarily applicable relations has been demonstrated in well over one hundred fifty RFT studies with a variety of different relations (such as relations of coordination, distinction, opposition, comparison, analogy, temporality, and perspective) and functions (such as elicited, conditioned elicited, discriminative, reinforcing, ordering, self-discriminative, and avoidance functions; for an overview, see Dymond, May, Munnelly, & Hoon, 2010). As one clear-cut empirical example of this phenomenon, consider an experiment by Dougher, Hamilton, Fink, and Harrington (2007) in which participants were first induced to derive relations of $A < B < C$, where A, B, and C were arbitrary shape stimuli, and in which stimulus B was then paired with mild shock. The experimenters found that six out of eight participants showed lower levels of physiological arousal (as measured by galvanic skin resistance) in response to stimulus A and higher levels of arousal in response to stimulus C than in response to stimulus B. The latter finding was particularly impressive. Normally, an arbitrary stimulus (such as stimulus C), which has not been directly conditioned itself, might produce at most (through association with the directly conditioned stimulus, for example) a level of arousal similar to that shown in response to the directly conditioned stimulus. The fact that stimulus C produced even more arousal than did stimulus B suggests a process alternative to that of associative conditioning and points instead to the process of transformation of functions through comparative relations. Results like these, in addition to the plethora of other studies, constitute strong evidence in favor of the RFT account of language. They also provide an impressive laboratory model of the kinds of transformation of functions, commonplace in human experience, whereby we experience emotional and other reactions through the relational frames responsible for language and thought.

For instance, as a naturalistic counterpart to the laboratory demonstration just described, consider a man who has a panic attack in a small local shop. As a result of this incident, he acquires a fear of that particular shop (direct conditioning) as well as of shops more generally (generalization). Now imagine that he reads in the newspaper about construction starting on a new superstore in his town. Thereafter, he experiences nightmares about the possibility of finding himself inside this store, and when he talks with a therapist, he suggests that instead of visiting this new store, he might prefer to return to the small shop where he had the panic attack. In this way, as a result of the transformation of functions through comparison relations (that is, the superstore is bigger than the local shop and is perceived as more dangerous and more frightening), he exhibits higher anxiety about a place that he has never seen before—a place that, in fact, does not yet even exist—than about the place where he directly experienced a panic attack. Such a pattern, facilitated by transformation of functions via relational framing, would not be unusual in someone experiencing anxiety. It is probably implicated, for example, in effects like *catastrophizing*, whereby someone's anxiety about things that could go wrong in the future is much greater than might seem warranted.

Thus, transformation of functions allows for a technical understanding of the influence of language on behavior, and of the generativity (capacity to allow novel behavior) and flexibility (capacity for adaptation) that characterize this influence. (We will consider both generativity and flexibility in greater detail later in this chapter.) It is also important to note, from an RFT perspective, that the transformation of function process is under contextual control that is separate from that involved in determining which variety of relational framing is occurring. Regarding the latter type of contextual control, recall that such contextual cues as "same," "opposite," "more than," and "less than" control which variety of relational framing is evoked. This is referred to as C_{rel} *contextual control*, where C stands for "context" and *rel* stands for "relation." In addition, RFT conceptualizes C_{func} *contextual cues*, where C again stands for "context" and *func* stands for "function"; these determine which functions should transform through the relation involved. For example, if I told you that X is bigger than Y, then you could derive the relation that Y is smaller than X. This is an example of C_{rel} contextual control for the relation of comparison. If in addition I told you that Y is a large quantity of gold and that X is an even larger quantity of gold, and if I then asked you whether you would like to own X or Y, you might choose X (the larger and therefore more valuable amount of gold), whereas if I asked you whether you would rather carry X or Y up a flight of stairs, you might choose Y (the smaller and therefore lighter amount of gold). The supplementary information conveyed by the C_{func} conceptual cue determines the function (value, on the one hand, or physical exertion, on the other) that transforms through the relation and thus determines how you will respond to the choice.

Relational Framing and Key Features of Language

Given the importance of transformation of functions and its role in the RFT explication of language, we will return later on to other examples of the concepts just discussed. For now, let's begin to explicitly consider four key aspects seen in language and how we can understand them in light of RFT, since they constitute important background information with respect to understanding the self in terms of RFT:

1. Reference
2. Generativity
3. Coherence
4. Rule following

Relational framing allows us to investigate and model these key phenomena, and each one is important in understanding complex human behavior, including self processes.

Reference

Relational framing, as already explained, allows us to perceive and express bidirectional or mutually entailed relations between stimuli (to see, for example, that if an object is related to a word, then the word is also related to the object). The capacity for bidirectionality that characterizes reference, and relational framing more generally, makes the human experience fundamentally distinct and differentiates us from other species.

UNIDIRECTIONALITY VERSUS BIDIRECTIONALITY

For other species, conditioning is unidirectional. Let's return to the phenomenon of respondent conditioning. For a dog, if an initially neutral stimulus (the spoken word "biscuit") regularly precedes an unconditioned stimulus (a dog biscuit), then the spoken word "biscuit" will gain the psychological functions of the actual biscuit and will become a conditioned stimulus. When the dog is presented with the conditioned stimulus (that is, the dog hears the spoken word "biscuit"), the dog may salivate. But this conditioning works only if the initially neutral stimulus (the spoken word "biscuit") *precedes* the unconditioned stimulus (the actual biscuit). Suppose that, instead of regularly presenting the dog with the spoken word "biscuit" *before* the dog receives the actual biscuit, you were to regularly present the dog with the spoken word "biscuit" *after* the dog had received the actual biscuit. Conditioning would be unlikely in that situation, which is to say that the presentation of the word "biscuit" by itself would elicit no reaction from the dog. But human conditioning, in contrast, is strongly bidirectional, thanks to relational framing. For example, if we present a child with a cookie first and only *then* tell him that this object is a cookie, then later on the child will still respond to the sound of the word "cookie," perhaps by smiling, salivating, remembering the look or taste of the cookie, or demonstrating interest. In other words, he frames the sound of the word "cookie" and the actual cookie as being the same. In this case, the psychological functions of the sound of the word "cookie" are transformed to include some of the psychological functions of the actual cookie.

BIDIRECTIONALITY: A DOUBLE-EDGED SWORD

Like some of the other features of language that will be discussed here, the bidirectionality inherent in relational framing has two facets. It can be hugely positive and beneficial, on the one hand, but can facilitate suffering and pathology, on the other.

The bidirectionality inherent in relational framing means that our species can remember and relive pleasant past events by discussing or thinking about them. We can analyze our past experiences and gain insight beyond that provided by operant learning alone. We can symbolize and think about aspects of our past and present environments in order to solve problems and plan for the future. We can verbally contact what it is that we most value in life (having friends, making a contribution, being healthy, and so forth), and our ability to do so can motivate us to pursue what we most value while it also guides our behavior more effectively as we pursue what we value. Of particular importance in the context of the topic of the self is the fact that the bidirectionality inherent in relational framing allows us to frame ourselves and our actions—to think about and reflect on who we are, what we do, and what we stand for. Nonhuman animals cannot do this, because they don't derive bidirectional relations, whereas this is something absolutely fundamental to and powerfully transformative for humans.

But just as the bidirectionality inherent in relational framing allows us to remember and imagine pleasant events, it also allows us to remember and imagine those that are unpleasant. And just as the bidirectionality in relational framing allows our past and present experiences to form the basis of our ability to plan for the future, it can lead us to worry about the future unnecessarily. We can think about ourselves and who we are in a positive light, but we can also become ashamed of who we are or imagine that the future holds only pain and suffering. And yet our ability to experience unpleasant thoughts and feelings via relational frames is not even the worst of it. Although such experiences are an aversive but unavoidable aspect of being a language-able organism, we may nevertheless attempt to avoid these experiences, and our "experiential avoidance" (Hayes, Strosahl, & Wilson, 2011) can interfere with our lives by undermining our pursuit of our values.

For example, consider a woman who has been involved in a terrible car accident and subsequently experiences post-traumatic stress disorder. The psychological effects of the accident severely interfere with her life, but she may also find it extremely difficult to talk to a professional about what happened to her (even though she knows that doing so might be able to help her) because she finds it too painful to talk about what happened. Given her ability to relationally frame, and to have functions transform through relational frames, the act of reporting what happened to her takes on functions of the accident itself. Therefore, speaking with a therapist about the accident would probably bring up aversive memories, including fear and pain. To avoid this unpleasant experience, the woman may avoid therapy, but she may also pay a price for that avoidance. Her symptoms may continue unabated or may even worsen, constraining her ability to live and fully enjoy her life; for instance, if socializing was a valued activity for her before the accident, she may now avoid going out so she can avoid driving and thus remembering the accident.

Generativity

Relational framing is extremely generative, accounting for the ability of language-able humans to produce and understand novel constructions of language. Indeed, it is our ability to relate any stimulus to any other stimulus, in accordance with any relational frame, that allows us to be generative. The repertoire of relational framing underlies the generativity and flexibility of human language and thought, from naming a pet dog to writing a best-selling novel to developing a comprehensive, empirically based theory of the origins of the universe.

At the heart of this generativity is transformation of functions through relational framing. In RFT, this is the core process underlying what we mean when we use the adjective "verbal." From this point of view, any objects or events that are relationally framed become verbal for us—they become part of the world as known through relational frames. In other words, we may imagine that we contact the world directly, without the mediation of our relational framing, but in fact everything around us is changed by this process, at least to some extent. For example, consider the fact that everything around us has a name (that is, everything around us is in a relational frame of coordination), and that when we think about (relationally frame) a named thing, we can also think about how it is related to other (named, relationally framed) things. Look around right now and consider where you are, what objects or people are contained in your surroundings, whether you like or dislike those surroundings, what your motivation is for reading this book in this particular place right now, and so forth. Anything you can see and name can be implicated as related either closely or more distantly to anything else as well as to you and your current activity. For you, then, all these things, and anything else you can think of, are parts of a relational network. As you reflect on this fact, also consider that by relating (comparing, contrasting, and so on) things to each other in this way through relational framing, you are transforming their functions. For instance, when you think of this book, you may ask yourself whether it is better or worse, along any specified dimension, than other books you may have read this year. And making that kind of comparison will immediately transform the functions of the book so that it seems slightly more worthy of your time (if you judge it to be better than another book or books) or less worthy of your time (if you judge it to be worse than another book or books). In everything you do, and in more or less obvious ways, this process goes on all the time.

As we frame objects, events, and people (including ourselves and our own behavior) through our interactions with our socioverbal community, we elaborate our network of related stimuli; and, through transformation of functions, the world increasingly takes on new, verbally derived functions. Our network of related stimuli begins to expand as soon as we start learning to frame words and objects as being the same, and this network probably continues to expand throughout most of the rest of our lives. The well-documented "language explosion" that occurs between the ages of two and three (typically, around the time when children are likely to have acquired the ability to frame in accordance with a few simple relations, such as coordination, distinction, comparison, and so forth), and that allows children to derive multiple novel relations from among an expanding set of named objects and events, is an obvious and salient example of the relational network's elaboration. As children grow into adulthood, continued verbal interactions produce an increasingly complex and multirelational network that involves vast numbers of different objects and events whose functions have been influenced by processes of transformation of functions. Everything that human beings encounter and think about—including ourselves, our thoughts and emotions, our prospects, other people, and our environment—becomes part of this elaborate verbal relational network. For human beings, then, the whole world, including ourselves, is verbal, and we can never get away from language except in very unusual circumstances. This all-pervasive and continuous framing and transformation of the functions of our environment is the key to understanding the generativity of human language.

Coherence

In RFT, *coherence* (or coherent relational responding) is defined as relating in a manner that is consistent with what was previously learned in a particular socioverbal community (Hughes & Barnes-Holmes, 2016). The human verbal community reinforces consistency of relational patterns under contextual control (if A is older than B, then B is younger than A, no matter what A or B looks like physically), and the human verbal community also punishes absence of consistency in this respect. For instance, if Jimmy reports that his friend Sally is older than he is but later states that he is older than Sally, then his caregiver may frown and provide corrective feedback, as the caregiver may also do if Jimmy refers to another friend as Toby after referring to him as Mark. Of course, there is an important context in which providing the wrong name or description for a person or thing may not be punished but instead reinforced. That context is humor, where deliberately using a wrong name may be reinforced by attention and shared amusement, as when a father playing with his daughters calls Sarah by Megan's name, and Megan by Sarah's name, causing both girls to laugh. But humor works on the basis of shared understanding of a lack of coherence in a particular local context, and this shared understanding in turn requires an understanding of coherent relations in the broader context. In the example just given, both girls know their names, and the source of their amusement is the contrast between their father's game and what they know to be the correct relations in the normal context. As such, ultimately even in humor, coherence is critical.

THE ADVANTAGES OF COHERENCE

Coherence is associated with successful problem solving in both the nonsocial and the social environment because coherence tends to allow better prediction and influence. For example, an accurate description of the environment ("I am playing chess"), combined with coherent derivations based on that description ("In chess there are particular rules for how to move pieces, and so I must move these chess pieces in accordance with those rules"), tends to lead to more successful engagement with the environment than would be possible if one or other of those elements were absent (by making legitimate moves, a chess player has a chance of winning the game, thereby obtaining social reinforcement, for instance). For these reasons, relational coherence, sometimes referred to in the contextual behavioral literature as *sense making* (Hayes et al., 2001), becomes a powerful conditioned reinforcer.

Sense making and problem solving are usually highly positive. Because sense making is a powerful conditioned reinforcer, it feels good in itself. In addition, however, it is often accompanied by resolution of a problem, so that one is subsequently able to achieve important goals connected with one's values. For example, figuring out how a piece of software works may be both a means of personal fulfillment and a means of accomplishing an important work assignment, an accomplishment that in turn is important in the context of pursuing one's values in regard to a career. And successful prediction of how the stock market will perform in the wake of a news story will probably be gratifying to a person as an example of her intelligence while also providing her a means of making money. As for the self specifically, coherence is particularly important across contexts. Having a coherent and consistent understanding of oneself, and of one's relationships with other people and the world, increases the likelihood of appropriate responding and effective planning regarding one's values and objectives.

THE DARK SIDE OF COHERENCE

Despite the importance and positivity, across domains, of seeking and achieving coherence, this aspect of our verbal learning history can be misleading. The pursuit of coherence in a particular context can sometimes interfere with effective and meaningful living in a broader context. It is our descriptions of ourselves and our place in the world that can cause this interference. When clients arrive for a first therapy session, they often bring with them coherent descriptions of what they do and don't do, what they will and won't do, and what is and is not possible for them. For example, if someone has experienced repeated failure, then concluding that he is a failure is coherent with his direct experience. Moreover, and all too often, someone's description of himself as a failure increases the likelihood of behavior that coheres with that description. Consider the case of a woman whose face was badly scarred in an accident. Her values may include creating intimate relationships and being loving within her eventual family, but after the accident she may avoid dating, reasoning that potential partners are likely to find her appearance disgusting, a conclusion that ultimately decreases her chances of finding a partner. Her self-description is relatively coherent with her experience, and her giving up dating will further strengthen that coherence. But this coherence is problematic if intimacy and love are important to her. It can be even more problematic if in the past she has defined herself, even in part, on the basis of her appearance. As a consequence, she may extend her evaluation of herself as disgusting until it applies not just to her appearance but also to her whole self (her personality, her character, and so forth), and then she may behave in ways consistent with someone who is disgusting, either by doing disgusting things or by making unreasonable efforts to be seen as pleasant. She may even begin to think of herself as fundamentally unlovable. A key point is that this woman, through coherent framing in one context—that of appearance, and of what is and is not likely in her romantic life—is engaging in behavior that, from the perspective of an observer, is incoherent, or inconsistent, with her broader values of meeting a potential partner and having a family, because this behavior makes achieving those things less likely.

Describing oneself as disgusting or unlovable may seem punishing and self-defeating, and therefore counterintuitive, but doing so may also be reinforcing. Self-descriptions like these, apart from apparently providing a coherent excuse for avoiding things that are difficult, are reinforcing in part *because* they are coherent, since, as we've said, coherence is itself a powerful conditioned reinforcer. In the long run, of course, simply attaining coherence is likely to be less psychologically fulfilling than acting in accordance with (being coherent with) one's values—in the case of the woman scarred in an accident, continuing to date despite her feeling that she is disgusting. Nevertheless, more immediate contingencies can be particularly influential with respect to behavior, and so people may cling to the feeling of being "right" while neglecting their longer-term values. In addition, beyond the original establishing of coherence as a reinforcer, the social dimension of these kinds of contingencies continues to be important. Our social community supports coherence and may provide a powerful supplement to the individual experience of coherence. In the example just used, social attitudes regarding the importance of beauty, and social norms regarding desirability, compatibility, and the like, are continuously conveyed through various media. Social influences of this kind may reinforce an avoidance decision. As suggested, however, this affirmation of coherence in a relatively narrower context may mitigate or suppress behavior that would be coherent or consistent with values pertinent to a broader life context.

Rule Following

Another important phenomenon facilitated by language is *rule following*. Whereas nonhumans learn primarily through respondent and operant conditioning, verbal humans act in accordance with verbally specified or rule-based (rather than directly experienced) contingencies. The rules involved are provided sometimes by other people ("Stay on the path") and sometimes by individuals themselves ("I need to get out more"). RFT provides a technical account of rules and rule following in terms of relational framing. Note, however, that, independent of this technical account, the concept of rules in contextual behavioral psychology and RFT is broader than the same concept in its more conventional uses. The word "rule" is conventionally understood to mean a verbal statement that explicitly prescribes (or proscribes) behavior ("Keep off the grass"), whereas in contextual behavioral psychology and RFT it means a verbal statement about events in the world (including oneself and one's behavior), one that can influence behavior more generally. In this approach, the statement "I am socially awkward" can be considered a rule because saying it to oneself can change the way in which one interacts with other people (it may make one more likely to avoid social contact).

THE ADVANTAGES OF RULE FOLLOWING

Following rules can be extremely advantageous. Research shows that rule following can allow more rapid and effective adaptation to one's environment than can contingency shaping alone (Allyon & Azrin, 1964; Baron, Kaufman, & Stauber, 1969; Weiner, 1970). For example, a child can learn a sequence of actions in a game much more quickly by having the sequence described than by having to learn it through trial and error, and rules (such as the rules for the repertoire of behavior needed to play a complex card game like bridge) can bring about more precise behavior than could occur through contingency shaping. Rules like "Study hard, and you'll succeed in your career" can also bring behavior under the control of greatly delayed consequences.

THE DARK SIDE OF RULE FOLLOWING

We also know that human behavior can come under the influence of rules to the exclusion of other sources of environmental control (Kaufman, Baron, & Kopp, 1966). Consider a university student who earns a number of bad grades on his midterm exams and generates the rule "I am stupid and will never achieve anything in academia." He may subsequently act according to this rule by disengaging from his academic work and perhaps ultimately dropping out. But if he is advised that there are ups and downs, and that he should continue to work hard despite temporary setbacks that leave him feeling bad, then he may improve his performance over time and experience progress. But behaving in accordance with his rule will prevent him from contacting this contingency. Much basic empirical work (Hayes, Brownstein, Haas, & Greenway, 1986; Matthews, Shimoff, Catania, & Sagvolden, 1977; McAuliffe, Hughes, & Barnes-Holmes, 2014; Shimoff, Catania, & Matthews, 1981) has documented the phenomenon of rule-based insensitivity to contingencies, whereby humans under the influence of a rule are much less likely to adapt to changes in their environment (see Hayes, 2004, for an overview).

This increased insensitivity to changes in direct contingencies is perhaps the most documented pernicious effect of rule-governed behavior. Rules can modify stimulus functions and override natural contingencies of reinforcement (Törneke, 2010). Rule-induced insensitivity is significant because many problematic kinds of behavior display this pattern of perseveration despite directly experienced adverse consequences (Hayes et al., 2011). For example, Monestès, Villatte, Stewart, and Loas (2014) conceptualized the perpetuation of delusions in the face of both overwhelming contradictory evidence and directly experienced negative consequences as a form of rule-based insensitivity to changing environmental contingencies. Accordingly, these researchers found that subjects with a history of delusional ideas demonstrated significantly greater rule-induced insensitivity to changing schedules of reinforcement than did control subjects. More generally, rule-governed insensitivity has been found to correlate with psychological rigidity as a pervasive response style (Wulfert, Greenway, Farkas, Hayes, & Dougher, 1994).

A FUNCTIONAL ANALYSIS OF RULES

As just discussed, rules have a substantial influence on human behavior, for better and for worse. Accordingly, we need a means of understanding rules and their effects in order to maximize the positive and mitigate the negative. This is where RFT is useful. As a functional analytic approach to language, in which rules are based, RFT can start to help us in this respect. RFT provides an analysis of rule-governed behavior in terms of both the relational frames involved and the cues (C_{rel} cues) that occasion the derivation of those relations, and also in terms of the psychological functions transformed through those relations and the cues (C_{func} cues) that occasion those transformations of function (see Barnes-Holmes, O'Hora, et al., 2001).

Consider the rule "Stand right outside the theater at 7:15, and I'll meet you there." This rule specifies spatial and temporal antecedents, the form and context of the response, and the nature of the consequence. In other words, it breaks behavior down into functional analytic units, thus facilitating scientific and practical understanding and influence. From an RFT perspective, this rule involves the following:

- Coordination relations between words ("the theater") and actual objects or events (the theater itself)

- Before–after relations specified in terms that indicate a temporal antecedent (the word "and")

- Deictic (perspective) relations based on cues such as the words "I," "you," and "there"

- With respect to transformation of functions, the words "stand right outside" alter the behavioral functions of the theater such that the listener is more likely to stand near it ("right outside") in the context ("at 7:15") specified in the rule

RFT suggests that an individual who is provided with a rule can determine whether the rule is being followed by the extent to which the rule coordinates with actual behavior. That is, for the rule follower (to put this idea somewhat more technically), the coordination between the relational network constituted by the rule, on the one hand, and the relations sustained among the objects or events specified by the rule, on the other, acts as an ongoing source of behavioral regulation. In other words, if the listener sees that events in the nonarbitrary environment specified by the rule are indeed in the relations specified by the rule, then the rule is being followed. In the example just given, if the listener sees that she is standing right outside the theater when her watch shows 7:15, then she is following the rule correctly.

In the example just given, someone is given a rule by someone else, but we can also follow self rules, meaning rules that we both provide and follow. It's likely that the typical verbally able person produces and follows vast numbers of self rules every day, ranging from the relatively simple and/or facile ("I should leave now if I'm going to catch the bus") to the relatively complex and/or profound ("I must decide what I'm going to do with my life—I need to choose a career in which I can really make a difference"). Given the number of rules that we derive for ourselves, and that subsequently influence our behavior both directly and indirectly, self rules are critically important in terms of the analysis of self.

FUNCTIONAL CATEGORIES OF RULES

Zettle and Hayes (1982) suggest three functionally different categories of rule following:

1. Pliance

2. Tracking

3. Augmenting

In each case, the process just outlined—that is, deriving a relation of coordination between a rule and one's behavior—occurs, but an additional pattern determines the behavioral effect.

Pliance

Pliance is rule-governed behavior under the control of socially mediated reinforcement for following rules. For example, if Julia follows her mother's rule about tidying her room because previous rule following has resulted in praise and attention, or avoidance of punishment, then this is pliance. To the extent that it is practiced, pliance requires subjugating one's behavior to someone else's rules for the sake of reinforcement by that other. As such, pliance is a pattern of rule following that undermines the development or expansion of the selfing repertoire (we'll have more to say about selfing in chapter 3). With respect to self rules, pliance is not really possible, since pliance relies on socially mediated reinforcement, and there is no "other" to fill this role.

Tracking

Tracking is rule-governed behavior under the control of a history of coordination between rules and the arrangement of the environment, independent of the delivery of those rules. For example, Julia may follow a rule provided by her teacher about which sections of the textbook to read for an upcoming exam because following previous rules delivered by teachers has allowed her to succeed in school. Where selfing is concerned, tracking is much more relevant than pliance, both because tracking of rules provided by either oneself or others is possible and because tracking either self- or other-generated rules involves following rules that are potentially relevant to or beneficial for the self.

Augmenting

Augmenting is rule-governed behavior that occurs because relational networks alter the degree to which events function as consequences. There are two forms of augmenting: formative and motivative.

Formative augmenting generates consequential functions for a previously neutral stimulus. An example of formative augmenting is being told in the context of a game that blue tokens are worth points. This information makes gaining blue tokens reinforcing in that context.

Motivative augmenting changes the effectiveness of a stimulus already functioning as a consequence. For example, you may already like the taste of chocolate, but if you see and hear, just before you go out to the grocery store, a TV ad that describes how good chocolate tastes, you may become even more likely to buy chocolate when you reach the store.

One way of explaining the effect of rules like these is that they function as verbal counterparts to the nonverbal behavioral effect of a particular type of motivational operation referred to as "reinforcer sampling." Recall the concept of a motivational operation as described in chapter 1. This is a procedure used in behavioral science to change the value of a reinforcer. One way of doing so is simply to allow a subject to briefly come in contact with the reinforcer. For example, animals pre-exposed to a reinforcer such as food will subsequently work harder for that reinforcer (hence the name "reinforcer sampling"). Motivative augmental rules may work in a similar way except that the name of the reinforcer ("chocolate") is presented instead of the reinforcer itself, and the psychological functions of the reinforcer (the taste or smell of chocolate) are thus presented via transformation of functions (Barnes-Holmes, O'Hora, et al., 2001). Given human language's ease and flexibility of use, and the demonstrated power of transformation of functions, motivation via relational framing in this way is potentially ubiquitous and thus quite influential and powerful, both for good (motivating one to act in accordance with one's values, for example) and for not so good (motivating one to buy things one doesn't want, for instance, or to vote for a politician who doesn't have one's interests at heart).

With respect to augmental control, relational frame theorists see motivative augmenting as the core process involved in valuing—namely, holding or pursuing particular values in life, which is important as regards selfing and, in particular, healthy selfing. Values (family, career, and so forth) are conceptualized in RFT as types of verbal relational networks. Again, motivative augmenting is rule-governed behavior whereby verbal relational networks alter the degree to which previously established consequences function as reinforcers or punishers. Consider how this definition might be mapped to a typical example of a value like "family." In this case, let's say that the previously established consequence is the verbal construct "spending quality time with my family," which can be thought of as the label for a domain of interpersonal experiences with particular people. A therapist's reminder of the value of family ("From what you say, I think your family matters to you") can serve to increase the degree to which particular events that the client typically associates with that domain (such as enjoying a family vacation) function as reinforcers for particular values-based actions (such as organizing a family outing). In other words, the therapist's reminder of the value of family may temporarily increase, for the client, the reinforcing function of spending time with his loved ones, which in turn may make it more likely that the client will do the things necessary for him to spend time with his family.

Dimensions of Relational Framing in Flight

We humans, uniquely, learn to relationally frame. Once we begin to do so, our capacity for learning profoundly increases, as does the complexity of our behavioral repertoire. We frame everything, on an ongoing basis—we can never stop doing so while we're alive and awake—and this ongoing activity continuously transforms the functions of our environment and experience. Therefore, scientist-practitioners, in order to understand, predict, and influence human behavior, need to understand the characteristics of relational framing in flight, so to speak—to understand, in other words, relational framing as it occurs in naturalistic conditions in someone with a relatively fully developed verbal repertoire.

One framework offered to facilitate RFT research by highlighting a number of potentially important aspects of relational framing in flight is the *multidimensional multilevel (MDML) framework* (Barnes-Holmes, Barnes-Holmes, Hussey, & Luciano, 2016). In the cited paper, the authors conceptualized the dynamics of relational framing in a three-dimensional space where, they suggest, framing varies in degrees of *derivation*, *complexity*, and *coherence*:

- Derivation involves the degree to which a particular pattern of relational responding has occurred previously. In other words, it can be thought of as involving the extent to which a particular relational response has already been practiced. When we emit a relational response for the first time, it is novel and highly derived, but as we continue to respond in accordance with this pattern, we become practiced in it, and it becomes correspondingly less derived. Increasing levels of derivation lend themselves to what might be described as automatic or unconscious responding. Reacting on autopilot can sometimes be helpful, as when we want to accomplish a particular task quickly and efficiently, but it can also be problematic, as when we rush to judgment about ourselves or other people.

- Complexity has to do with the ways in which patterns of relational responding may differ with respect to such properties as number of stimuli, relations, transformations of function, and types of contextual control. It can be thought of as the intricacy or density of elements and/or relationships in a pattern of relational responding. For example, generic *mutual* entailed relational responding can be thought of as being less complex than generic *combinatorial* entailed relational responding, since the former involves two stimuli and two relations, whereas the latter involves more than two stimuli and more than two relations. Our capacity to respond in complex ways allows us to gain an increased understanding of the world and of ourselves, and to adjust our responding in line with complex contingencies.

- Coherence, as explained earlier, marks the extent to which relational framing is consistent with what was previously learned in a particular socioverbal community. In our earlier discussion of coherence, we mentioned consistency between a relational response and what was previously learned, and theorists also refer to the predictability of consequences for a particular relational response. These go together because if a particular relational response is highly consistent with what has been learned before, then reinforcement will be strongly predicted for that response. For example, the relational pattern "If A is similar to B, then B is similar to A" is highly consistent with what is learned in our society, and so we can predict reinforcement for deriving responses in accordance with this pattern. As already mentioned, coherence is a powerful reinforcer that can be a helpful guide but can also sometimes trap us.

When relational framing in the natural environment is understood in these terms, scientists and practitioners alike may be able to distinguish patterns of functional relations that may be helpful in allowing prediction and influence over behavior.

Barnes-Holmes, Barnes-Holmes, Luciano, & McEnteggart (2017) have suggested a possible additional dimension, *flexibility*, conceptualized as the extent to which a relational response is modifiable on the basis of context. For instance, in RFT research using the Implicit Relational Assessment Procedure, participants are required, under time pressure, to relate stimuli in ways that are both consistent and inconsistent with their relational learning history; thus, for example, participants are asked both to respond "Spring comes before summer" (consistent) and to respond "Spring comes after summer" (inconsistent). The more readily a person can do this with respect to a particular relational response, as required by the context, the higher the participant's level of flexibility with respect to that response. Flexibility is crucially important to mental health, and so understanding and supporting flexibility is a key task of the practitioner.

The point of the MDML framework is to explicitly highlight the importance of the dimensions of relational framing just described as well as to foster investigation into their effects and, in particular, to note how they covary and interact with each other. An example offered by Barnes-Holmes et al. (2016), which implicates the three original dimensions, is that "a relatively complex relational network, such as a story, may require less derivation, appear more coherent, and seem less complex with repeated exposures to the network" (pp. 156–157). Although the example in question does not touch on flexibility, it is possible that flexibility can decrease on the basis of repeated exposures, which can make someone more likely to hold a particular story literally than to be able to see it as a verbal product.

Apart from the dimensions just discussed, the MDML also refers to levels of behavioral development to which the dimensions apply, including those listed here:

- The relational response
- The relational frame
- The relational network
- The relating of relations
- The relating of relational networks

For example, the dimension of derivation can be applied to each of these levels. Take the level of the relational response: as we continue to derive a response such as "If A is opposite to B, then B is opposite to A," this response becomes better practiced and less derived each time. The same reduction in derivation through practice and/or exposure applies to each of the other levels. For example, the frame of opposition ("If A is opposite to B, and B is opposite to C, then B is opposite to A, C is opposite to B, A is the same as C, and C is the same as A") as a unit also becomes better practiced and less derived every time we encounter or engage in this pattern. As an example at the level of the relating of relations, empirical evidence suggests that children become better at this relational pattern as they get older, and so this unit, too, may become better practiced and less derived with increased exposure (see Stewart & Barnes-Holmes, 2004). And as these repertoires, from simple to more complex, become well practiced, we become increasingly verbally adept, and the world simultaneously gains increasingly complex verbal functions.

According to Barnes-Holmes et al. (2016), "The [MDML] framework generates a plethora of potential units of analysis…each [of which] may be conceptualized as a verbal or relational response class…thus allowing for direct manipulation via…contingencies of reinforcement.… In effect the MDML serves to highlight the intensely operant but wholly verbal nature of RFT, with a focus on the impact of direct acting contingencies on its (verbal) operant units of analysis, from the most simple or basic relational responses to the most complex" (pp. 157–158).

We will turn to the MDML framework again as we discuss aspects of the RFT conceptualization of self. When we do, we will focus mainly on the dimensions rather than on the levels, since we view the dimensions as particularly important to an understanding of the dynamics of relational framing. As an example of how the MDML framework might be used to analyze different classes of verbal behavior, consider two individuals with anxiety about exams: Peter, who freezes or panics as he enters the exam room, and Jane, who experiences intense anxiety that results from her ruminating about the exam the day before. These two scenarios are functionally different. More traditional conceptualizations might see Peter's behavior as a nonverbal or respondent response, and Jane's as reflecting an obviously highly verbal pattern, but in the MDML framework they are both verbal patterns in that both involve relational framing, although the two patterns of verbal behavior occupy different areas within the multidimensional space of the model. Peter's response is indeed verbal, but it is probably a low-derivation, low-complexity, high-coherence, low-flexibility relational response. Jane's response is more clearly verbal (relational), but it is a high-derivation, high-complexity, high-coherence, low-flexibility relational response. Thus, there are important functional differences between these two patterns of behavior, and knowledge of the MDML dimensions may prompt different interventions. It should be noted that both patterns share the feature of high coherence and low flexibility, which is to say that for both Peter and Jane, the pattern of relational responding is consistent with other experiences of exam anxiety, and that they are both unable to modify their responses as needed in the situation. The key point is that these are functional analytic distinctions that facilitate the analysis of relational framing in flight, in terms of separable and potentially manipulable operant units. Relational framing is key to understanding the development of the complex and multifaceted human self. As such, the concepts of the MDML framework may be useful with respect to conceptualizing and examining self responding, and so we will return to these concepts in our discussion of selfing.

CHAPTER 3

Relational Frame Theory and the Self

In chapter 1, we introduced functional contextualism, the set of fundamental philosophical assumptions underlying the contextual behavioral science (CBS) approach, and we laid out the core nuts and bolts of this approach's realization in psychological science, which centers on explaining psychology in terms of environment–behavior relations, most specifically in terms of the operant. In chapter 2, we presented relational frame theory (RFT), the specific CBS approach to human language and cognition, building on what had come before by focusing on one critical operant in particular—namely, arbitrarily applicable relational responding (AARR), or relational framing, which humans alone seem specialized to learn, and which, as explained earlier, has profound effects on our psychology. Together, chapters 1 and 2 constitute the building blocks on which the RFT analysis of self—the core of the CBS approach to self—is based (McHugh & Stewart, 2012).

This chapter introduces the CBS approach to the self and, more specifically, the RFT approach to the self. The chapter features the key ingredients of self, as RFT sees them, and provides the foundation for an exploration of more advanced concepts in chapter 4. First we consider a basic operant definition of the self that was proposed by B. F. Skinner, and that provides a functional but nonverbal concept of self. Then we consider how RFT extends this basic idea into a verbal model by adding in the concept of relational framing.

Self as Responding to One's Own Responding

Self is not a technical term in traditional operant psychology. A term is technically defined in this approach if it's explicated in terms of environment–behavior relations. Terms such as *stimulus, response, reinforcement,* and *relational framing* are all technical terms in this sense—they all point to this dynamic interaction. But *self* does not do so. Indeed, the idea of the self, as it has been conceptualized in some mainstream psychological theories, is philosophically incompatible with operant psychology. For example, humanistic psychologists explicitly conceptualize the self as an executive mental agent that makes decisions and causes action, while cognitive psychologists imply the same concept by referring to the idea of executive function, a kind of control center of the mind. Skinner and other operant psychologists reject this type of concept for the purposes of scientific psychology because it assumes an entity or force that stands outside behavior and can wholly determine that behavior, independent of the scientist or any other outside influence. Recall that Skinner's approach was about determining variables that allow for prediction and influence over behavior. If one assumes that there is an inner mental agent that, by itself, can completely determine a person's behavior, then the scientist or practitioner is powerless to have any influence over it. That is why, from Skinner's perspective, this way of conceptualizing behavior is not useful.

Skinner rejected the kind of concept of self proposed in mainstream accounts, but he did not reject the idea itself; rather, he provided the outlines of an operant conceptualization of the self when he wrote, "There is a difference between behaving and reporting that one is behaving or reporting the causes of one's behavior. In arranging conditions under which a person describes the public or private world in which he lives, a community generates that very special form of behavior called knowing" (Skinner, 1974, pp. 34–35). Here, Skinner suggests that "self" has to do with responding to one's own responding or, in more everyday terms, reporting on or describing one's own behavior. For example, if someone asked you what you do in your spare time, you might say that you enjoy going to the movies. If someone asked you whether you prefer chocolate or vanilla ice cream, you might say you prefer chocolate. To answer these two questions accurately, you would have to discriminate some aspect of your own behavior (in the first case, an activity in which you often like to engage; in the second, your reactions to the flavors available in a particular type of food). In both cases, you would be reporting on your own behavior, thus demonstrating insight into your behavior, and this is what would seem to be meant by the term *self-knowledge*. As in these two examples, the behavior that someone reports on can be either overt (publicly observable, as in the first example) or covert (private, as in the second example). Recall from chapter 1 that in Skinner's approach, overt and covert behavior are equally legitimate subjects for study. The admission of covert behavior into the realm of what can be studied is particularly important in the context of the human self because much of what we consider relevant to the self is private experience, and of course such experience is of core importance in human life.

Training Self-Discrimination

As you may recall from chapter 1, an antecedent (that is, discriminative) stimulus can set the occasion for a particular pattern of responding. Responding to one's own responding is referred to in behavioral science as *self-discrimination* because it involves responding under the discriminative control of one's own behavior. In other words, when one responds to one's own responding, it is one's own behavior that is the discriminative stimulus for a particular response. For example, if you enjoyed a movie you just saw, you might say, "I enjoyed that. When's the sequel?" But if you didn't enjoy it, you might say, "I hated that. An hour and a half of my life, wasted!"

The idea that self is based on self-discrimination is one aspect of Skinner's approach to this concept. Another aspect is that this behavior comes about as a result of conditions set up by the community. In Skinner's words, "self-knowledge is of social origin" because "it is only when a person's private world becomes important to others that it becomes important to him" (Skinner, 1974, p. 35). Questions such as "How are you?" and "What are you doing?" help young children establish the ability to discriminate different forms of their own behavior.

Training a repertoire of self-discrimination pays dividends for the verbal community. This is because members of the community can gain useful access to an individual's behavior by asking appropriate questions. For example, if you ask a child how she's feeling, and she tells you that she feels unwell, then you may be able to guide her in ways that are helpful. You can offer sympathy or ask her what kind of discomfort she is having or ask where she feels the discomfort so as to learn more about the problem; and, according to her answer, you may decide that it would aid her recovery if she stayed home instead of going to school. Learning self-discrimination will also be useful to the individual herself. Once a person has been trained to be aware of herself, she'll be better able to predict and control her own behavior. An older child who feels unwell, for example, may know enough to tell someone before being asked, or she may ask permission to stay home from school.

One issue that arises regarding the example just given is how children are taught to accurately answer questions that concern their private behavior. Our private events (such as feeling unwell) are, by definition, inaccessible to the external world, but the verbal community nevertheless shapes our labeling of such events. Skinner (1945) suggested a number of means by which the community can teach a child to accurately label (or, in Skinner's terminology, "tact") private experiences. One means is to train on the basis of publicly observable events, including stimuli (such as a cut arm) as well as the responses (such as grimacing) that are correlated with those private events. For example, if a child enters a room bleeding, crying, and holding his hand over his knee, his caregiver can say, "You got hurt" and then ask him about the level of his pain. Children also learn through the correlation of private stimuli with publicly trained verbal discriminations. In these instances, the private stimuli become more central as the public behavior fades. Reading, for example, is initially taught by means of shaping reading aloud. This process eventually results in silent reading, wherein private stimulation (a flow of verbal meaning) dominates. Finally, children learn to label private events through stimulus induction, or metaphorical extension. In this case, when there is a physical similarity between two private experiences, the child can learn to label one of them through correlation with a public event, and that labeling facilitates the labeling of the other event (for example, the private sensation of "pins and needles" feels somewhat like being jabbed by hundreds of actual little pins and needles).

An Unusual Approach

Skinner, as we have just seen, provided a behavioral interpretation of self (self-awareness) as involving discrimination of one's own behavior. At this point, it is worth thinking about how unusual this conception is by comparison with the common everyday idea of the self. The conventional idea of the self is that of an agent of consciousness, or perhaps (for many) even spirit, that has autonomy and makes decisions, and this conventional concept has been adopted—more or less, and in one form or another—by mainstream psychology. But Skinner's concept is completely different. There's no agency or consciousness invoked. Just like everything else in Skinner's approach, his concept of self has to do with responding under the control of the environment. In the case of self, however, the environment to which one is responding consists of instances or aspects of one's own previous or ongoing behavior.

This may seem unusual and maybe even too simplistic. Some may want to claim that there's more to self than simple learning as just described. Indeed, as you will see, from an RFT point of view there is something more to it, something very important. This something is derived responding, or AARR, the core process involved in language, which, as explained in chapter 2, significantly transforms functions of one's environment and experience. Even if that process is not invoked, however, there is still something profoundly insightful and parsimonious about this (Skinner's) concept of self that is typical of the behavioral approach. Self-awareness, at its core, is really about responding in some way to one's own behavior. As we have seen in the examples already offered in this chapter, when people are asked about themselves or think about themselves, they answer or act, to some extent, under the influence of their own behavior. Of course, the process involved can range from the relatively simple (answering a question like "Did you like the taste of that hamburger?") to the profoundly complex (answering a question like "Do you consider yourself to have lived a moral life?"); at the heart of the process is discrimination of one's own responding.

A Nonhuman Model of Self?

Behavior analytic researchers have taken the opportunity to model Skinner's basic concept, with a view to building on it. This work, as is typical of much initial investigation of psychological concepts in behavior analysis, has been done with nonhumans, and it has been successful in that it has indeed demonstrated responding under the control of subjects' own responding. The majority of such studies have used what are called *reinforcement schedules*. In this paradigm, reinforcement is provided not for every single response but only when a particular pattern of responding is displayed. For example, reinforcement may be provided for every five responses, or if responses are performed at a certain predesignated rate. Training subjects in this way induces them to display a particular pattern of behavior. Experimenters interested in modeling responding to one's own responding have often started out by training the nonhuman subject on such a schedule and have then provided an additional conditional discrimination task in which the animal must correctly discriminate the pattern previously displayed. For example, Lattal (1975) trained pigeons in a conditional discrimination task to peck a red key if they had made a response within a previously designated window of time, and to peck a green key if they had not. In effect, these pigeons learned to respond to ("report on") their own responding and could thus be said to have demonstrated an important component of self-awareness, according to the Skinnerian definition. This paradigm has been employed with a variety of other behavioral patterns as well (Pliskoff & Goldiamond, 1966). Research such as this might seem to suggest that nonhumans can demonstrate rudimentary (and even not so rudimentary) self-awareness.

The RFT Approach: Verbal Responding to Responding

The suggestion that nonhumans may have basic self-awareness is not confined to behavior analytic researchers. It has also been made by mainstream researchers (see, for example, Gallup, 1977). This suggestion is often allied to the argument that the difference between human and nonhuman is *quantitative* (a difference of degree rather than of kind in that nonhumans can do the same basic things that we can do, but we can do more of them, or we can do them faster) and has to do with a vaguely defined idea of complexity of responding (maybe our responding ultimately becomes more complex because we can do more things or can do things faster). Nevertheless, despite evidence apparently supporting this argument, including the experimental demonstrations already mentioned, it can be argued that there is at least one important difference between humans and nonhumans that makes human self-awareness *qualitatively* different (different in kind) from that of nonhumans. This difference is the capacity to use symbolic language or, in RFT terms, to relationally frame.

The Verbal Self

From an RFT perspective, once the individual begins to relationally frame through her interactions with the socioverbal community, the functions of her environment will be transformed in increasingly complex and diverse ways as she elaborates her relational network. In other words, the world becomes increasingly verbal, and this "verbalness" becomes integral to everything she does. The person's own behavior becomes part of this network of relationally transformed stimuli. Indeed, in the case of the typical individual, given how much access she has to her own experience, directly and through the reflection of that experience by other members of the verbal community, verbally responding to her own responding will become a core aspect of her world. For example, a young adult will typically be aware of her likes (chocolate ice cream, horror movies) and dislikes (small talk, shock radio). She may also note changes in her patterns of behavior (such as improved feelings of health and vitality, which make the running club she's joined more reinforcing). She may recognize her tendency to rush when she's feeling worn out and may, as a result, deliberately try to slow down the next time she's had a long and stressful day. She may observe her struggles in math, conclude that she is just not a math person, and delegate tasks that include calculations to her coworkers. In these ways, her descriptions and evaluations of her own response patterns become part of her verbal network and can influence her subsequent responding.

We can also imagine how she might derive more generalized functions of self. For example, if, according to her learning history, being healthy means being good, then the healthier she gets, the better she is. And if being independent means being good, then the more she delegates, the worse she is, at least in some respects. Thus she, or her self, continues to evolve via the transformation of functions. We all engage in these kinds of patterns, thus contributing to the creation of our "self."

As for how children learn to accurately tact their private behavior, RFT extends Skinner's analysis by suggesting that the correlations between private and public stimulation may be further reinforced through derivation of relations between experiences, such that relational networks are formed as caregivers and others talk to children about themselves. For example, a child who can respond in accordance with basic relations (including relations of coordination, distinction, and causality) can be warned off a possibly dangerous activity through reference to a private experience: "Don't go into that nettle patch—you'll get stung, and that's so painful!"

In addition, as the child's repertoire of derived relations expands, private events are incorporated into increasingly complex relational networks, including metaphorical networks. In this way, Skinner's concept of metaphorical extension—which, as originally laid out, is closely tied to physical or nonarbitrary similarity—can be greatly extended through transformation of functions. Thus, joy can be described as overflowing, and sadness can be described as being kept down or depressed.

Therefore, verbal responding to one's own responding, on the basis of transformation of functions, is how the self is conceptualized from a CBS/RFT perspective. This conceptualization may seem a little unusual at first glance, but hopefully it will make sense when you consider some of the examples we've given. In fact, the current conception reflects important aspects of mainstream theories, but it has a fundamentally important advantage over other theories in that it is based on functionally defined processes and thus facilitates research and, in particular, practical intervention.

A Preliminary RFT Model of Self

To quickly recap, the RFT concept of self involves transformation of functions through relational framing of one's own responding. Of course, it's one thing to theorize about psychological processes that may or may not be involved in the self. Many approaches in psychology do this. The psychodynamic approach talks about the ego, and humanists refer to actualization, while cognitive psychologists describe cognitive self schemas. It's another thing, however, to specify manipulable processes that can allow for effective influence on selfing behavior. The RFT account is a functional analytic one wherein the processes involved boil down to behavior in context, specified such that behavior can in principle be predicted and influenced by manipulation of aspects of that context (that is, specifiable environmental variables). In other words, this is a pragmatic account of self, one with which we can directly do potentially useful things. That said, it's one thing to simply talk about this concept; it's another to provide an empirical demonstration of it. Providing such a demonstration is an important step forward because it lets us see the process in action—to see that it makes sense, and how it might work. But has this kind of demonstration been done?

The RFT approach to self has been demonstrated a number of times in a series of papers by Simon Dymond and Dermot Barnes-Holmes. The first demonstration is reported in Dymond and Barnes (1994).

Recall the two key elements that need to be combined in order for selfing processes to be modeled:

1. Relational framing (derived relational responding)

2. Responding to one's own responding

Dymond and Barnes started with relational framing. The initial part of their study involved inducing coordinate ("same as") relational framing between arbitrary nonsense-syllable stimuli. Four participants were first given baseline match-to-sample training in which relations between particular nonsense words were taught. Given the comparisons B1, B2, and B3, they were taught to choose B1 when A1 was the sample, B2 when A2 was the sample, and B3 when A3 was the sample. Similarly, given C1, C2, and C3 as comparisons, they were taught to choose C1 when A1 was the sample, C2 when A2 was the sample, and C3 when A3 was the sample. Thus, training produced the following six directly taught relations:

1. A1-B1
2. A2-B2
3. A3-B3
4. A1-C1
5. A2-C2
6. A3-C3

Participants were then tested for and successfully demonstrated the following three untrained or derived relations:

1. B1-C1
2. B2-C2
3. B3-C3

The demonstration of these untaught performances suggested that the participants had derived three coordinate relations, as follows:

1. A1-B1-C1
2. A2-B2-C2
3. A3-B3-C3

Empirically established and controlled coordinate relational responding, as described here (also referred to as *stimulus equivalence*), has been extensively studied. In this case, however, it was only the first of the necessary elements. A second element was also needed, namely, responding to one's own responding. This is where Dymond and Barnes capitalized on previous work by Lattal (1975).

Recall that Lattal had previously taught pigeons to respond to their own responding. The next part of the study by Dymond and Barnes (1994) was quite similar in key respects to Lattal's procedure. For this part of the study, the four participants were first taught how best to respond in order to maximize reinforcement (gain points exchangeable for money) in two different time-based tasks (reinforcement schedules). The key pattern that they had to learn was that in one task, making a response (a button press) within a certain time window would earn points, whereas in the other task, *not* making a response within a certain time window would earn points. In addition to learning this pattern of responding, however, the participants could also earn points by choosing one of the two arbitrary stimuli B1 or B2. Specifically, if they had *not* responded within the particular time window, then choosing B1 was reinforced, whereas if they *had* made at least one response within that time window, then choosing B2 was reinforced. In this way, just as in the Lattal study, the participants learned to respond in ways that were contingent on their own previous responding. But Dymond and Barnes subsequently showed a critical extension of this effect, an extension that represents the key difference between the two demonstrations. They included a final test that probed for a combination of the "responding to one's own responding" effect and the "coordinate-derived relations" effect, which is the core of the RFT approach to self. That is, they tested for transformation of the functions of stimuli in derived coordinate relations with B1 and B2, respectively—namely, C1 and C2, such that C1 should be chosen if no response were emitted, and C2 should be chosen if at least one response were emitted. All four participants showed the predicted transformation of functions. In so doing, they demonstrated discrimination of their own behavior via stimuli (C1 and C2) that had not been directly trained, and they did so by way of derived relations, the RFT definition of a verbal response. In other words, they *verbally* discriminated their previous behavior. This effect, as such, provided a basic empirical model of verbal self-discrimination (that is, self-discrimination based on transformation of functions through relational framing).

Dymond and Barnes (1994) thus provided a very basic empirical demonstration of self as conceptualized from an RFT point of view. Two subsequent studies by the same authors (Dymond & Barnes, 1995, 1996) extended this basic model by showing transformation of self-discrimination functions via alternative frames, including comparison (more/less) and opposition. In the first of these two later studies, Dymond and Barnes (1995), instead of training and testing a network consisting solely of equivalence relations as in the earlier study (Dymond & Barnes, 1994), trained and tested a network that also included comparison (more than/less than) relations such that participants derived relations of "same as," "more than," and "less than," respectively, between one particular stimulus (B1) and three others (C1, B2, and C2) in the network. They then trained participants to engage in a task in which the participants sometimes had to press a space bar once, sometimes had to press it twice, and sometimes did not have to press it at all, and the participants were also taught to engage in self-discrimination such that they had to pick B1 if they had pressed the space bar once. The participants then showed transfer of functions via a sameness relation such that, without any further training, they also picked C1 if they had previously pressed the space bar once; and, more important, they showed a transformation of functions via comparison relations such that they picked B2 if they had not pressed the space bar at all and picked C2 if they had pressed the space bar twice. This demonstrated not just verbal (derived) discrimination of their own previous behavior but derivation based on comparison relations, modeling processes involved in self-comparison, and self-evaluation.

At this point, let's remind ourselves why empirical demonstrations such as these are important. When we demonstrate the key processes involved in any behavioral phenomenon, we show that our functional analytic conceptualization makes sense, in principle, as a means of trying to understand that phenomenon (for example, by way of its origins and characteristics), but we also provide a foundation for further research, both basic and applied, that uses the model and that may be able to afford new theoretical and/or practical insights. The patterns of self behavior modeled in the studies just described are relatively simple, as suggested, but we might also use them as a launching pad to model and investigate more complex phenomena, such as self-evaluation or self-esteem, both having applied significance. For example, as mentioned earlier, the study by Dymond and Barnes (1995) that showed transformation of functions through comparative (more/less) relations gives us a clue to how we might conceptualize self-evaluation. Perhaps this phenomenon involves transformation of functions such as the goodness (or worthiness, or ability, and so forth) of "I" or "me" along a comparative dimension with respect to other people. As another possible direction for future research, the model described here could also be used as the basis of research investigating the origins and effects of self-understanding in children. For example, it might be used to examine both how readily transformation of self functions occurs in children and whether training particular patterns of transformation of self functions (in accordance with before–after relations, for example, which might be predicted to be involved in anticipation of future rewards) might make particular patterns of behavior (such as self-control) more likely.

Verbal Versus Nonverbal Self-Discrimination

To return to and extend our recap, the RFT perspective on human self-awareness is that a person does not merely respond to his own responding; he responds to his own responding via the process of transformation of functions through relational framing. RFT sees the latter process as the defining characteristic of verbal behavior. A more elegant and concise way of putting this is to say that a person is "not simply behaving with regard to his behavior, but is also behaving *verbally* with regard to his behavior" (Hayes & Wilson, 1993, p. 297). The studies by Dymond and Barnes showed transformation of self-discrimination functions via relational frames and thus have provided simple models of verbal self-knowledge, or the symbolization or description of one's own behavior, the core of the RFT approach to self. In one sense, this approach reflects traditional theories of self that suggest the importance of self-description. In another sense, however, as explained earlier, this approach advances beyond those theories in a very important way, by allowing empirical modeling of this process at a basic level. Thus, this approach potentially facilitates new insights and functional analytic interventions through progressive refinement of the models involved.

From the RFT perspective, verbal self-knowledge requires relational framing. What this means, logically speaking, is that self-knowledge is confined to entities that can relationally frame, which in turn means that self-knowledge, at least as far as we know now, is confined to human beings. As discussed in chapter 2, this human capacity is a double-edged sword. It can be important and beneficial, but it can also be a cause of psychological pain and suffering (see Hayes & Gifford, 1997).

Verbal self-knowledge is potentially important because a verbal description of one's own behavior, and especially the contingencies controlling it, can alter relevant behavioral functions. Consider a positive example of behavior change brought about through relational framing of one's own behavior. In developmental tests of delayed gratification, young children are typically told that they can have one edible reinforcer (often something sweet, such as candy) immediately, or two if they wait for several minutes. RFT would suggest that a sufficiently verbally advanced child might relationally frame this situation in accordance with "if-then" frames in such a way that waiting is coordinately framed with "more," and not waiting is coordinately framed with "less." This framing may transform the functions of the choice situation and make the child more likely to wait. Alternatively, imagine a child who takes the smaller amount of candy even though she is told that she can have more if she waits. This child's capacity to describe her own behavior and compare its outcome with the alternative outcome ("I didn't wait, and now I have less candy than I could have had") may well make the edible reinforcer less reinforcing through transformation of functions. Furthermore, as a result of this experience, the next time the child has a choice of either taking a smaller reinforcer now or waiting for a larger one, she may take the latter option. Learning to do so is an important step in terms of self-awareness and self-regulation, with all the potential benefits of this repertoire.

This analysis suggests the verbal processes that may be involved in self-regulation of behavior. The analysis is consistent with the Skinnerian idea that "a person who has been 'made aware of himself' by the questions he has been asked is in a better position to predict and control his own behavior" (Skinner, 1974, p. 35). But relational frame theorists argue that the verbal quality of this self-awareness is critical. The relational entailment (derivation of new, untaught relations) and the transformation of functions (change in behavior following derivation) that characterize relational framing mean that individuals who are verbally self-aware may derive new relations with respect to their situation so that their subsequent behavior becomes more effective than could otherwise happen. An illustration of this idea is the child's framing as a facilitator of delayed gratification. Nonverbal self-awareness, which does not have qualities of relational entailment and transformation of functions, should not allow for self-regulation. In other words, the ability of pigeons to report on their own behavior, as in the study by Lattal (1975), does not make those pigeons more effective at responding to future contingencies. The lack of any capacity to derive new relations, or the impossibility of subsequent behavior to be affected by transformation of functions via those relations, means that, in the nonverbal case, responding to one's own responding is a limited and inflexible pattern of behavior that adds nothing beyond itself.

Now that we've considered how relational framing of one's own behavior can be potentially beneficial, let's consider how it may contribute to a negative outcome. As noted earlier, verbal self-knowledge, despite its powerful advantages, can be a cause of suffering. The relational entailment and transformation of functions that characterize relational framing mean that giving a description of a painful event that one has experienced can itself be painful. For example, if someone has come close to death in a car crash, then a description of that event will be in coordinate relations with the event itself, and so negative functions of the traumatic event (such as intense fear) will be transferred to the description of the event, with the result that every time the person thinks about the event, he psychologically relives something deeply aversive. In order to avoid the suffering involved in recalling this traumatic event, he may attempt to avoid thinking or talking about it, even with a therapist. He may also attempt to minimize or avoid traveling in cars or other vehicles, or he may try to avoid revisiting the place where the accident occurred. Response patterns like these can have a negative impact on the quality of his life by restricting his activities ("Commuting by car is too dangerous") and may support negative self-perceptions derived since the accident ("I'm no longer the man I was"). Avoidance per se, then, can be problematic. Moreover, even the attempt to avoid or suppress private experiences like thoughts and feelings is typically futile and counterproductive (Hooper, Saunders, & McHugh, 2010; Stewart et al., 2015; Wegner, 1994), and so such an attempt is likely to increase rather than decrease the availability of these private events (that is, thoughts and feelings). As a result, attempts at avoidance would act to strengthen a negative down-spiral involving ever higher levels of negative experience accompanied by increasingly self-defeating and life-stultifying avoidance.

It is more useful to deliberately engage in describing an aversive event than to avoid describing it, since describing it can help decrease the aversiveness of the stimuli (such as cars, for someone who has been in an auto accident) connected with the event and thus facilitate psychological recovery. In other words, recovery can be facilitated through *verbal extinction* of the functions of the event (Dougher, Augustson, Markham, Greenway, & Wulfert, 1994; Wilson & Blackledge, 2000). For example, if the person who has experienced a traumatic car accident directly associates the thought of his car with the thought of an accident and then generalizes this association to all cars, he may come to find that cars produce high levels of fear and anxiety in him. Furthermore, as a result of transformation of functions, talking about things associated with the accident (such as cars) will present the conditioned aversive functions of those things in the present moment, and this also will be painful or aversive. At the same time, however, talking about the accident presents words in derived relations with accident-related stimuli (such as cars) but in the absence of unconditioned aversive events (such as a car crash or other trauma). This can lead to direct extinction of the psychological effects of those words, which in turn can lead to *derived extinction* (Dougher et al., 1994) of the effects of the events to which those words refer, including cars among other things. This phenomenon probably contributes to the generally beneficial effects of talk therapy as well as to the beneficial effects of a variety of other psychotherapeutic techniques, such as desensitization.

As we have seen, the RFT-based approach to self has things in common with traditional approaches, but it also provides novel contributions to the study of self-development. With respect to the initial development of self-awareness, the RFT-based approach is in agreement with previous approaches on the importance of discriminating self behavior from other aspects of the environment. However, the RFT-based approach is unique in that it highlights and empirically models the *verbal* dimension of this self-discrimination (that is, its basis in transformation of functions through relational frames), which is critical for the acquisition of the highly complex self repertoire seen in humans. But perhaps the most important, novel, and unique aspect of the RFT-based approach, at least in comparison with non-behavioral approaches, is that, in accordance with its underlying philosophical assumptions, it can specify potentially manipulable variables that facilitate prediction of and influence over the development of appropriate self-descriptive behavior.

CHAPTER 4

Acquiring Selfing

Most of us take the idea of having a sense of self for granted. The experience of the self is so well developed and so well integrated into our everyday existence that we can't remember and can barely imagine what it would be like *not* to have a sense of self. A sense of self, learned through interactions with one's social environment, is fundamentally important and life-changing in terms of our ability to understand ourselves and our environment, including our needs and values, and our ability to understand how we can navigate the world, and in particular our social environment, in order to live a fully human and fulfilling life. But some individuals do not receive adequate training or the teaching needed to develop the sophisticated sense of self with which most of us are familiar. Because of developmental delays, an impoverished social environment, or some combination of the two, a relatively complete or typical sense of self is not acquired.

This chapter examines the contextual variables that may have an impact on the development of a healthy selfing repertoire as well as what contextual behavioral science (CBS) can offer in terms of intervention. In order to understand how a healthy selfing repertoire is acquired, it's necessary to further explore the developmental context from which the self emerges. To that end, the chapter examines the two processes involved:

1. Learning to accurately tact (Skinner's term; see chapter 3) one's experience

2. Learning to engage in deictic relational responding (that is, perspective taking) on the basis of a distinction between one's own and others' behavior When the social environment is rich and an individual is developing typically, awareness of the self and awareness of

others develop in tandem. We will look in turn at the emergence of each of these repertoires.

Optimal Environment for Acquiring a Selfing Repertoire

A relatively ideal environment for the development of a healthy selfing repertoire is one where there is frequent interaction, and where discussions include plenty of references to feelings and emotions as well as plenty of distinctions between *I* and others (*you, he, she,* and so forth). In this environment, adults and peers talk to and ask children about themselves and their feelings and about what they like and don't like, and they ask and answer questions involving deictic relational cues.

We are not born with the ability to talk about ourselves (or others), and so we need to acquire skill in this behavior. This skill is acquired via relational framing more generally, and through interactions with others in the socioverbal community. For example, we may ask a young child showing obvious signs of sleepiness (yawning, eyes closing), "Are you tired?" The child may reply, "No." Accordingly, he is allowed to stay up a bit later. But if he then starts misbehaving, he may receive socially mediated consequences (such as no screen time the next day), and his mother may say, "When you're tired, you throw tantrums—you need to go to bed earlier." These kinds of consequences will eventually produce more accurate reporting of his behavior by the child, which in turn will allow for more accurate prediction of his behavior, both by the child and by others.

The things we point out to children, and the questions we ask them about themselves, are numerous and span three dimensions:

1. *Interpersonal.* "I'm the opposite of you" or "Do you like the same one as your sister?"

2. *Spatial.* "I see you here" or "Do you like it over there?"

3. *Temporal.* "You did that really fast!" or "Did you remember to put the trash out?"

And one common property spans all the things we point out to a child, and all the questions we ask—we are looking for responses from the child's perspective. That is, when the child responds to questions about his own behavior ("Where are you going?" or "What are you doing today?"), the answer is always from the perspective of *I*.

The acquisition of perspective-taking framing requires that the child receive exposure to multiple exemplars of the relations involved. In an optimal environment, rich and relevant questioning about the child's behavior and experiences will provide such exemplars:

- How are you feeling now?
- What are you doing tomorrow?
- Would you like ice cream?
- Are you sad?

These kinds of questions help establish a strong and well-practiced repertoire of deictic relations, needed for the acquisition of a solid, healthy sense of self as well as for development of the ability to take the perspective of others. In other contexts, however, such questioning may be more limited, which may hamper the development of these important repertoires. This may happen, for example, in some institutionalized environments where there are low levels of interaction. Even outside such institutions, however, children with developmental delays may be slower to respond to questions, and as a result fewer questions may be posed to them, so that the number of potential training exemplars is reduced. Thus, fewer exemplars are provided when more are needed, and any deficits in the child's learning to self are compounded.

Typical social interactions in typical social environments establish two skills foundational to selfing:

1. *Accurate tacting of experience.* We need to be able to discriminate and label our internal experiences in order to be sensitive to contextual influences. If we cannot discriminate what we are feeling (hurt, excited, angry, happy) about particular experiences, then it will be very difficult for us to learn from those experiences about what is important to us.

2. *Deictic relational framing.* When we can say, for example, "My perspective *here* and *now* is different from yours *there* and *then*," we can describe experiences as happening to "I," not to someone else. Development of this perspective supports an increasingly sophisticated idea of who we are, what we enjoy, and what is important to us.

Tacting Private Events

The ability to discriminate and accurately label our thoughts, feelings, and internal experiences is critical to understanding our own behavior, and to behaving effectively as circumstances change. It is easier to learn to be in contact with (mindful of) our current experiences when we have accurate labels for these experiences. When we are able to notice our thoughts and feelings as they emerge, we are also able to notice the context contributing to these experiences. For example, if we notice that we feel excited one morning, we may also notice that the excitement showed up after we realized that we were scheduled to see a friend at lunch that day. If we are able to notice feeling frustrated, we may also notice that we often feel frustrated when we encounter a certain kind of challenge at work.

In addition, if we identify and label situations in which we feel certain emotions (happiness, excitement, anxiety, fear, and so forth), we can better understand and predict how particular contexts impact our overt behavior. If we are particularly productive after lunch, for example, then our awareness of our excitement may help us notice that refreshing lunches have a positive impact on our productivity. If we tend to withdraw after challenges at work, then our awareness of our frustration may help us recognize that repeated challenges are having a negative impact on our relationships.

Further, identifying how particular contexts impact our private experiences and our overt behavior can help us engage in more effective behavior. Remembering our excitement and subsequent productivity after lunch, we may be more likely to schedule another lunch with a friend very soon. Recalling our frustration and social withdrawal after a challenge at work, we may seek additional training on how to handle such challenges. In these ways, knowledge of our internal experience is important for contextual sensitivity and flexibility.

Individuals vary in their awareness of their current experiences. For some, simply being aware of thoughts or feelings is a challenge. One person may report that she struggles to know what she thinks about things that happen to her, and her lack of awareness may be disruptive: her behavior changes with her changing mood or thoughts, but it changes outside her awareness. Someone else, anxious about an upcoming presentation, may find herself speaking rudely to her coworkers, ignoring phone calls, and skipping a gym class, but she may not connect this kind of behavior to her upcoming presentation. However, if she were able to acknowledge her anxiety, she could also take the opportunity to ask her coworkers for support, to exercise, or to take time to practice her presentation.

Still other people mislabel their thoughts and feelings, which is to say that they label their thoughts and feelings in ways that are different from how people in their culture generally label their own thoughts and feelings. For example, one person, planning to lunch with someone to whom he's attracted, feels his heart pound and his face get hot and gives his private experience the label "humiliation," whereas others in his culture would probably label similar feelings "anticipation" or "arousal." This man's labeling of his private experience can be problematic because he may avoid the very person he is attracted to, and to protect himself from further humiliation he may express dislike for that person or avoid going out to lunch altogether. But if he could acknowledge his anticipation and arousal, he could take the opportunity to explore the attraction and get to know someone new. Many forms of mislabeling can occur—confusing excitement with fear, for example, or embarrassment with anger—and such mislabeling can cause someone to be insensitive to the context of his or her own behavior.

Discrimination of private experiences is critically important for the development of sensitive and flexible responding to the constantly changing context. For instance, if an individual has poor repertoires with respect to her internal experience, then she will have great difficulty predicting and understanding the causes and consequences of her behavior. As a result, she may increase her pliant behavior (that is, behavior reinforced by socially mediated consequences rather than by her tracking of her own experience), and so she may demonstrate increased rigidity and insensitivity to her changing world.

Clearly, then, a deficit in our ability to accurately discriminate our internal experiences can have problematic consequences. How does such a deficit arise? For an explanation, we must look at how we learn to discriminate and accurately label our experience.

By definition, our private events (feelings, thoughts, sensations) are inaccessible to the external world, but our verbal community must nevertheless shape (train) our labeling of these events. As discussed in chapter 3, the verbal community does so by providing appropriate discriminative training with respect to external and thus publicly accessible correlates of internal experience. Nevertheless, even with the advantages of very careful and attentive caregivers and the potential of language for teaching precise and subtle discriminations, the fact that our private experiences are available only to ourselves means that the training of accurate tacting is an inexact process. Despite adequate resources and the best intentions, difficulties can emerge. And when caregivers and other members of the verbal community neglect, impede, or deliberately distort learning, accurate tacting of internal experiences is undermined, with potentially serious consequences for children's psychological development.

Deictic Relational Framing

The ability to describe our own experience, which we have just discussed, is one of two key skills foundational to the development of self-awareness. The other is deictic relational framing, or perspective taking. Once a child can relationally frame, she can begin to relationally frame behavior, including her own and that of others. This ability facilitates the emergence of deictic responding.

There are three key deictic frames (see Hayes, 1984):

1. *I–you*

2. *here–there*

3. *now–then*

One characteristic of deictic frames is that they do not have straightforwardly formal or nonarbitrary counterparts. Some fundamental frames have very obvious, nonarbitrary counterparts; coordination and distinction, for example, are based on physical sameness and difference, respectively, between related events. Things are less straightforward with spatiotemporal frames, such as *in front of–behind, left–right, above–below, before–after,* and *inside–outside*. These frames have nonarbitrary counterparts (thanks to the fact that events can be physically positioned in relation to each other), but even at the nonarbitrary level, the physical characteristics of the relata themselves are either largely or wholly irrelevant; it is the relationship between them that matters. For example, regardless of the physical properties of two objects, one of them can be located physically above the other.

Frames that require perspective taking, of which the deictic frames are the key examples, are the most unusual with respect to their relationship with the nonarbitrary environment. In this case, a discrimination must be made on the basis of the locus of particular activity: in the case of *I–you*, between responding done by the current speaker and responding done by someone else; in the case of *here–there*, between activity occurring at the location of the current speaker and activity occurring elsewhere; and in the case of *now–then*, between current and noncurrent responding. Thus, the response patterns that need to be learned in this case are particularly abstract and require demonstration via extensive multiple-exemplar training of the relational pattern, with minimal reliance on formal properties. Barnes-Holmes, Hayes, and Dymond (2001) argue that "abstraction of an individual's perspective on the world, and that of others, requires a combination of a sufficiently well-developed relational repertoire and an extensive history of multiple exemplars that take advantage of that repertoire" (pp. 122–123). In the course of interactions with the verbal community, the child will gradually learn to appropriately respond to and ask questions such as these:

- What are you doing here?
- What am I doing now?
- What will you do there?

As in the case of learning other relational frames, these patterns will be abstracted over time as long as consistent and appropriate contingencies are applied with respect to the required relational patterns—in this particular instance, the patterns of *I–you*, *here–there*, and *now–then*.

According to RFT, once the deictic frames of *I–you*, *here–there*, and *now–then* are established in a person's behavioral repertoire, they become an inherent property of most verbal events for that person. In other words, no matter what particular thing we say or do, we either explicitly (by actually using deictic cues) or implicitly (because we could use the cues if needed) say or do it within a deictic relational frame of reference. It should be said, of course, that the terms "I," "you," "here," "there," "now," and "then" themselves are not defining features of deictic relational framing. For example, one doesn't have to use *I* to be engaged in deictic framing of one's own behavior. One could also use *me* or *myself* or possibly one's own name. Similarly, *you*, as used to describe deictic framing, covers all cases of behavior enacted by someone other than me, including not just my interlocutor but also third parties who might be referred to, for example, as *he*, *she*, *it*, and so forth, as well as by names, possessive pronouns, or other ways of referring to the behavior of any such characters. In addition, the same applies to the other terms used to classify deictic framing. For example, instead of saying *here*, I might say *in this place* or give the name of my present location to any degree of specificity; instead of saying *now*, I might say *today* or *this week*. It is the functional pattern that is important, not the particular contextual cue (C_{rel}) terms employed at any particular time. *I, you, here, there, now,* and *then* are simply (arguably) among the least ambiguous and thus most useful terms for purposes of scientific communication.

In RFT, whenever an individual talks to another person, it is from the perspective of *I*, located *here* and *now*, and that perspective never changes, no matter what is being described. Thus, if the person is asked about aspects of his or her perspective itself, the person will always describe himself or herself in terms of *I*, *here*, and *now*. For example, if someone is asked about himself, he will reply with *I* or something equivalent (such as *me* or *myself*); if he is asked about his location, he will use *here* or something equivalent (such as *this place*); and if he is asked about the current time, he will use *now* or something equivalent (such as *the present moment*). In contrast, the way in which one frames what is being described can vary. Any particular event or person that one describes may be *here* or *there*, and it may be *now* or *then*; it depends on exactly what one is describing. For example, if the speaker is referring to another person at a shared location, then the speaker might say, "We are both here." But if the speaker is referring to someone at a different location, then the speaker might describe that person as *there* in contrast to *here*. If you start to talk to another person about something that happened to her or to someone else yesterday, then you will talk about what happened *then* as distinct from your (and your interlocutor's) perspective *now*. Thus, events that one talks about can be *here* or *there*, and they can be *now* or *then*, but one's perspective as one describes those events is always *here* and *now*. This leads to the development of the consistent locus or sense of perspective seen as a core feature of the human experience of self. This locus is experientially central, and, supplemented by hierarchical and metaphorical relational framing, it also can provide a conceptual vantage point from which to respond flexibly to one's own experience so as to facilitate psychologically healthy selfing. (These concepts are discussed in more detail in chapter 5 and later chapters.)

There is evidence that deictic relational framing shows increases in accuracy, fluency, and complexity from childhood to adulthood (see McHugh, Barnes-Holmes, & Barnes-Holmes, 2004). A number of follow-up studies have demonstrated that deictic frames can be trained in typically developing children (see Heagle & Rehfeldt, 2006; Weil, Hayes, & Capurro, 2011) as well as in children with autistic spectrum disorder (ASD; see Rehfeldt, Dillen, Ziomek, & Kowalchuk, 2007; Jackson, Mendoza, & Adams, 2014) and adolescents with Asperger's syndrome (Lovett & Rehfeldt, 2014).

Inaccurate Tacting of Internal Experiences

Children can develop a distinct and rich sense of themselves and their qualities and preferences when they are able to acquire both the capacity to accurately discriminate and label their own internal experiences and the capacity to compare and contrast their own behavior with that of others through the development of deictic relational framing. They then become able to reflect on, share, and learn more about these experiences, meanwhile learning more about who they are and what they value. In some cases, however, there may be deficits in one or both of these repertoires that will impede this development of selfing.

A number of different types of circumstances can lead to inadequate tacting of private experiences. Not unexpectedly, the most serious and long-lasting effects are produced by nonoptimal learning environments, but particular (dysfunctional) strategies for coping with unwanted private events may also produce such problems. In what follows, we consider four different circumstances that may give rise to these types of problems:

1. Dominance of pliance

2. Absence of emotional talk

3. Deliberate distortion

4. Avoidance

Dominance of Pliance

One situation that can lead to poor discrimination of internal experiences is growing up under the shadow of an authoritarian type of caregiver. This person's demands for compliance and provision of particular consequences that depend on compliance or its absence may shape behavior whose function is to please the caregiver. As a result, once the child grows up, his behavior and sense of who he is will probably be rooted in pleasing others rather than guided by his own experience. Many such people do not know much about themselves in terms of what their preferences are, what matters to them, or what they want to stand for. Instead, their lives have been guided predominantly by strong compliance with what others (such as parents, or representatives of religion or of society at large) want for them. They learn to predominantly reference *you* rather than *I* as a determinant of their preferences, wishes, and desires, and in this way they fail to contact their own experience as a guide. This is a type of rule following known as *pliance*.

Pliance, which we met in chapter 2, is defined as "rule-governed behavior under the control of apparent socially mediated consequences for a correspondence between the rule and relevant behavior" (Hayes, Zettle, & Rosenfarb, 1989, p. 203). If a parent tells a teenager to empty the dishwasher, and if the teenager does so because the parent has provided reinforcement in the past for complying with instructions—because, that is, there is a history of consequences for rule following per se, mediated by the verbal/social community—then this is an example of pliance.

In chapter 2, pliance-type rule following was contrasted with tracking-type rule following. Törneke (2010, p. 206) defines tracking as "rule-governed behavior under the control of the apparent correspondence between the rule and the way the world (environment) is arranged." For example, imagine that a teenager starts to empty the dishwasher in order to live in a clean house. In this case, she makes contact with the consequences of emptying the dishwasher and specifies the rule that emptying the dishwasher helps create a clean house. It is this rule that guides her behavior. She is following the rule because she has a history in which following that rule has worked to change her environment in helpful ways. In addition, the more her experience reflects the perception that rule following in general is helpful in particular contexts, the more likely she may be to follow rules in general in those contexts.

As we also saw in chapter 2, research suggests that once control is established on the basis of a rule, subsequent behavior is likely to be in accordance with that rule and is less likely to change when the contingencies specified by the rule change (see Kaufman et al., 1966). In such circumstances, behavior is said to be "insensitive" to the contingencies, and a frequent result is that the individual misses out on life-enhancing opportunities. This type of insensitivity can happen with either pliance or tracking, but it is particularly likely in the context of pliance, since this form of rule following is completely divorced from any kind of contact with the environment. For example, if someone is given the rule "Don't eat sushi, because if you eat raw fish you'll get sick" and then avoids eating sushi, the result is that he never gets to eat sushi and never experiences consequences that would inform him about the truth of whether sushi will make him sick. In this case, his behavior becomes relatively divorced from contact with the environment.

Children naturally engage in more pliance than adults do because children are still learning about the world and are under the direction of their caregivers. But moving from pliance to tracking is critical for the development of a healthy sense of self, and for the facilitation of meaningful life choices. As we grow out of childhood, rules provided by well-meaning others, such as parents or educators, may continue to be useful to us, but it is important that we follow a rule because of its current utility and not because of its source. In other words, it is important that we maintain flexibility and sensitivity regarding rules so as to best take advantage of their potential utility with respect to our goals.

Clients who have been limited by the influence of an overly authoritarian caregiver may find it difficult to track their own experiences and be guided by them. Instead, they may tend to navigate the world via excessive pliance. Clients for whom pliance dominates over the inclination to follow their own wishes and desires are sometimes described as people pleasers. They have negotiated their way around the world by playing a passive role in their relationships with others (such as parents, teachers, and partners) in order to keep those others happy.

In the applied context, clients presenting with a repertoire dominated by pliance will have trouble connecting their actions to any sense of meaning or purpose. When they describe their beliefs about why they do the things they do, those beliefs are likely to be inconsistent or no longer relevant. For example, a client may work excessively, causing problems with his family and his health, because of a belief (that is, a rule) that his worth depends on his ability to provide, and despite the fact that his children are grown and his family is financially sound. He is likely to express pointlessness or a sense of emptiness but will struggle when he attempts to make efforts in other directions because his experience of what is important to him (other than providing for his family) will be limited.

Individuals whose repertoire is dominated by pliance will be confused by questions like "What do you want from therapy?" or "What matters to you?" or "What goals do you have?" Nevertheless, they often do not admit confusion, and often they don't even seem confused. Instead, they are likely to respond with pliance-based rules about what they *should* want or try to achieve. For example, they may report strong opinions about changes they'd like to make as parents, with clear emphasis on what they believe they should do ("I should cook more often and be more attentive and keep a cleaner house") instead of on what they want to do.

Clients who struggle with problematic pliance may also respond to such questions by trying to seek the therapist's approval, particularly if they have strong regard for the practitioner. For example, such a client may report to the therapist that she feels more accepting or more present because she believes that this is what the therapist wants to hear. A client who engages overly in pliance should be guided in learning to track her environment so that she is behaving in line with consequences that are chosen and desirable for herself and not just in the service of following a rule as such.

Absence of Emotional Talk

Growing up in an environment in which emotions are rarely discussed can mean that a child has an impoverished emotional vocabulary and is unlikely to appropriately tact her own internal experiences. To some extent, Western culture on the whole promotes deficits in this area because we do not generally encourage talking about emotional experiences, particularly uncomfortable emotions. It is often seen as weak to succumb to certain emotions (such as shame, sadness, or guilt) and even rude or inappropriate to express them when they do arise.

Children who grow up in environments in which emotions are not discussed have a learning history that is less than adequate with respect to the labeling of their own emotions. Without feedback on his or her private experiences, a child will not learn to tact them accurately. This can result in the child's having trouble discriminating particular feelings from each other, or from the whole of his or her experience. For example, if caregivers never acknowledge when they themselves feel sad, or if they never reinforce the appropriate expression of sadness, then the child is unlikely to learn to discriminate sadness.

In the context of therapy, clients who have never been trained to use emotional talk may have trouble discriminating certain emotions. They may confuse more vulnerable emotions like sadness or fear with emotions that are generally seen as more acceptable to express. For example, expression of anger may be reinforced so reliably in childhood that any sort of uncomfortable feeling actually comes to be experienced as anger. Clients with deficits in emotional talk may present as *alexithymic*, or seeming to lack the skills to discriminate any feelings at all. They may report feeling numb and distant and not understanding other people's emotional expressions. They may express their feelings in terms of somatic complaints (for example, reporting a racing heart or an upset stomach instead of expressing anxiety).

When a client has difficulty discriminating emotions, the challenge to the therapist is to train the client to discriminate subtle shifts in emotion. In other words, the therapist provides the training opportunities that were not provided during the client's development. For example, the therapist can introduce brief in-session exercises that involve the client in contacting her current experience. The exercise that follows gets the client present to her current experience of her breath and to how blocking her breathing may change how she is feeling—a relatively nonchallenging fluctuation for the client to notice and acknowledge:

> *Therapist:* Close your eyes. Sit so that your back is away from the Cchair, or straight and upright. Gently become aware of your breathing. You don't need to try to control it. Just let your breath flow in and out, allowing yourself to notice how it feels. Observe your breath. Try to be with your breathing for one minute. If at some time you think that this is silly or boring, just notice that, and see if you can continue to sit there with the intention of noticing your breath. Now hold your nostrils closed with your thumb and your index finger, and notice what that feels like. Now let go of your nose, and notice if your sensation changes.

The therapist can build from simple examples of changing sensations (from being able to breathe to not being able to breathe) to emotions (shame, embarrassment, anxiety, and so forth) that are more difficult to discriminate or acknowledge. The therapist can use in-session exercises that require the client to label her internal experience during a session. For example, if the therapist notices the client looking down at the floor, the therapist might say, "I notice that you looked down at the floor. What is your experience in this moment?" Initially, the client may well find it tricky to identify her experiences. When this occurs, the therapist can ask the client to discriminate any physical sensations that she can notice, and eventually the therapist can help the client notice changes in her internal experiences not only during a session but also over time.

Deliberate Distortion

There are situations in which a child does receive emotional training, but the training is deliberately distorted or inaccurate. In some cases, a caregiver who believes that particular types of feelings are inappropriate may label those feelings "bad" or "wrong" when they arise in the child. For example, Martin's caregiver may believe that anxiety indicates weakness, and so she teaches Martin to ignore anxiety or express it as anger. Martin, as an adult, may be subject to inappropriate outbursts of anger as well as to interpersonal problems because he has learned to express anger anytime he feels anxious. Or Susan's caregiver, believing that homosexuality is disgusting, and recognizing Susan's disposition toward homosexuality, teaches Susan to experience disgust and shame when sexual urges come up. As an adult, Susan is likely to feel disgust toward any person or situation that arouses her sexual interest, and she may struggle with interpersonal closeness with other females, especially when there is a potential for sexual attraction.

In other cases, a caregiver may teach a child to be more sensitive to others' feelings and stated experiences than to the child's own. For example, Bethany's caregiver may differentially reinforce Bethany's responses according to how consistent they are with the caregiver's own feelings. Suppose the caregiver asks Bethany if she wants ice cream. Bethany may have already discovered the effectiveness of discriminating that her caregiver is the one who wants ice cream, and of giving an answer ("I'd love some, Mommy") that is consistent with the caregiver's feelings, since if Bethany were to express her own feelings ("Nah…I don't really feel like ice cream"), that expression would meet with disapproval ("Bethany, you never appreciate anything I try to do for you") or another aversive consequence. And so Bethany learns to discern her caregiver's desire and then experience and express that desire as her own. In some situations, the caregiver's feelings may be functionally important in terms of the child's ability to discriminate a whole class of types of behavior that will and won't be effective. For example, if Bethany's caregiver is physically abusive when in a low mood, then Bethany is likely to learn far more about discriminating her caregiver's feelings than about discriminating her own. As an adult, she is likely to struggle with healthy relationship boundaries, experiencing others' distress as her own and working to manage others' distress as if it were directly harmful to her.

An even more serious and potentially damaging type of distortion occurs when an adult intentionally mislabels an experience in an attempt to disarm a child for purposes of victimization. For example, Ben's football coach began sexually abusing him when Ben was about ten years old. Prior to the abuse, the coach had been effusive in his expression of love and admiration for Ben. As a result, Ben had felt proudest and most sure of himself when his coach was around, and so Ben had pursued the relationship. Once the abuse began, however, Ben's coach began withdrawing some of his affection, making it contingent on Ben's expressions of love and his compliance with the sex acts. For Ben, this deliberate mislabeling has resulted in a distortion of the meaning of his own reactions (for example, when he feels disgust, he labels it "love"). In cases like this one, there can be serious consequences with respect to the victim's subsequent psychological health. For instance, Ben, as an adult, will be likely to avoid typical relationships, in which the contingencies for acceptance and love are not explicit, and to express himself sexually (sometimes inappropriately) when emotional closeness comes up, and perhaps also to seek abusive relationships in which he will be able to allow domination in order to feel loved. When clients mislabel their emotional experience, the challenge to the therapist is not just to sensitize them to their emotions but also to train them explicitly in how to use bodily sensations and elements of a situation in order to label their emotions appropriately.

Avoidance

The examples discussed so far pertain mainly to childhood learning experiences (not exclusively, however, since these repertoires can need work in adults who have developmental delays). There are also conditions in which inaccurate tacting of internal experiences emerges later in life. Our emotional experiences are fundamentally important to our human experience. They color our existence, making our lives sometimes intensely pleasurable and sometimes immensely painful. We learn to tact certain emotions as positive and other emotions as negative, and we learn that we should pursue the emotions we regard as positive and try to avoid those that we regard as negative. Avoidance of negative emotional experiences seems particularly important in our society. Feelings like anxiety and sadness are seen as threats to our well-being, and we are bombarded with messages about how to be happy, as if feeling happy were the only means to having a more satisfying life.

Some people may adopt an avoidance strategy to deal with unwanted emotions. James, for example, a software engineer, was twenty-three years old when he began to suffer from social anxiety. He desperately wanted to get away from his anxiety because it was hampering his social life and causing him significant distress. Whenever his social anxiety peaked, James applied a suppression strategy to help him cope with it. He adopted a stance that involved responding to each of his internal experiences with an attitude that essentially said, "I don't care." This strategy seemed to work for him, since his social anxiety was significantly reduced before long. Therefore, James continued to approach life with this strategy. And when anxiety continued to show up for him in a number of social situations, he began to apply his strategy of shutting down his feelings in *all* social situations. He also had to apply this strategy to the emotions of others because acknowledging others' feelings made him very anxious (he thought, for example, that if other people were angry, their anger must have been caused by something he had done, and that if other people looked displeased, they must not like him, and so forth). As James continued with this strategy, his understanding of his own and others' internal experiences became weaker and weaker. Then, when James was thirty-three years old, his partner became ill, and James responded, as usual, with his "I don't care" strategy. His apparent lack of concern ended the relationship, and James could not understand what had happened—namely, that he had spent nearly a decade failing to acknowledge any of his own or others' emotions and, as a result, didn't have the repertoires that would have allowed him to respond sensitively to his partner when his partner got sick.

How to Teach Tacting of Internal Experiences

When individuals show impairments in the ability to interpret their own emotional states and the emotional states of others, the result can be impaired social behavior (LeBlanc et al., 2003). The inability to label (tact) private events has been linked to inappropriate behavior (Durand, 1993). Therefore, it is important to develop training procedures to remediate these difficulties. A child with ASD has limited ability to label emotions provoked by particular situations (Harris, Johnson, Hutton, Andrews, & Cooke, 1989). Testing for this repertoire involves presenting the child with a story and asking him to predict the emotional expression of a particular character on the basis of the character's circumstances. A number of studies have found that children with ASD, by comparison with their age-matched, typically developing counterparts, were less able to recognize emotional reactions in certain situations (Downs & Smith, 2004).

McHugh, Bobarnac, & Reed (2011), using corrective feedback, successfully trained children diagnosed with ASD to tact situation-based emotions ("happy," "sad," "angry," and "afraid"). These researchers' approach provided empirical evidence that tacting of internal repertoires can be trained in clients when such repertoires are deficient or absent. This work has been adapted as a game of tic-tac-toe and used with other individuals (typically children, adolescents, or adults with developmental delays) whose capacity to tact their internal experiences was deficient (see Gordon & Borushok, 2017). It involves facilitating the client's use of language to describe his or her internal experiences. For example, the therapist can show the client a piece of paper on which a simple drawing of a face expresses a simple feeling. Starting, say, with a "happy," smiling face, the therapist asks the client, "What feeling is this?" If the client responds correctly with the word "happy," then this correct response is reinforced; if the client responds incorrectly, then he or she is first given corrective feedback and then given a description of how the emotion in question might feel. After the therapist has described the emotion, the client is asked about a time when he or she felt that emotion: "When was a time you felt happy?" If the client still cannot answer, the therapist can provide an example of a relatable time when the therapist was happy: "I remember when I got an iPad for my birthday—I was happy then." The therapist can then build this out and draw a few different faces with different expressions on a sheet of paper. Then, in gamelike fashion, the therapist can select one of the faces, without telling the client which one (the client can take a turn doing the same with respect to the therapist), and describe an incident when he or she experienced this feeling, with the client guessing which face the therapist has selected. This game can be adapted to fit the client's age and context.

Training Verbally Advanced Individuals to Tact Their Emotions

When a verbally sophisticated individual has difficulty tacting internal experiences, the challenge to the practitioner is to get the client back in mindful contact with his or her current experiences. Exercises that involve contacting internal experiences at this point may be met with strong resistance because this will be unfamiliar territory for the client. Therefore, it is important that the practitioner take a slow pace to help orient the client to getting back into contact with his or her experiences. This will begin with simply starting to label external stimuli or sensory experiences that are easy for the client to identify. What is easy to identify will differ from client to client, of course.

Discriminating Sensory Experiences

Self-discrimination work may begin with teaching the labeling of elements of experience that are not particularly threatening—that is, sensory experiences. Clients will vary regarding which aspects of their sensory experience are appropriately innocuous for this purpose. A person struggling with issues related to body image may find it extremely difficult to attend to and notice her breath.

Similarly, a person with social anxiety may struggle with noticing other people in a crowded room. The individual who struggles with body image, however, may benefit greatly from an exercise in which she sits in the waiting room simply noticing the people around her—what they are wearing, how they hold their bodies, how they move, their facial expressions, and so forth. Likewise, the individual with social anxiety might benefit greatly from practicing sitting and noticing what it feels like to breathe—noticing the air around his nose or mouth, all the muscle movements that pull air in and push air out, the feeling of clothes shifting as the client inhales and exhales. Often the client, if given the opportunity, can explicitly assist the practitioner in creating exercises likely to be effective.

Another consideration involves the integration of two skills—discriminating and labeling. Early in this work, the therapist might simply have the client notice an experience while labeling it for the client: "Notice a place in your body where you feel warmth coming in with each breath." Later, however, the therapist might provide more vague instructions ("Notice if the temperature in your body changes or varies from one body part to the next") and might instruct the client explicitly to label the experience ("In one word, tell me what you notice now"). Eventually, the therapist will instruct the client to notice the sensory experience, to label that experience, and to notice labeling that experience: "With each new experience that enters your awareness, let one word come up to label it, and then move on once that label is applied."

The therapist might also begin building these capacities in very brief exercises lasting between two and five minutes, and supported by much guidance. Initially, this work may involve the therapist guiding the client's attention: "Take a moment now to notice how the muscles in your chest or belly move to pull air in." At-home practice can be facilitated with brief recordings posted on a website, sent via email, or provided on a thumb drive. The exercises may eventually be as long as twenty or thirty minutes, with the client guiding his or her own attention without instruction, both in the therapy session and at home.

Practice outside the therapy room is particularly important for generalization of these capacities but can be difficult to facilitate. Some clients do well with setting aside time to practice regularly with a recording or an unstructured exercise. Others struggle and may benefit from being assigned an exercise in which they use an existing daily activity as an opportunity to pay attention and notice their sensory experience. For example, a client might be assigned to notice the sensations in her hands every day when she washes the dishes. Another client might be assigned to attend to the green spaces he passes on his commute. There should also be some practice bringing these skills to bear in multiple contexts. For example, clients might set an alarm to alert them to notice and label their sensory experience at different points throughout the day. Early on, having a single assigned sensory experience to attend to (such as the way his feet feel, or the brightest bit of light in the room) may help the client be successful with this practice.

Discriminating and Labeling Emotions

Once a client has developed some skill in noticing and labeling sensory experiences (and, to some extent, noticing the process of labeling), the next step is to bring these skills to bear on more vulnerable experiences—emotions. This phase of self-discrimination work might be introduced with emotions that are easy to discriminate, and that the client is not likely to resist. Again, this will vary across clients. For one client, excitement may be an excellent place to start. For other clients, excitement may be too closely associated with anxiety and can be saved for later, after some foundational skills have been developed. Eventually, the therapist will want the client to be noticing and labeling the full range of emotions, from subtle to intense, including those that are sought and those that are unwanted.

As with sensory experiences, the therapist may initially provide more explicit instruction in structured exercises and then gradually withdraw this support. For example, initially the therapist may ask the client to talk about something that the therapist knows makes the client happy—for example, "How is your son Jack doing?"—and then have the client pause throughout his or her account, noticing different aspects of the experience of happiness. The therapist might say, for instance, "I noticed your face changing just then as you started talking about watching Jack play with the other kids. What was it that happened for you just now?" The therapist may then probe for increasing amounts of detail: "What shifts are you noticing in your movement?" or "Do you hear your voice changing as you speak?" Eventually the therapist may prompt the client to notice and express happiness or whatever other feeling he or she is experiencing: "I think I see some happiness coming up here. What do you notice?"

Advanced work may also involve having the client identify dynamic emotional experiences and their connection to the changing context. Here is an exercise that can be used in session to promote contact with the client's current emotional and sensory experience:

Therapist: Think about how you are feeling here and now (*pause*) really go there in your mind (*pause*) and, as you do, become aware of any changes in your body (*pause*). Do you notice any particular physical reactions in your body as you focus on here and now? (*pause*) If you do notice a particular reaction or feeling, become aware of it as a physical sensation (*pause*). Become aware of exactly where in your body you experience this feeling or sensation (*pause*). Imagine a spotlight shining on the sensation, helping you identify exactly where in your body it sits (*pause*). Even if the sensation or feeling is unpleasant, just notice it for a moment for what it actually is—a physical sensation, not something you have to get rid of or struggle with (*pause*) bringing some curiosity to your feeling or sensation, as if you haven't noticed it in this way before (*pause*). As you continue to think about your current feeling, imagine that your sensation or feeling is now a physical object that has popped out of you and is sitting there in front of you (*pause*). If this sensation or feeling were a physical object, what kind of shape would it take on? (*pause*) What would it look like? (*pause*) What color would your feeling object be? (*pause*) What kind of texture would your feeling or sensation have if it were an object? (*pause*) If the object could move, how fast do you think it could move? (*pause*) How heavy does it look? (*pause*) Just imagining, for a moment, this feeling or sensation, as if it had physical properties (*pause*) think about what this sensation or feeling would look like if you could step back from it (*slightly longer pause*). And now (*pause*) I'd like you to *welcome back* your feeling object, back inside your body, where it belongs (*pause*) just noticing any thoughts or emotions that show up for you as you're returning this object back inside yourself (*pause*) and once again spend a few moments identifying where in your body you experience this sensation (*pause*). Where is it in your body, exactly? (*pause*) What is it, exactly? (*pause*) Just experience your feeling as a physical sensation, nothing more and nothing less (*pause*) and imagine a spotlight pinpointing the feeling you are experiencing, helping you identify where it sits in your body (*pause*). And now, shift your awareness back to current sensations and the movement in your stomach as you breathe in and as you breathe out (*pause*) and then expand your field of awareness from the sensations in your stomach to the sensations throughout your entire body (*pause*) again developing a strong sense of your entire body in the present moment (*pause*). I'll bring the exercise to a close in a moment, but before I do, take a moment to congratulate yourself on taking the time today to practice being mindful of feeling and sensation (*pause*). And bringing your attention back into the room (*pause*) remember where in the room you are sitting (*pause*) and imagine what you will see when you open your eyes (*pause*). Whenever you feel ready, open your eyes, and stretch or do whatever feels natural for you (*pause*).

This "deepening contact with emotions and sensations" exercise allows the therapist to use whatever current experience the client has as an exemplar for labeling his or her current feelings and sensations. Such exercises can help clients accurately discriminate experiences that they may previously have been unable to tact or with which they may have been out of contact. Once the repertoire of discriminating internal experiences is in place, it will ideally be rehearsed on an ongoing basis, perhaps via formal and informal mindfulness practices, thus facilitating healthy selfing.

Acquiring Deictic Relational Responding

The other major repertoire needed for the development of selfing (the first being tacting of internal experiences) is deictic relational framing. Like tacting of internal experiences, a repertoire of deictic relational framing (perspective taking) is critical in acquiring a selfing repertoire. From the CBS point of view, deictic relating perspective taking is a key language-based skill that underpins the development of empathy, a sophisticated sense of self, and mindful awareness. As mentioned earlier, children learn to relate their own behavior as different from that of others by learning three key deictic or perspective relations:

1. *I* as opposed to *you*

2. *here* as opposed to *there*

3. *now* as opposed to *then*

They learn to respond appropriately to questions like "What are you doing here?" or "What am I doing now?" or "What was I doing then?" As children gradually learn to respond appropriately to these questions, they will also learn that whenever they are asked about their own behavior, they always answer from the point of view of *I*, *here*, and *now*, and they will learn that this perspective is consistent and different from that of other people. For example, if you ask me about my behavior, I will always answer from the position of *I*, *here*, and *now*. *I* is always from this perspective *here*, not from someone else's perspective *there*. A sense of perspective is therefore abstracted through the process of learning to talk about one's own perspective in relation to others' perspectives. Deictic relational responding allows one to describe experience as happening to *I* rather than to someone else (*you*). It also allows us to develop the sense of a continuous *I*, which is a consistent aspect of all our experiences, and which allows perspective taking on those experiences. This repertoire allows us to develop an increasingly sophisticated idea of who we are, what we enjoy, and what is important to us.

RFT studies have identified deficits in deictic relational responding among individuals with ASD (Rehfeldt & Barnes-Holmes, 2009), social anhedonia (Villatte, Monestès, McHugh, Freiza i Baqué, & Loas, 2008), schizophrenia (O'Neill & Weil, 2014), pathological altruism (Vilardaga & Hayes, 2011), and subclinical narcissism (Almada, 2016). Rehearsing deictic relational responding has been shown to enhance empathy toward an outgroup member (Vilardaga et al., 2009), and to reduce the fundamental attribution error (the predisposition to attribute someone else's behavior to the dispositional characteristics of that individual rather than to situational causes external to the individual) (Hooper, Erdogan, Keen, Lawton, & McHugh, 2015) in typical adults.

How might we go about remediating deictic deficits? This is a key question. A growing body of research suggests that it is possible to use multiple-exemplar training to train deictic relational responding skills. Studies have been successful in establishing these skills in typically developing children (Davlin, Rehfeldt, & Lovett, 2011; Heagle & Rehfeldt, 2006), individuals diagnosed with schizophrenia (O'Neill, 2012), an individual with Down syndrome (Montoya-Rodríguez, McHugh, & Molina, 2017), and children with ASD (see Weil et al., 2011; Jackson et al., 2014; Rehfeldt et al., 2007).

Training Deictic Relational Responding

Yvonne Barnes-Holmes (2001) developed a protocol for training the three deictic frames of *I–you*, *here–there*, and *now–then* across three levels of relational complexity:

1. A *simple* relational response

2. A *reversed* relational response

3. A *double reversed* relational response

Table 4.1 provides a schematic representation and examples of the repertoires targeted in the testing and training protocol (for a review of evidence in the area of deictic relational responding, see Montoya-Rodríguez, Molina, & McHugh, 2017). Historically, this protocol has been used in a discrete-trial format for learners with a narrower repertoire. Discrete-trial formats involve a method of teaching that uses simplified and structured steps. The skill, instead of being taught in one trial, is broken down and established with the use of trials that teach the steps one at a time. In training, deictic relational trials are standardized, with questions presented sequentially, correct responses prompted, other aspects of the environment highly controlled, and correct responding reinforced. This protocol can also be adapted to a more natural-language conversational type of format, for those who have the skills to benefit from it. For a full set of testing and training trials, see McHugh et al. (2004).

Guidelines for Training Deictic Relational Repertoires

Before deictic relational responding can be trained, certain skills need to be in place in an individual's repertoire. These include joint attention (and other forms of mutually responsive orientation), tacting, relations of coordination, and relations of distinction. The practitioner should test for these prerequisite skills and then specify whom *I* and *you* refer to. This can be made explicit in trials (for example, "I, the teacher, have the red brick; *you*, the student, have the blue brick"). Actual names can be inserted here, too. It is important from this point on to keep the perspective constant. For example, when the practitioner says *I* on a test item, this must always be a reference to the practitioner, and when the practitioner says *you*, this must always be a reference to the student. Constancy of perspective facilitates the correct abstraction of *I* as referring to the self and of *you* as referring to the other.

Table 4.1. Types of Deictic Relational Tasks

Relation type	I–you	Here–there	Now–then
Simple	I have a green brick and *you* have a red brick. What do *you* have?	I am *here* playing golf, and *you* are *there* swimming. What are *you* doing? What am *I* doing?	*Yesterday* I was reading. *Today* I am watching television. What was I doing *yesterday*? What am I doing *today*?
Reversed	I have a green brick and *you* have a red brick. If I were *you*, and *you* were *me*, what would I have? What would *you* have?	I am *here* playing golf and *you* are *there* swimming. If *here* were *there* and *there* were *here*, what would I be doing? What would *you* be doing?	*Yesterday* I was reading. *Today* I am watching television. If *today* were *yesterday* and *yesterday* were *today*, what would I be doing *today*? What would I be doing *yesterday*?
Double reversed	I am *here* playing golf and *you* are *there* swimming. If *here* were *there* and *there* were *here*, and if I were *you* and *you* were *me*, what would I be doing? What would *you* be doing?	I am *here* at the university and *you* are *there* at the coffee shop. If *here* were *there* and *there* were *here*, and if I were *you* and *you* were *me*, where would *you* be? Where would I be?	*Yesterday* I was reading. *Today* you are watching television. If *yesterday* (*then*) were *today* (*now*) and *today* (*now*) were *yesterday* (*then*), and if I were *you* and *you* were *me*, what would *you* be doing? What would *you* be doing?

The training sequence should go from simple to complex. With respect to relational frames, interpersonal *I–you* should be trained first, followed by spatial relations (*here–there*) and then temporal relations (*now–then*). This order is based on the fact that interpersonal relations are the key foundation of perspective taking itself; as for the remaining relations, temporal relations are more complex than spatial relations because temporal relations involve a more abstract discrimination that is relatively more difficult to demonstrate and learn. Levels of complexity should progress from simple relations on to *I–you*, *here–there*, and *now–then* reversed relations and then on to *I–you/here–there* double reversed relations and *here–there/now–then* double reversed relations.

To aid the learner, physical prompts can be incorporated and then gradually withdrawn. Prompts may include pointing to *I* (the teacher) and *you* (the student), using items (such as a red brick and a green brick) for what *I* have as opposed to what *you* have, and using objects (such as a table and a chair) to represent where *I* and *you* may be. Prompts for temporal relations may include pictures (of the zoo, for example, or of someone sitting at a table and working) showing activities performed at one time or another (*today* or *yesterday*). They may also involve actual sequences of activities in which the client is prompted to take part during the session (for example, clapping *right now* versus pointing *a minute ago*). The mastery criterion for progression to training of the next relation or level of complexity should be set to at least six consecutive correct answers produced without additional prompts. Before the practitioner moves on to more complex tasks or new relation types, he or she should always ensure that generalization to novel sets has been tested. For example, if a child has been trained on *here–there* spatial relations, with *I* sitting on a chair of one color and *you* sitting on a chair of another color, then other locations (such as *at the beach* or *in the office*) should also be probed, to test the child's flexibility and ability to generalize in responding beyond the trained items. Traditionally, deictic relations have been trained with the use of tabletop procedures, but a more recent development is software applications that provide interactive cartoons. The more interactive the tasks, the more likely they are to keep the learner engaged.

Training Deictic Fluency When the Basic Repertoires Are in Place

Even when deictic relational repertoires are in place, an individual may still benefit from deictic relational training by becoming more flexible with respect to awareness of self and others. For example, think about someone you know who is having a difficult time. Take a few moments right now to imagine that you are this person. Where would you be? What would you be feeling? What would you be thinking? What might you need? As you do this, you may notice yourself experiencing a broader awareness of the other person's perspective. This exercise can also be applied to taking perspective on our own experience. Many mindfulness and acceptance exercises involve engaging in deictic relational framing of our own experience. For example, *I here now* notice that I am having the feeling of mild anxiety, the thought *I hope I don't make a mistake*, and the sensation of tingling in my fingers. Indeed, various therapeutic exercises across a number of different therapeutic approaches actively promote flexible deictic relational responding (see table 4.2).

Table 4.2. Examples of Therapeutic Exercises from Different Therapeutic Traditions That Involve Deictic Relational Responding

Exercise	Approach
Imagine yourself ten years from now, reflecting on your life. What would you like to see?	Acceptance and commitment therapy
If you were your best self, what would you do now?	Positive psychology
What would you advise your best friend to do if he were feeling the way you feel right now?	Cognitive therapy
What is your wise mind telling you right now?	Dialectical behavior therapy
If you were the most compassionate person you know, what would you say to a person who's feeling the way you are feeling right now?	Compassion-focused therapy

| Chair work | Emotion-focused therapy (Gestalt) |

Adapted from M. Villatte, *A Manifesto for Clinical RFT*, Keynote address presented at the 10th conference of the Association of Contextual Behavioral Science, Australia and New Zealand chapter (ANZ ACBS), Melbourne, November 2016. Used with permission.

In a study on social judgments, Hooper et al. (2015) demonstrated that accurate responding to items included in a deictic relational responding task was associated with significant reduction in the incidence of the fundamental attribution error. Participants in the study were not directly required to take the perspective of the individuals about whom they were making social judgments; rather, the participants were responding to trials that involved rehearsing reversed and double reversed deictic relational tasks such as the ones shown in table 4.1. It appears, then, that simply engaging in complex levels of deictic relational responding can change a key pattern of interpersonal perspective taking in someone who already has the appropriate repertoires in place. Moreover, shifting a client's interpersonal perspective is something that therapists across a number of traditions have been doing for many years (refer again to table 4.2).

As we've seen, the acquisition of a healthy sense of self depends on an optimal developmental environment as well as on the repertoires of discriminating internal experiences and engaging in deictic relational responding. With these two basic selfing repertoires in place, the individual is in a position to acquire additional, more complex selfing repertoires.

CHAPTER 5

The Three Selfing Repertoires

In previous chapters, we introduced relational frame theory (RFT) as the core of the contextual behavioral science (CBS) approach to language or verbal behavior. We examined the basic theoretical and empirical foundations of the RFT approach to the self as verbal responding to one's own responding. We considered the acquisition of repertoires of self-discrimination and perspective taking. In this chapter, we discuss the CBS conceptualization of the relatively fully developed verbal self, focusing on three emergent selfing repertoires. The core idea is that as humans learn to relationally frame about the world, including ourselves and our environment, these three separate repertoires of selfing—or, in more conventional phraseology, these three senses of self—are acquired, and thereafter they play a psychologically central role in our lives. This chapter describes these three repertoires in some detail.

The Three Selfing Repertoires

In the previous chapter, we described the acquisition of perspective taking or deictic relations (*I–you, here–there, now–then*). RFT suggests that the acquisition of perspective taking—in combination with an extensive relational repertoire involving multiple different types of relations (in other words, an extensive linguistic repertoire)—contributes to establishing three functionally different selfing repertoires, or senses of self (Hayes, 1995):

1. *Self-as-content:* the conceptualized self, or self as the content of verbal relations

2. *Self-as-process:* the knowing self, or self as an ongoing process of verbal relations

3. *Self-as-context:* the observing self, or self as the context of verbal relations

In what follows, we will discuss these three repertoires.

Self-as-Content (the Conceptualized Self)

Self-as-content, or the conceptualized self, consists of elaborate descriptive and evaluative relational networks that people construct over time about themselves and their histories. As soon as verbal humans become self-aware, we begin to interpret, explain, evaluate, predict, and rationalize our behavior. Coherence is a powerful reinforcer, and incoherence is a powerful punisher, and so we strive to organize our descriptions and evaluations of our personal histories and tendencies into a coherent network—a consistent presentation of a self that generally persists across time and situations. For example, Tom might describe himself as a generous person, basing this self-description both on a noticeable pattern in his behavior over time, whereby he frequently gives money, time, or assistance to other people, and on feedback and praise from other people who have noticed the same pattern in Tom's behavior. This self-description, which he may sometimes use when he is thinking about himself or describing himself to others, is a coherent network in that it groups together functionally similar instances of behavior consistent with the concept of generosity as Tom has learned it. Acts that may not fit in this category, or that may at least be ambiguous (as when he fails to donate to an arguably deserving charity when he is solicited by a street volunteer), may be interpreted by Tom in such a way as to fit in with the self-concept of generosity ("I've already given to several other charities; even generous people have their limits") and avoid a perceived inconsistency.

The conceptualized self is a well-elaborated relational network, one that includes every verbally known aspect of life and integrates one's knowledge of one's current and historical feelings, sensations, preferences, abilities, thoughts, interactions, and learning. In fact, this network includes the entirety of one's conscious experiences. It's also multilayered, since contingencies support different depths of self-knowledge in different contexts. For example, someone might explain a given instance of behavior to her boss very differently from the way she would explain it to her therapist. In addition, on the basis of differences in her history with different individuals (friends, family members, work colleagues), she may present herself or even think of herself very differently.

Consider Cliona, who has many different relationships and experiences of different people across different contexts. She's a loving, devoted mother who goes out of her way to make time for playing and interacting with her two children, and she does her best to be as empathetic and understanding with them as possible. She divorced the children's father after discovering that he was having an affair. She loved her ex-husband and felt deeply betrayed at the time of the divorce, and she still feels resentment when she talks to him. At the same time, she has surprised herself with how she's coped and managed to get on with her life, including getting back into the dating scene. She recently started seeing someone new, and this is exciting. Despite having more experience and maturity now, she feels somewhat the way she did in high school, when she first started dating. She loves both her parents, but she has a different relationship with each of them and is much closer to her mother, in whom she has always found it easy to confide, whereas with her father she is a dutiful and respectful daughter. She is also close to her older sister, who always protected her at school, and Cliona continues to look up to her sister; they're both adults, but Cliona still feels like the little sister. Her friends from school always saw Cliona as a bit of a joker; she's laid back with them and enjoys getting back into "joker" mode when they meet. At work she's a midlevel manager, and the people who report to her see her as hardworking and strict but also fair. Meanwhile, she has worked hard to show her bosses that she's professional and ambitious; recently, her years of hard work paid off in a promotion. Thus Cliona has many different relationships and many different experiences of different people across different contexts. In these different contexts she fills different roles—(loving and devoted) mother, (betrayed) ex-wife, (loving and respectful) daughter, (little) sister, (comic-relief-providing) friend, (strict) manager, (hardworking) employee—and she has quite different experiences of self (self content repertoires) based on these roles. Some of these roles are more intimate and rooted in deep emotional connections (her roles with close family members, for example), whereas other roles involve relative shallowness and less connection with others (such as her roles with her boss and her direct reports).

In trying to understand conceptualized selfing at a functional level, one theoretical system we can draw on is the multidimensional multilevel (MDML) framework, introduced in chapter 2. Recall that the MDML framework analyzes relational framing along four dimensions:

1. Derivation
2. Coherence
3. Complexity
4. Flexibility

We've already noted that the conceptualized self repertoire is high in complexity, given the extent of relational networking involved, and the fact that we reveal differing depths of selfing knowledge across different circumstances. It has also been suggested that the conceptualized self repertoire is generally well elaborated, meaning that it is well practiced and thus would typically be low in derivation. For example, many of the ways in which we might describe ourselves (generous, outgoing, conservative, and so forth) are well-established, well-practiced patterns of framing. Of course, this varies according to the content. Whereas Tom, whom we met earlier, has thought of himself as generous for many years, only within the last few months has he begun to describe himself as a bit overweight, perhaps since he started noticing differences in his body's shape. In addition, we continue to learn new things about ourselves. Nevertheless, many if not most such things tend to be assimilated into already well-established relational networks, and thus to extend or elaborate those networks. Mary, for instance, may learn that she likes a new band, and this is obviously a new thing she finds out about herself, but her liking this new band is probably consistent with older and better-established relational patterns, such as her knowing that she likes particular genres of music and music in general.

The self-concept may also be described as having relatively high coherence. Coherence tends to be correlated with derivation, at least to the extent that low derivation (whereby a pattern of relational framing is well practiced) predicts high coherence (because multiple exposures to the same pattern will strongly establish that pattern). Thus, core patterns of selfing are low in derivation and will also seem highly coherent. Coherence with respect to relational framing in general is reinforced from an early age by the social environment, whereas incoherence is punished, and so coherence becomes a strongly conditioned reinforcer. Therefore, we work to maintain coherence for our selfing networks, and any information that appears to contradict such well-established patterns may be resisted, distorted, or denied rather than accepted, lest change in those networks be forced. The rigid pursuit of coherence in this way can ultimately become problematic and undermine psychological health.

The issue of flexibility with respect to self content is particularly important and is at the heart of the psychological struggle of many individuals who seek therapy. Self content involves descriptions of behavior at varying levels of abstraction and complexity, both of which not only result from but also facilitate navigation of the socioverbal world—and, indeed, such content is inevitable and ubiquitous for humans raised in a typical socioverbal environment (recall the example of Cliona). But one aspect of this selfing activity that should be noted is that we rarely attend to the process of describing as it happens in the present moment—we rarely attend, in other words, to the fact that this process is itself an act of relational framing. Engaging in self-as-process undermines the typical pattern of transformation of functions and facilitates a wider array of responses than does simply acting in accordance with the literal content of the description. As such, engaging in self-as-process enables flexibility with respect to the relational framing involved.

Let's take a closer look. If, on the one hand, a person has the thought *I'm worthless* and responds to it as an objectively true description, then this makes it more likely that there will be particular, logically coherent emotional and behavioral transformations of function (such as feeling bad or avoiding company, respectively). This represents inflexibility. If, on the other hand, the person responds to this thought as simply a relational act, then emotional and behavioral consequences such as those just suggested are less likely, and so the person's behavioral options are less restricted. This represents a more flexible response. Inflexibility with respect to many of our self-descriptions (especially relatively mild or positive descriptions, such as "I'm standoffish" or "I'm generous," respectively) can be innocuous much of the time. But inflexibility regarding our self content can result, to varying degrees, in dysfunctional or maladaptive behavioral outcomes (such as experiential avoidance). This is especially the case with respect to negative self-descriptions like "I am worthless" and even more so if such self-descriptions occur with relative frequency. In the contextual behavioral–based psychotherapy known as acceptance and commitment therapy (Wilson, Hayes, Biglan, & Embry, 2014), this phenomenon is referred to as *cognitive fusion* and is seen as a major causal element in behavioral problems ranging from nonclinical interpersonal and intrapersonal challenges right up to full-blown psychopathology.

In addition, the topic of flexibility with respect to self-as-content overlaps in an important way with another key topic for selfing: values. Acceptance and commitment therapy views explicitly stated overarching values as particularly important in guiding a psychologically healthy and vital pattern of selfing. Values in this sense are described as the highest points of a hierarchical relational network (which is part of one's network of self content), serving to guide aspirations and goals, which in turn motivate particular patterns of behavior directed toward achievement of those aspirations and goals.

For example, if a person values intellectual stimulation, then she might aspire to a certain type of career (say, working as a researcher), engage in particular hobbies (such as reading or learning a second language), and look for a partner who also values intellectual stimulation and perhaps shares her intellectual interests. Each of these aims or goals might be considered a supporting node in the hierarchical relational network of the value of intellectual stimulation. Furthermore, each of these aims or goals might in turn be supported by certain activities; that is, attaining a position as a researcher might involve this person's getting into one or more good universities, working to obtain several degrees (including a PhD), building up a network of research contacts in her area, applying for positions, and so forth. Thus, the overarching value at the top of the hierarchy transforms the functions of those activities lower down that help her work toward that value so as to make the activities more reinforcing.

An important point is that this type of hierarchical relational network is how RFT conceptualizes values—as a type of self content. Hence, in an important sense, values can be considered under the rubric "selfing-as-content." Like other types of self content, however, values should ultimately be rooted in accurate discrimination of one's own ongoing experience, especially one's likes and dislikes. This is in contrast with values that, for instance, might be received or imposed from outside. One example is caregivers' imposition of the value of a particular career on their child, who then internalizes the idea of that career as something that he personally values when in fact it was imposed from elsewhere. For example, John loves sports and yearns to become a professional athlete, but he convinces himself that he wants to become a lawyer because this is what his father wants him to do. Acting in accordance with an imposed value like this one, while ignoring or not fully exploring one's own personal preferences, constitutes a pattern of inflexibility. Instead, ideally, a person would base his values, as much as possible, on his ongoing personal experience of what is fulfilling to him (for John, this might be his love of physical activity and his athletic skill) and subsequently choose to act in accordance with these experience-rooted values (by becoming a professional athlete, for example, despite parental disapproval). Thus, flexibility is essential for healthy valuing. Values as self content need to be rooted in personal historical experience and preferences, and valuing can become inflexible if it is cut off from such experience and preferences.

Self-as-Process (the Knowing Self)

Self-as-process, or the knowing self, is the repertoire that supports ongoing verbal discrimination of our behavior as it occurs in the moment. Statements that reflect the self as a process of knowing, or ongoing awareness, typically begin with phrases such as "I feel...," "I think...," "I wonder...," and so forth. Chapter 4 discussed the emergence and initial training of this capacity, which provides the wellspring for the entire adult selfing repertoire. The knowing self feeds the conceptualized self; that is, in order for a person to know that she is "a depressed person," she must first know that she frequently feels sad and has low energy across many contexts. In addition, as we will see later, the knowing self plays a key role in supporting the third sense of self—self-as-context (the observing self)—because a self-monitoring repertoire is critically important for this.

Self-as-process occurs in the context of the repertoire of self-as-content, and so it is easy for us to slip from self-as-process into self-as-content. For instance, when Tania verbally discriminates her sadness while watching a film, she may also think of herself as someone who cries during films or is emotional in general. Thus her verbal discrimination of an experience may itself immediately be co-opted into a relatively well derived, complex, coherent network. Indeed, given the pull toward coherence that characterizes all relational framing, this will certainly happen, at least to some extent. The more consistent (and thus better practiced) we are in verbally discriminating our ongoing behavior, the less likely this is to happen. Sessions of deliberately temporally extended practice in self-as-process (which might be categorized as a species of mindfulness exercise) might be particularly helpful. Beginners may find it difficult to maintain such activity for an extended period, but, over time, those who continue to practice relatively regularly will strengthen the operant skill of verbally discriminating their current behavior. A well-practiced repertoire facilitating extended selfing-as-process makes it less likely that we will slip into inflexible self-as-content during deliberate practice of this skill as well as more generally.

Using the MDML framework to analyze self-as-process, we might say that this responding tends to be relatively higher in terms of derivation than self-as-content, and relatively lower in terms of level of complexity and coherence. It tends to be relatively higher in terms of derivation because experiences in the moment are new and can sometimes be quite different from previous experiences in certain aspects. For example, Tania may feel sad when she watches a particular scene in a film, and she may think about and categorize this experience in a particular way. Her current sadness is similar to other moments of sadness but is also unique. It's something felt and labeled with respect to a particular on-screen moment involving a particular character and a particular actor. Maybe she finds the soundtrack uniquely moving, or perhaps the leading actress reminds her of a friend of hers. Hence, particular experiences that Tania may label in the current moment are similar to previous experiences but are also unique, and so characterizing such experiences is generally higher in derivation than responding in accordance with (generally well-rehearsed) self content.

Complexity may be relatively lower in self-as-process than in self-as-content because self-as-process is generally focused more on particular or specific experiences and less on extensive overarching concepts. Self-as-process also seems relatively lower in coherence, both because things in the moment are new and because they are particular. Both of these features would seem to push against coherence, at least to some degree, because coherence pertains to elements already embedded in a relational network, and new or particular phenomena are less coherent, by definition, because they have yet to be categorized or classed. Finally, self-as-process would also seem to lend itself to higher flexibility because engaging in self-as-process is already a reflexive type of response involving the verbal discrimination of previous verbal responding (for example, one has the thought *I am anxious*), and so verbally discriminating a self-as-process response itself (such as "I just had the thought that I just had the thought *I am anxious*") is in the same functional category.

Having described the characteristics of self-as-process in this way, we must remember that we are describing it in comparison with self-as-content, and not in some absolute way. Therefore, we are not suggesting that self-as-process is high in derivation, low in complexity, low in coherence, and high in flexibility, but only that it will probably tend to be so in comparison with self-as-content. According to the particular situation, self-as-process, just like the other selfing patterns, will vary in levels of each of these dimensions.

The self-as-process repertoire is extremely useful in behavioral regulation, both for the socioverbal community and for the individual. With respect to the socioverbal community, the self-as-process repertoire allows members of the community who have no knowledge of a person's learning history to predict that person's behavior. For example, if an individual says that she feels anger toward someone else, then this may allow other people to predict how she might act toward that person in particular contexts. Self-as-process is also a critical guide for the individual herself. In order to respond effectively to her own responding, she must first be aware of the response and its impact. For example, the capacity to understand and respond fluidly and flexibly to her thoughts and feelings about other people's behavior is critical in the context of establishing and maintaining personal relationships.

Self rules would also be much less effective without self-as-process. From the RFT perspective, self rules are an important topic because verbal humans probably produce vast numbers of self-directed rules that guide daily behavior. Some of these self-directed rules are simple and trivial ("I should take a left turn at the shop"), whereas others are complex and profound ("I must do something meaningful with my life"), but the effect of self-directed rules is undoubtedly significant. To a great extent, the production of useful self-directed rules for living relies on accurate selfing-as-process. This is because we need to be aware of how we feel about particular situations, and aware of the likely results of particular actions we might take in those situations, in order to develop appropriate rules to guide us. For example, we need to be able to discriminate our responses to particular types of activities (say, discriminating that we like being with people and dislike being by ourselves) in order to develop useful rules regarding what kind of career we might prefer ("I want a job involving people"). Of course, even when we can discriminate our reactions well, the rules we develop may not be useful. Thus, the rules we develop with respect to feelings of anxiety in an important situation, such as a job interview, may be relatively useful ("anticipate and accept such feelings as they arise while continuing to perform as needed"), or they may be disadvantageous ("avoid such feelings at all costs, even by avoiding situations where they typically arise, if possible"). In this case, connecting with values may be useful: "Even though I feel anxious during interviews, I should persevere because I really want the job."

Self-as-process is also of central importance with respect to values. Earlier, we suggested that awareness of current experience is foundational for flexible, psychologically healthy valuing. As also suggested earlier, a person's values may sometimes be based on sources other than his or her own experience (caregivers' taught values, for example, or received social wisdom) and thereafter adopted as his or her own. As indicated, however, such received or impersonalized values may not cohere perfectly with one's own personal experience or one's perspective on oneself. Ideally, values should be based on ongoing experiential contact with one's own responding, and it is in this way that the consistent practice of self-as-process is of fundamental importance for healthy valuing.

In chapter 4 we explored threats to the development of the self-as-process repertoire. These include inadequate training by the verbal community, as when one's awareness and expression of emotions, thoughts, and sensations are punished, ignored, denied, or contradicted. This is frequently observed in the case of child neglect or abuse. A neglected child may not learn to accurately describe the sets of emotions and sensations he experiences as "hunger" or "boredom" or "fatigue" if there is no one to ask him questions and teach him to label these experiences in a way that allows him and others to respond to these experiences effectively. Similarly, a child who experiences pain and fear at the hands of a parent and is told, "Mommy loves you and would never do anything to hurt you" may not learn to accurately predict or describe her psychological experience.

Weak self-knowledge may also be the result of experiential avoidance, or the tendency to avoid or escape difficult psychological events even when doing so results in negative consequences. As a result of transfer of function through bidirectional relations, self-knowledge regarding aversive events is itself aversive, which means that humans cannot always avoid or escape pain by avoiding or escaping from the situation in which the pain was actually encountered. Since we can't escape our own psychological experience, we often attempt instead to avoid awareness of the experience. Chronic experiential avoidance of this nature results in difficulty observing and describing one's thoughts, emotions, and sensations (as in alexithymia, anhedonia, and amotivation), a difficulty that is characteristic of such psychological disorders as depression, post-traumatic stress disorder, and borderline personality disorder, with obvious implications for the self. Other difficulties linked to deficits in the self-as-process repertoire include an inability to persist in or change focus (attention disorders, obsessive self-focus leading to phobic anxiety); the dominance of a conceptualized past and future, whereby the present moment is lost to worry and rumination (anxiety and depression); and the dominance of framing events involving judgments that have affective relevance for the self (narcissism, depression, anxiety, personality disorders). We will look at some of these conditions in more detail in later chapters.

Self-as-Context (the Observing Self)

At its core, the repertoire of self-as-context pertains to a critical pattern that characterizes deictic relational framing, which is that someone engaged in such framing is always responding from a perspective of *I–here–now*. In this sense, self-as-context can be understood as the abstracted invariant in all self-discriminations. Because it is an abstraction from the content of verbal responding (or, more specifically, deictic relational responding), it is free of content and thus constant and unchanging from the time it first emerges. It is a product of verbal responding; yet, as a verbal category that applies to everything a person has ever done, it incorporates both the nonverbal self (the behavioral stream resulting from direct psychological processes) and the verbal self (as both object and process of knowledge gained through relational framing). Thus, self-as-context has been described as providing the experiential link between nonverbal and verbal self-knowledge.

Self-as-context in this narrow sense—as pure perspective—has sometimes been referred to as the *transcendent self* because it is difficult to describe or contact verbally, even though it is a product of relational framing. One's perspective cannot be experienced as an object, because experiencing it would necessitate adopting a perspective on it that is not one's own, and this is impossible. As such, one's perspective is not thinglike and thus can be described as limitless, unchanging, and ever present; therefore, it is linked with spiritual and religious concepts and experiences. Direct experience of one's own perspective is impossible. Nevertheless, aspects of the "contentlessness" of perspective taking per se can be approached through meditative practices, which are indeed often explicitly promoted in some religious and spiritual traditions. For example, exercises that involve consistent ongoing verbal discrimination of one's own relational framing (a type of selfing-as-process) can create a context in which transformation of function is greatly reduced, and in this context the sense of perspective taking per se, as the invariant background to all such behavior, may be amplified.

Transcendental experiences such as might be achieved through meditation can be therapeutic and potentially even transformative in certain circumstances. Such experiences are potentially important and psychologically beneficial, but they represent only one potential outcome of self-as-context, broadly conceived as the verbally produced experience of having a perspective. According to Steven Hayes (discussion on the electronic mailing list of the Association for Contextual Behavioral Science, 2011), self-as-context involves "the coming together and flexible social extension of a cluster of deictic relations (especially I/Here/Now) that enable observation and description from a perspective of point of view" that facilitates as outcomes "many different experiences, including theory of mind, empathy, compassion, acceptance, defusion, and a transcendent sense of self." In this sense, self-as-context subsumes the entire process and experience of relationally framing one's own experiences as distinct from those of others. The core of this repertoire is the verbally produced experience of perspective taking. Different outcomes, such as those just listed, can be facilitated via different patterns of (typically metaphorical) relational framing. These are brought to bear in such a way as to transform the functions of the perspective-taking experience itself as well as other elements of one's environment and behavior. For example, outcomes such as acceptance (of negative private experience), defusion (from linguistic influence), and transcendence (of typical experience) are supported via metaphorical framing of an observer as the container for, or at least as separate from, one's own private behavior (such as feelings, thoughts) and thus one is free to respond in various ways to this behavior (that is, framing it in this way facilitates behavioral flexibility). As suggested, the use of such metaphorical framing helps transform the functions of one's behavior and environment in potentially helpful ways. Self-as-context exercises of this kind can also play a central role in the applied arena, as we will see in later chapters.

At the core of self-as-context in the sense just described is hierarchical framing. This framing involves relating elements (parts or members) to a unity of those elements (the whole or a class). In the case of the self, the elements are all the things one does (thinking, feeling, and so forth), while one's perspective provides the consistent context for their unity in the self. In this sense, engaging with selfing-as-context involves hierarchically framing one's activities as contained within the overarching context of *I*. Framing my behavior in this way can transform the functions both of the behavior and of the self or *I* that subsumes it. Doing so allows me a sense of my behavior as simultaneously both linked to me and separable from me. As such, I can accept or own any aspect of my behavior or experience, even a seemingly negative or aversive aspect, and thus acknowledge and learn from it while also seeing that no aspect of my behavior or experience defines me, and that my choices are not limited or constrained by any aspect of my behavior or experience. Framing my behavior in this way confers a flexibility that is particularly important for psychological health.

Self-as-context in the broad sense is so all-encompassing and diverse that it varies along all four dimensions of the MDML framework. Meanwhile, self-as-context in its narrower sense is an unusual repertoire, and so it can be argued that using the four MDML dimensions with self-as-context is less appropriate than using the MDML dimensions with other, more conventional repertoires. Nevertheless, if the MDML dimensions are applied, we can see this repertoire as low in derivation (because it has been practiced so often), low in complexity (because even though it is abstracted from complexity, the phenomenon itself is a simple one), and high in coherence (because it's highly predictable). Finally, this repertoire can be viewed as highly inflexible because one cannot disengage or step back from this experience. The last point may seem surprising because, as suggested earlier, the observer self can be viewed as supporting psychological flexibility. It is indeed true that engaging a sense of self as pure perspective can help facilitate behavioral flexibility with respect to other behavioral repertoires (such as self-as-content), but it may be suggested that the response of self-as-perspective itself is inflexible, since one cannot, by definition, take perspective on this response itself.

Self-as-context, especially in the narrower sense of pure perspective, has important implications for how humans experience and regulate psychological pain because this sense of self is not threatened by aversive content in the way that the conceptualized self or the knowing self can be. This selfing repertoire allows a person to confront deep emotional pain, and it facilitates willingness, compassion, and intimacy. If I am experiencing particularly aversive emotional responding, perhaps in the context of a diagnosis like anxiety or depression, then I will probably find it helpful to cultivate my sense of self as pure perspective so as to facilitate separation from my own negative framing, thus undermining the typical patterns of transformation of function that accompany such framing. Conversely, a weak self-as-context repertoire results in a variety of social and psychological problems, including an unstable identity or sense of self (as seen in borderline personality disorder and the dissociative disorders), fear of annihilation in the face of aversive private experiences, difficulties with intimacy or trouble connecting with others, social anhedonia, stigmatization or objectification of others, and lack of empathy and self-compassion.

The Three Selfing Repertoires and Other Perspectives

The three different selfing repertoires, or senses of self, that have been described so far characterize the verbal adult repertoire. These three repertoires are logical conceptual extensions of the empirically supported RFT analysis of selfing. As such, they can facilitate new, pragmatically oriented insights into this key domain. The use of these concepts to explore psychological suffering and psychotherapy will be the subject of some of the ensuing chapters of this book.

Meantime, in the concluding section of the current chapter, we will briefly explore how these concepts compare with approaches to self within alternative psychological approaches.

The conceptualized self (self-as-content) can be seen as corresponding to the "me" or "empirical self" of James (1981), to the self-concept of humanistic psychology (Rogers, 1961), to the self schemas of mainstream cognitivist psychology, and to the narrative self of Gallagher (2000) and Dennett (1991). In addition, the suggestion that psychological problems can result when the conceptualized self becomes rigid and guides behavior in unhelpful ways has important similarities to the humanistic concept of incongruence, whereby the self-concept diverges from the "true" self and causes psychological maladjustment. In contrast with humanistic and other approaches, however, the approach described here offers functional analytic explanations of the early origins of self, and of self-related psychological maladjustment in adulthood, that can facilitate research and intervention to a unique degree.

Many religious and psychotherapeutic traditions seem to emphasize the importance of self-as-process (the knowing self) in the name of openness, sensitivity, or wholeness. One of the aims of a therapeutic relationship, for example, is to help clients get in touch with their feelings or, in RFT terms, to establish framing with respect to emotional terms that coordinate more generally with those operating in the wider verbal community. This emphasis on the knowing self was originally confined to the humanistic psychology movement, but it is now also recognized as important in other psychological approaches, both therapeutic (cognitive behavioral therapy) and nontherapeutic (industrial and organizational psychology).

Evidence from neuroscience supports the distinction between self-as-content and self-as-process. For example, Farb et al. (2007) found evidence for two neurally distinct but habitually integrated forms of self-reference. These researchers describe the narrative (conceptualized) self—which integrates experiences across time (*now–then*) and place (*here–there*) from a single perspective (*I*)—as a higher-order mode of self-reference that may be overlearned and made automatic through practice. Meanwhile, they found the "experiential" self (self-as-process), derived from neural markers of transient body states, to be a more basic mode of momentary self-reference characterized by neural changes that support awareness of the psychological present.

A core aspect of self-as-context is the capacity to take perspective on one's own selfing processes; hence, one corresponding concept is the cognitive psychological concept of metacognition, or executive functioning. Both concepts have been linked in turn with mindfulness meditation (Teper, Segal, & Inzlicht, 2013). There is a growing body of empirical evidence, both at the level of basic science (Farb et al., 2007) and at the level of practitioner research (Miller, Fletcher, & Kabat-Zinn, 1995), showing that mindfulness meditation is a practice that can promote psychological health and provide the basis for increased insight into one's own psychological processes. From our perspective, simple mindfulness meditation exercises, in which one focuses on one's own breathing or experiences of the environment, involve self-as-process responding (see Foody, Barnes-Holmes, & Barnes-Holmes, 2012). This strengthens the operant behavior of taking perspective on one's own behavior as well as weakening the functional context for cognitive fusion (that is, as mentioned earlier, dominance of transformation of function through relational frames leading to dysfunctional outcomes). It does so with the kinds of ongoing thoughts that might otherwise simply become part of the increasingly expansive self-as-content relational network. Both of these processes probably increase the generalized repertoire of perspective taking involved in self-as-context.

As mentioned earlier, one outcome of self-as-context is self-transcendence, relevant to spiritual and religious experience. A related concept in psychology is the peak experience (Maslow, 1964), described in humanistic and transpersonal psychology, and characterized by those to whom it happens as mystical, revelatory, and personally illuminating. Humanistic psychological perspectives describe an increase in the frequency and quality of such experiences as an important characteristic of self-actualization (Maslow, 1964). In addition, proponents of transpersonal psychology (such as Wilber, 1997) have advocated the deliberate exploration of such experiences to enable continuing psychological development. As suggested earlier, such experiences can be interpreted in the RFT/CBS approach as temporary amplifications of pure perspective taking itself, in the context of the reduction of typical levels of transformation of function. Thus, the nature and origins of a peak experience are explained in terms of processes of perspective taking that are themselves forms of relational learning. In this way, the RFT/CBS approach can provide a bottom-up understanding of peak experiences and other forms of revelatory insight that is supported by an empirical program of research. This kind of specification is arguably unique to the RFT/CBS approach and can facilitate further research into and refinement of our understanding of these experiences as well as, more generally, the domains of mindfulness and self-as-context with which they are associated.

Perhaps the most important, novel, and unique aspect of the RFT/CBS approach to selfing described over the last several chapters is that—in accordance with the approach's underlying philosophical assumptions, and through the advance of concepts like the MDML framework—the approach can specify variables that facilitate prediction and influence over the development of appropriate self-descriptive behavior. Examples of such variables include contextual cues for relational responding (coordinate, deictic, and analogical) and (typically social) reinforcement for accurate self-description at different levels of the development of self (as in discrimination of self from environment, discrimination of self from other, and discrimination of content from context).

This pragmatically oriented feature of the approach means that it readily facilitates interventions that have to do with self-related problems, whether these involve delayed development of self and perspective taking in autistic populations, for example, or self-related psychotherapeutic problems. It also allows ongoing research to refine theory and thus yield improved interventions. For example, there has already been a considerable amount of empirical work on perspective-taking frames with respect to assessment and training of the basic frames in young children (see Rehfeldt et al., 2007; Weil, Hayes, & Capurro, 2011) and with respect to investigations into therapeutically relevant patterns of behavior, such as empathy in adults (see Vilardaga, 2009). Therefore, in view of the RFT/CBS approach's pragmatic orientation, the remaining chapters describe the uses of the approach in understanding and treating psychological suffering.

CHAPTER 6

Self Content Issues

In chapter 5 we discussed important senses of self that characterize the typical selfing repertoire. The first and, arguably, most common and easily understood of them is self-as-content. This sense of self includes descriptions and labels as well as stories or narratives about who we are. Of course, as suggested especially by the discussion in chapter 5 about the other two senses of self, we are more than the descriptions and labels that we subscribe to (or that are ascribed to us), and we are more than the stories we tell about ourselves. At times, however, we can focus so rigidly on certain labels and descriptions (especially negative ones, such as "depressed," "obese," or "alcoholic"), or get so caught up in our stories, that we can forget that we are more than these stories.

A number of phenomena can contribute to our getting stuck on or entangled in our self content in this way. To begin with, three separable but interrelated phenomena—*coherence*, *literality*, and *rule following*—which are involved in complex human language (that is, relational framing) can contribute to problems, especially if we are unaware of them. These are features of language use in general. But there are four additional phenomena—*inappropriate ideals*, *inaccurate rules*, *simplistic labels*, and *assignation of roles*—that are not so much features of language use as products of the human socioverbal community. Although the latter four phenomena are in addition to the three features of language mentioned earlier, they interact with those three features so as both to be supported by them and to amplify them.

Properties of Language

Coherence

As discussed in chapter 2, the multidimensional multilevel (MDML) framework sees coherence as a key dimension of language. The language community teaches us that our relational framing should be internally coherent, or noncontradictory. As a result, coherence itself becomes automatically reinforcing and a central feature of our languaging about ourselves and the world. Of course, there are good reasons why the community teaches us to be coherent in our relational framing. With coherence, we as individuals and as a society can organize our environment and our own behavior, which can greatly facilitate effective interaction with our world. At the same time, we should be aware that the pursuit of coherence can sometimes be misguided. Because of the powerful conditioned reinforcement value of coherence, we can end up seeking coherence in limited contexts, to the neglect of coherent responding in overarching and potentially more important contexts.

For example, imagine that Alan buys a new software program but is finding it difficult to use. He may remember previous occasions when he also had trouble using new software, and so he may conclude that he has difficulty with software and even that, more generally, he's not very bright. This conclusion would be consistent with empirical evidence concerning this particular strand of his experience, and perhaps it would also tally with an article he once read, whose author suggested that people who are bright are able to use software with relative ease. In light of that notion, Alan's conclusion would be relatively coherent in that it would be aligned with these two converging strands of evidence. In reaching this conclusion, however, Alan would have focused on a limited number of facts. Perhaps he temporarily forgot certain things that are true in the more extended relational network to which he potentially has access, such as the fact that he is a talented writer and that several of his colleagues and friends have praised his writing. If Alan were to add this information into the mix, and if he were to reach a coherent conclusion based on a consequently larger dataset, his conclusion that he is not very bright would probably have to be revised. Given this expanded information, his revised conclusion might be that even though he is more talented in some areas than in others, overall he is quite bright.

This is a relatively simple example, offered solely to illustrate the concept of coherence in a limited context, and to show how expanding the context can change the conclusion. Coherence is a critical aspect of language, and it is powerfully useful in solving problems, but coherence is still always a function of a particular context, and so the pursuit of coherence in and of itself, without sufficient awareness of context, may be misguided.

Coherence, as we've seen, is highly reinforcing, and lack of coherence is punishing. This fact applies to the self as verbally created, just as it does to other verbal contexts. Indeed, given the central place of the self in our verbal worlds—for example, an individual describing his own experience typically uses the words "I" and "me"—coherence tends to become even more important in the context of the self than in other contexts. Therefore, when I (as subject) want to describe and evaluate myself, I want to create a logical and consistent sense of who I am.

For another example of how coherence in a limited context can be unhelpful, imagine someone who makes impulsive decisions. Maybe she has a habit of buying expensive items that she cannot afford, or taking recreational drugs despite negative outcomes. Imagine as well that she notices this behavior as a problematic pattern. Perhaps from this behavior she derives the rule *I am impulsive* and wonders why she is this way. She may then begin reading about impulsivity and, on the basis of what she has read, deriving reasons for why she is impulsive. She may conclude, for example, that her parents were overly strict, and that once she got to make her own decisions, she wasn't very good at pacing herself. Alternatively, she may infer that she was born with a temperament that predisposed her to impulsivity. Or perhaps she derives the idea that her condition is based on some kind of interaction between her upbringing and her temperament. These or other reasons that she comes across or formulates can begin to function as a coherent explanation for her problematic pattern of behavior. As a result, she can now justify her impulsive behavior by the nature of her upbringing, her temperament, or some combination of the two. She need not feel so bad about her behavior, because, after all, behaving in this way is her unavoidable destiny, given her background. In addition, her deriving the self label "impulsive" can become powerfully reinforcing in and of itself because it provides verbal validation of her having achieved a coherent understanding of her situation. In this way, the feature of coherence can help her explain her behavior, and it feels good to her to be "correct."

But a problem arises with respect to the possibility of her actually changing her impulsive pattern of behavior. Remember, she has already noticed that her behavior is problematic, and so she may want to change it. And yet she can't change how her parents were when she was younger, and she can't change her temperament, so how can she reduce her impulsive behavior in the future? Again, she can't change the past, and so she may just conclude that her impulsivity is unavoidable. In this way, she uses her (unchangeable) past to explain and justify her future unhelpful patterns of behavior, and this justification in turn can make such behavior more likely.

Again, all derived coherence is derived from a particular context, and so when one steps outside that context, more helpful alternatives may begin to appear. Even someone whose history predisposes her to impulsivity can take steps to minimize or eliminate unhelpful habits. But the apparent coherence achieved in a relatively limited context can make doing anything at all about one's situation seem all the more difficult. Thus, the pursuit of coherence in such a context makes it less likely that one will be able to break out of a destructive pattern of behavior.

Coherence seeking can happen even when a label is very strongly negative—for example, "unlovable." Even in a case such as this, the reinforcement value of coherence means that a person may seek out confirmatory evidence and coherent explanations regarding the label. For instance, someone could look to all his past failed relationships, instances of rejection, and ways in which his relationships with his family are lacking and see all these things as confirmatory evidence that he is unlovable. This apparent evidence can come to influence his future behavior. He may select partners who are abusive, perhaps in order to compensate for his lack of lovability, instead of selecting them in accordance with his core values. Buying into verbal content to an excessive and potentially problematic degree is referred to within CBS as *fusion with content*. If a selection is made on the basis of fusion with the rule *I am unlovable*, rather than on the basis of what matters to him, he may actively select away from something important (such as an equal, honest, and intimate partnership). In addition, this type of move will also be self-reinforcing (that is, it will embody a self-fulfilling prediction) because the relationship will be less likely to work if it is chosen on this basis, and so the conclusion *I am unlovable* will be supported by yet further evidence.

In addition, although it seems obvious that misguided coherence may be problematic when it involves obviously negative self content (*I am selfish* or *I am a failure*), it can also be so with ostensibly positive self content (*I am smart* or *I am hardworking*). For example, maintaining coherence with the belief *I am hardworking* may mean putting in longer hours than other people do, including evenings and weekends, and thus sacrificing time that could have been devoted to more genuinely valued activities.

The pursuit of coherence in limited contexts can be self-limiting and stultifying. Seeking coherence with our self content (labels, evaluations, and judgments, for example) in a limited context can trap us in ways that influence us to behave as though our self content were all of who we are rather than just a part of who we are. This can result in self-related problems. To counteract this process, we need to be able to be aware of the ways in which the pursuit of coherence in a limited context can be problematic. The pursuit of coherence in a more functional way, in a context of values, can promote a healthy selfing repertoire. In moving toward this more functional agenda, we need to question rather than accept absolutes in our thinking, especially when it comes to making important decisions about our future and what may help us achieve our goals. For example, in the case of the person carrying the label of impulsivity, it is important that she see this as simply a label that she uses for herself. The label may make sense in many ways, but there are many additional variables that can affect her behavior and her future; no single explanation is or can be the be-all and end-all. Viewing "impulsive" as a label rather than who she is will make it less likely for her to get stuck in a trap created by her verbal behavior (that is, the behavior of using the label "impulsive" to describe herself as all that she is, can be, and will be).

Literality

Literality is another very central and ubiquitous aspect of language. This is the extent to which verbal descriptions of the world appear to represent the way things are in themselves rather than simply being descriptions. In other words, literality is the extent to which a linguistic description appears as truth. From an RFT point of view, this is based on contextual control over relational framing and the extent to which particular contexts facilitate transformation of function through relational frames. Many typical linguistic contexts (sometimes called *contexts of literality*) allow extensive transformation of function so that our behavior tightly conforms to the description involved. In other contexts, however (for example, contexts in which we become aware of language itself as a process), there is much less extensive transformation of function, and our behavior may not conform to the verbal description.

Like coherence, literality is a product of language training and, to a degree at least, it is important to the proper functioning and utility of language. If we constantly questioned the truth of our verbal descriptions in every situation, then language would not exert control over our behavior with respect to our environment, and thus it would not have the power to guide and orient us and allow us to get things done. But even though literality in some situations is useful, literality in all situations is not. The latter scenario would mean that we could never stand back and become aware of language as a behavioral process and become aware of when and how this process can blind us to important contingencies. As such, the issue of relevance, in this case, is what has been referred to in the MDML framework and elsewhere as *flexibility*. Much of the time in life, high levels of transformation of function are useful and welcome, in everything from following a cake recipe to reading a novel, but not always (as when one buys into negative or limiting self-descriptions). Ultimately, flexibility with regard to language use, in terms of this dimension, is the capacity to engage and disengage with language as a process so as to maximize pursuit of one's valued objectives.

Fusion with content, self-related or otherwise, can be thought of as strongly and consistently buying into that content without taking any perspective on the process of thinking. For example, Jane has been struggling with her weight her whole life. She is forty-two years old and desperately wants to get married and start a family. She is fused with the thought *I'm unlovable*, and she buys into that thought completely. She treats that thought and all the additional derivations to which it is related (*I'm unattractive, I'm a bad person, I'm weak, I'm unreliable, I'm unworthy of being loved*) as real and true. As a consequence of buying into derivations such as these, Jane also experiences associated painful emotions (regret, sadness, shame, and so forth). In addition, certain patterns of her overt behavior are increased. She avoids going out, dating, and going for a promotion (or doing anything in which she is visible), and she engages in comfort eating. In other words, when she holds what she perceives to be a negative thought (such as *I'm unlovable*) as true, she is likely to think, feel, and act in accordance with the content of that thought. In the language of RFT, we say that a high level of transformation of function occurs.

Also, as explained in the case of coherence, it's not just negative self content that presents problems. When we hold any self content (positive or negative) as true in this way, it can create problems. For example, the thoughts *I am unlovable* and *I am the best* are not true descriptions of who we are; rather, they are evaluations about who we are, even if we believe them to be true. Fusion with such content on an ongoing basis undermines our ability to be flexible with respect to our situation.

One other issue to consider with respect to literality is its relationship with coherence. There are important similarities as well as differences between these concepts. Both are ubiquitous and powerfully influential aspects of language, and they are also likely to be strongly correlated. This is because experiencing high levels of coherence in one's beliefs is likely to support belief in their truth, while a stronger belief in literal truth will probably underline the importance of seeking coherence in one's understanding of reality. At the same time, there is also at least one important difference: literality, although it is useful in amplifying the effect of language, is not strictly necessary in order for language to function. This is obvious from the fact that worldviews such as contextualism, for example, eschew literality for a pragmatic perspective on truth. In contrast, coherence is arguably essential to the functioning of language. Without some minimal level of coherence, language would become nonfunctional. Of course, pursuit of coherence in a limited context can lead a person astray, but ultimately coherence must be achieved in some context. In CBS, striving for so-called functional coherence is an important aspect of psychologically healthy selfing.

Rule Following

As we saw in chapter 2, a rule describes relations among events and can influence the behavior of people who understand it. Society can give us rules, and we can also derive rules ourselves. Rules can be accurate and helpful or inaccurate and not so helpful. When accurate, they are significantly and extensively useful. When they are inaccurate, but for particular reasons we choose to follow them anyway, this can cause problems for us.

A stereotypical example of a rule is *Don't walk on the grass*, as seen in a park, or the *No diving* sign found at the swimming pool. A person encountering such a rule may follow it (by not walking on the grass in the park, or by not diving into the shallow end of the pool)—nothing new or surprising there. But CBS broadens the concept of rule following in important respects and explains in detail how and why rules affect us.

In CBS, the term "rule" covers much more than stereotypical rules. Instead, the term "rule" means any sort of potentially behavior-regulating relational network. For example, a contingency like *If I just stop feeling sad, my depression will go away* can be a rule (that is, an "if-then" rule), just as a self-description like *I have attention deficit disorder* can function as a rule. Although these sorts of relational networks don't look like stereotypical rules, they can still regulate or influence behavior (hence the term "rule," since it functions to rule or regulate behavior). In other words, we can pay attention to rules and modify our behavior to be consistent with them, typically without even seeing that this is what is happening. In the case of the person with the rule *If I just stop feeling sad, my depression will go away*, she may act in accordance with this rule by trying to do things that will remove her feelings of sadness (and thus her depression), such as drinking alcohol, distracting herself, or seeking reassurance from others. In the case of attention deficit disorder, this is a label that someone may start to use for himself only after having received this diagnosis. Categorizing himself in this way, he may now begin to act in accordance with this diagnosis. He may label himself in this way when he meets new people, or he may derive the notion that there is something wrong with him or that he is different from others. Imagine that before this diagnosis, he thought of himself as spontaneous. This repertoire of behavior may have been one that worked well in many social situations. After the diagnosis, however, this individual may view that aspect of himself as part of what is wrong with him, and he may try to stop being spontaneous, despite the fact that spontaneity is a repertoire that has worked well for him in many situations. (As an aside, the fact that CBS defines rule following as behavioral control via a relational network means that this phenomenon, like both coherence and literality, may also be approached via the MDML framework. By contrast with coherence and literality, however, rule following is not a dimension of the MDML framework; instead, rules as relational networks fall within the ambit of one of the key levels of this framework.)

CBS also highlights the effects of rules. These effects can be either positive or negative. Rules can be tremendously useful by allowing us to adapt to or change our environment in helpful ways. At the same time, rules can lead us astray by making our behavior insensitive to contingencies, and by promoting the maintenance of maladaptive patterns of behavior. For example, the person whose rule specifies that she should change her feelings (that is, stop feeling sad) may try to do things (such as drinking) that remove her feelings of sadness and that seem to work in the short term but that undermine or remove longer-term opportunities (by damaging her health or longevity, or by negatively affecting her relationships or career prospects). As for the person with attention deficit disorder, his belief that there is something wrong with him may prompt him to formulate a further rule, such as *I am unworthy of love*. He may then begin to avoid other people. Once again, this avoidance may remove important opportunities for him to experience life in a more vital and enriching way.

In both cases, the person rigidly follows the rule rather than staying in contact with direct experience and thus perhaps producing a different outcome. In the case of the person who is sad, rule following leads to avoidance of the direct experience of her feelings, despite the damage this avoidance does with respect to living a meaningful life. In the case of the person with attention deficit disorder, rigid following of a rule leads to avoidance of the direct experience of interacting with others, an experience important to his growth and development as well as to his having a rich experience of the world. To counteract the maladaptive effects of rules in particular contexts, CBS aims to reduce the influence of rules in those contexts, thus bringing people back into greater contact with direct experience and facilitating the possibility of more values-based action instead.

Socioverbal Community Issues

Apart from the phenomena just described, which are aspects of complex language, there are also four phenomena that contribute to rigidity of self content and that are features of the behavior of the socioverbal community rather than of language per se:

1. Society holds up certain ideals that we can conform to.

2. Society gives us inaccurate rules regarding our psychology.

3. Society assigns and encourages labels.

4. Society organizes roles, deliberately and otherwise, for us, and to which we conform.

These four phenomena combine with the features of language described earlier to facilitate rigidity of the self-concept. In what follows, we describe these phenomena and illustrate them with examples, including examples of how they are exacerbated by the properties of language already discussed.

Society Holds Up Inappropriate Ideals

Society (in the form of caregivers, family, friends, peers, community, authorities, and so forth) can exhort us to uphold certain ideals, and we may then strive to do so, even though this may not always be useful or psychologically healthy. Carl Rogers often talked about how parents or other caregivers provide conditional positive regard to children, meaning that they offer children positive regard only if the children conform to certain ideas that the parents and caregivers hold up as appropriate. Perhaps parents want their child to take after them with respect to particular interests or attitudes. Alternatively, a child may be taught that he should aspire to be a good or upstanding person, as defined in a particular religious tradition. In cases such as the latter, the parents may make their wishes explicit through verbal exhortations, whereas in other cases they may make their wishes known through more subtle feedback, perhaps without even being fully aware themselves of their own behavior or its effects. In any case, the child may see particular behavior as a model to be adopted and followed as closely as possible. The child may subsequently evaluate himself as good only to the extent that he adheres to this model; conversely, he may see himself as bad to the extent that he deviates from the model.

Society Can Teach Us Inaccurate Rules

As noted earlier, rules can be accurate and useful, but they can also be inaccurate and thus distract or undermine us. One such problematic rule, deeply rooted in our culture, is that feelings cause behavior. One example of a subtype of this rule is that one must feel confident before taking on a difficult task; another is that feelings of anxiety can stop a person from performing well or even performing at all. Rules like these can affect our behavior in such a way that when we feel certain types of emotion (such as sadness or anxiety), we may believe ourselves unable to engage in particular types of behavior (such as performing well in a presentation). We may make decisions accordingly (for example, deciding to avoid an upcoming event in which we may have to make a presentation), even though such decisions may affect us adversely. Everyone experiences negative emotions like sadness and anxiety, and so, in this sense, everyone can be adversely affected by this kind of inaccurate rule. Things are even worse, though, for someone who experiences such emotions regularly. In that case, the person may be even more likely to make decisions that may narrow rather than open up opportunities in life. In addition, the person may be more inclined to judge himself—a person who experiences negative emotions more frequently than others—as being generally incapable.

Society Assigns and Encourages Overly Simplistic Labels

Since 2010, in a social experiment called the *What I Be Project*, the photographer Steve Rosenfield has been asking people from the general public to write down their deepest and darkest insecurities (see http://whatibeproject.com). Participants' insecurities have included self-evaluations related to body image, substance abuse, mental illness, race, and sexuality. The self-identified labels are written in bold black letters on a participant's arms, chest, or face, and then the participant is photographed with the label prominently shown. Each image serves as an empowering statement against being reduced to one's insecurities, fears, and negative labels. The project does not function to deny the labels that the participants may have given themselves or inherited from others; instead, it suggests that people should accept every tender and dark part of themselves. The physicalization of insecurity in Rosenfield's images works to illustrate that who we are, and who we can be, is more diverse and dynamic than the thing we like least about ourselves. In this way, Rosenfield's project suggests that we are not just our labels. Culturally, we recognize how constricted our world can become when we are pigeonholed by ourselves or others as mediocre, unlovable, stupid, and so forth. Attachment to labels can be problematic and can exacerbate self-loathing and shame, and so this project's focus on exploring the vast edges of self is significant. For example, one young participant wrote "mental" across her forehead in heavy black ink. "Mental" may have been the story in light of which everything else in her life made sense. "Mental" may have been the rule that guided her life. "Mental" may have been her identity, the only role she was allowed to play. As we know from our own work as practitioners, a label like "mental" can have a devastating impact on someone's relationship to herself and others. If all she can see of herself is colored and narrowed through the lens of the term "mental," then "mental" can devour her life whole; that is, her behavior can become rigidly consistent with the story told by the label "mental." Other parts of her, parts that are dynamic and complex—her fondness for sarcastic jokes, her meticulous care of her garden, her compassion toward her grandmother—can be eclipsed by "mental"; that is, her capacity to engage more fully with life can be limited. Rosenfield's photography project thus illustrates the problem of labels and points to their powerful nature. Labels can be extremely constricting in terms of the way we see ourselves and the decisions we make. We are more than the labels we ascribe to ourselves. At times, though, we can focus so rigidly on certain labels or descriptions (such as "depressed," "obese," or "homeless") that we forget that we are more than labels and descriptions. Attachment to labels can be limiting and may lead to self-related problems.

Society Organizes Us into Roles

Society organizes people into roles, both formally (with the assignment of roles like manager, police officer, teacher, pupil, supervisor, soldier, husband, or wife) and informally (with the acquisition of roles like clever student, passive housewife, hardworking husband, hypersexualized girlfriend, or domestic goddess). This kind of organization can be socially useful; and, in the case of formally assigned roles, it is often necessary for the functioning of society. Nevertheless, a particular role may be not be the most appropriate one for a particular individual, and yet that individual can be pressured to conform anyway.

A role can provide a certain level of stability with respect to the sense of self. Consistency in a role makes us more predictable. But a role can be limiting. Many roles are what might be considered stereotypes—they're useful at times, but they can tend to box people in. That is, a person can become inflexible in her relational framing as it concerns what a particular role suggests she should be. For example, the role of domestic goddess can put extreme pressure on a woman to achieve difficult if not unachievable standards (such as a perfectly clean house and perfectly well-behaved children), and it can set up unrealistic expectations on the part of men looking for female partners.

Certain idealized roles can be seen in mass media. The movie *The Stepford Wives* examines the idea of the model wife who plays her role perfectly. The perfect wives in the movie—submissive and domesticated—turn out to be robots. This suggests, among other things, the artificiality and narrowness of roles such as this one. In addition, and of particular importance, it suggests how the human self can be lost in the adoption of a role. The roles we adopt or with which we identify are very much products of the culture we inhabit. To take another example, Western society stresses the importance of participation in a monogamous relationship, and those who are single may be categorized in certain ways, with age and gender adding key dimensions, so that a single person can be variously classed as a player, a slut, or an old maid. And in the case of two celebrity marriages, and as a reflection of how single men and single women are branded by the media in particular and by Western society more generally, the movie star George Clooney is said to have been tamed by marriage, whereas Jennifer Aniston is said to have been saved (Freeman, 2014). Moreover, the greater the number of the characteristics that determine a role, the more appropriate that role can seem for those who have those characteristics (thus if I am a single, middle-aged woman actively looking for a relationship, I must be a cougar).

Although certain aspects of idealized roles may be functional (for example, by establishing expectations for what kind of mother I want to be), stereotyped roles taken literally can override our own experience as a guide to how we want to be and behave. Imagine a twenty-nine-year-old woman who feels that she is viewed as occupying the role of the tragic single woman, despite the fact that she actually feels satisfied and enjoys many fulfilling relationships. She may begin to disregard her feelings of satisfaction if the discrepancy between how she actually feels and how she is supposed to feel leads her to think that there is something wrong with how she is feeling, and to pursue a relationship she does not want. Indeed, clients caught up in inauthentic, limiting roles lack contact with their internal experience, just as they lack perspective on their situation, and they view their conceptualizations of themselves as true.

The alternative to adopting a role is to accept ourselves as we are, in the here and now, in all our complexity and nuance. Rather than trying to distort our "self" by fitting into a role so as to follow an ideal that is an oversimplification, we can accept our complex, multifaceted sense of ourselves. Once again, awareness of how language works, combined with flexible responding as it concerns our own languaging, can facilitate this kind of outcome.

CHAPTER 7

Toward Healthy Selfing

Jim lost his job as an accountant one week ago. As he peeps out from the curtain in his living room, he feels a sense of loss of the independent and self-sufficient man he was before he lost his job. He is ashamed of who he is now and of anyone finding out he has not left his house for the past week, since hearing the news. He has avoided phone calls and just texts people to keep them off his back and prevent them from finding out the truth. He is disgusted that this is how his life is. He feels hopeless and cannot see a way forward. He believes that he is a loser and that nobody will want to employ a loser. He is scared to spend his severance package, in case he doesn't get a new job. He notices a neighbor, Billy, walking down the street, and he closes the curtain so as not to be seen.

* * *

Jim lost his job as an accountant one week ago. He is out for a run because fitness is something he cares about, and he can spend more time running now that he is temporarily unemployed. Losing his job has raised thoughts of being a loser and feelings of shame. Jim allows these thoughts and feelings to arise and also notices that these are just experiences that will come and go. As he connects to where he wants to take his life, he notices that accountancy was really only a means of paying the bills, and that he would actually prefer to have a more social job. He feels scared and yet hopeful about moving in that direction. As he runs down the road, he bumps into his neighbor, Billy. He stops and talks to Billy, telling him about his recent job loss. Billy is supportive and suggests that Jim have dinner with him later in the week. Jim agrees to meet Billy later in the week and notices that friendship is something that is important to him. As Jim continues on his run, he notices himself having negative thoughts about his job loss but continues to run anyway.

In these two examples, we start Jim off from the same point (losing his job), but then we imagine how he may cope with this event, given two very different selfing repertoires. In the first example, his repertoire is narrow and rigidly attached to his conceptualized self, whereas in the second one it's broad, flexible, and values-focused. It is likely that all practitioners reading this chapter can identify that Jim's relationship with himself in the first scenario is problematic. What can a practitioner do to help foster the kind of broad and flexible selfing repertoire seen in the second scenario? Answering this question is the focus of this chapter, which aims to help readers apply theory and concepts from the earlier chapters as a means of promoting flexible (healthy) selfing.

Before considering the contextual behavioral science (CBS) concept of healthy selfing, let's start by revisiting the CBS conception of selfing. According to Hayes, Barnes-Holmes, and Roche (2001), "Self is not simply behaving with regard to [one's] behavior but is behaving verbally with regard to [one's] behavior." This definition allows the concept of selfing to include a very wide array of possibilities, from the relatively simple (a young child verbally discriminating his likes and dislikes from those of others) to the relatively complex (a verbally sophisticated adult making an important life-changing decision in accordance with an extensive selfing repertoire that includes selfing-as-content, selfing-as-process, and selfing-as-context).

As we've seen in previous chapters, there can be deficits even in an otherwise relatively verbally advanced individual's selfing repertoire, such as the inability to tact internal experiences (not being able to discriminate different emotions) as well as weak or absent deictic (*I–you, here–there, now–then*) relational responding. These are serious deficits that require training as remediation to allow development of a more typically comprehensive selfing repertoire. Even given the development of the latter, however, there are of course serious issues that still need to be addressed (such as low self-esteem and persistent self-criticism). Aspects of language itself, as well as of the typical socioverbal environment in which the average selfing repertoire is acquired, allow the emergence of such issues. It's in the context of a repertoire such as this—that is, a more typically comprehensive selfing repertoire—that the question of establishing processes of healthy, flexible selfing becomes particularly relevant.

Healthy Selfing

From the CBS point of view, healthy or flexible selfing essentially involves consistent practice of a combination of selfing-as-process and selfing-as-context, facilitating minimal inflexible relational framing with respect to self-as-content and maximizing values-concordant behavior. All three selfing repertoires (self-as-content, self-as-process, and self-as-context) are involved in a typical verbally able adult's repertoire of self. Self-as-process involves verbally discriminating (labeling) ongoing experience (for example, "Right now I feel anxiety"). On the basis of self-as-process activity over time, and in conjunction with relational framing of our behavior by others, an increasingly complex network of self content will be derived, including descriptions, labels, and rules that summarize and organize (coordinately and hierarchically frame) previous experience. For example, John feels anxious often, and in various situations. He has noticed that he seems to feel more anxiety than some of his friends. His best friend, Marty, teases John about being easily scared. John has derived the concept that he is an anxious person and thinks of himself in that way. The derivation of such content is inevitable and, indeed, important for purposes of understanding, communication, and self-guidance. But how we relate to that content is critically important in determining our psychological health. To the extent that we rigidly coordinate ourselves with elements of content, we will operate on the basis of self-as-content, which is psychologically stultifying and limiting. The key way in which we can minimize doing so is by consistently and frequently engaging in a combination of selfing-as-process and selfing-as-context. Self-as-context is the locus from which one engages in all selfing activity, and to the extent that we verbally engage with this aspect of our experience, it can be transformative. In terms of relational frame theory (RFT), engaging with selfing-as-context involves hierarchically framing one's selfing activity as contained in the overarching context of *I*. This activity, sometimes referred to in more casual terms as taking the *observer perspective*, facilitates appropriate contextual control over the relational framing of one's ongoing experiences (selfing-as-process) so as to guide one's behavior in maximally beneficial ways with respect to the achievement of one's values.

In discussing further the concept of flexible selfing as maximal engagement in the combination of selfing-as-process and selfing-as-context, let's examine each element, as well as their interactions, in a bit more detail. Self-as-process involves relationally framing current experiences. Such activity need not be done consistently or on an ongoing basis. But the more consistently one does engage in this activity, and the greater its extent, especially where that engagement is deliberately and flexibly applied, the more one can be described as being mindfully aware, and the less likely one is to be under the control of particular content not based on the framing of current experience (self-as-content).

Self-as-process is a central aspect of the developmental emergence of selfing as the young child learns to relationally frame his experiences over time. As he engages in framing his experiences in this way, this also provides a basis for the creation (derivation) of self content. This is one reason for the importance of self-as-process, because in order for there to be accurate self content (coherent with mainstream social convention), there needs to be regular accurate contact with (verbal discrimination of) one's current experience. Another reason for the importance of this sense of self is that self-as-process is much more variable than self-as-content and thus strongly encourages behavioral flexibility, which is fundamentally important for psychological health.

Self content itself is not problematic. It is simply a repertoire based on one's learned verbal descriptions of oneself. It can be inaccurate or imprecise (by which, from a functional perspective, we simply mean unhelpful with respect to achieving our goals), to some extent, in particular contexts. But so is a lot of our verbal content, to some extent. Nevertheless, with continued learning about ourselves, that content may continue to be refined and adapted so as to be more helpful. The problem, therefore, is not our self content but how we respond to it. If we respond with flexibility, we can change and adapt our behavior in spite of it. To the extent that we respond inflexibly, self content can distort our experience and pull us away from values-oriented activity. This state of inflexibility with respect to self content is what we sometimes mean by the term *self-as-content*.

Therefore, responding in accordance with self-as-content can be problematic because it is inherently rigid and inflexible. One way of thinking about this is that in this case, self content is framed in deictic relational framing terms as *here* and *now*, which facilitates high levels of transformation of function (that is, we buy into it, and it strongly influences our subsequent behavior). In addition, we respond to much of our self content repeatedly, thus facilitating strong levels of coordination between self and content (in the MDML framework, such responding is both low in derivation and high in coherence). This further strengthens transformation of function in accordance with that relation. By contrast, in the mode of self-as-process, in which we frame our ongoing current experience, self content can be framed either as *here* and *now* (as when we accurately discriminate our current emotional state, but without taking any perspective on our discrimination itself) or as *there* and *then* (as when we consider a thought we've just had and wonder why it popped into our head). Even if content is typically experienced as *here* and *now* (that is, even if we don't often take perspective on it), that content, as part of our ongoing experience, will be relatively variable (because our psychological state changes over time), which will act to limit the strength of coordination between any particular content and *I*. As such, this is one way in which this mode of selfing supports the kind of flexibility that is critically important for healthy selfing. In addition, however, the more consistently we engage in self-as-process practice, including discrimination and deliberate labeling of that behavior, the more likely we are to be aware of and be able to take perspective on any particular content (feelings, sensations, or thoughts) that may arise, and to act flexibly with respect to that content. The extent of such deliberate practice will be amplified by a person's engagement with self-as-context framing.

Because individuals (typically, at least) are trained by the verbal community from an early age to engage in selfing-as-process, all typically verbally able individuals continue to engage in selfing-as-process, at least to some extent, on an ongoing basis throughout their lives. But the extent and depth to which people engage in this process will vary according to their individual histories. For example, some individuals whose training in self-discrimination may have been relatively inadequate are not always able to accurately or precisely discriminate aspects of their own subjective experience. Imagine a child growing up in a household where anxiety is seen as weakness and is never discussed, and who thus never learns to properly discriminate when she feels anxiety. In contrast, verbally typical adults who have also received training in mindfulness or meditation will probably score higher than most others in terms of the consistency, comprehensiveness, accuracy, and precision of their selfing-as-process activity. Ideally, people would receive training in this repertoire throughout their lives, so as to amplify their level of psychological flexibility; and, indeed, such training is useful in the context of psychotherapy. Now, however, such training, whether in psychotherapy or elsewhere, is relatively rare and therefore not something to which many individuals are exposed. Thus, for most even verbally typical people, self-as-process as a practice is less deliberate, less consistent, and less comprehensive than may be desirable for full psychological health.

Currently experienced self content frequently tends toward feeding the conceptualized self and contributing to a relatively more static and limited sense of self. For example, if I trip and immediately describe myself as clumsy, this may make it just a little more likely that I will thereafter think of myself as a clumsy person. Feeding the conceptualized self occurs more readily in circumstances where engaging in self-as-process is not consistent or well practiced, but it can and will occur often, even given relatively frequent self-as-process practice. This will tend to happen in particular with well-rehearsed content that strongly coheres with already established self-as-content (referred to sometimes as *sticky content*). The latter is one way in which even a relatively well-developed repertoire of self-as-process may fail to prevent inflexible engagement with problematic self content. Another situation is the presence of negative self content (such as aversive emotions) that may be relatively more difficult to stay present to, potentially supporting deliberate avoidance. The greater the avoidance, the less one will be in contact with one's experience, and the less accurately one will be guided by it, and hence the greater the potential distortion of one's self content.

One other aspect of engaging in selfing-as-process that is relevant to the current discussion is its relative variability. Although this property can promote flexibility (a key advantage), it is also something that makes it relatively unstable. Constantly changing experience is not, in and of itself, enough of a guide to living a fulfilling life in the long term. This is at least partly why a repertoire of self content becomes important. Self content is produced and supported by the reinforcing effect of coherence (such as the coherence of the story of who I am, what I like and don't like, and so forth), and in turn this coherence can facilitate stability. This is because coherence supports prediction, and the more reliably I can predict what I will like or dislike, the less chance there will be of my making choices that prove disappointing or confusing. Of course coherence does not guarantee stability, since self content, even the most seemingly stable, is subject to change (when someone changes his career, for example, his description of himself in terms of his job will also change). In addition, even the relative stability provided over a particular period of time is not guaranteed to be a good thing all the time. As we saw in chapter 6, stability afforded by self content can be rigid and limiting. At the same time, stability in the form of values, for example, can indeed be positive, guiding us over the longer term and ensuring that we establish and maintain patterns of behavior that allow us to contact relatively more satisfying and more fulfilling experiences. For example, Jim's value of health orients him toward regular engagement in physical activity, which he finds fulfilling and energy-boosting.

Although the practice of self-as-process is beneficial, engagement with self-as-process alone is not enough. A critically important way in which a practitioner needs to support a client's engagement with self-as-process is by promoting self-as-context. Operating from self-as-context can facilitate perspective taking on one's own experience. Such perspective taking allows one to see that this experience (whether positive or negative) is contained in the *I* but does not define it, thus allowing one to be guided by that experience without getting rigidly attached to it. In terms of deictic relations, such perspective taking ensures that psychological content is consistently framed as *there* and *then* rather than as *here* and *now*. As such, for any and all types of experience (positive or negative), this allows one to be psychologically distant from those experiences so as to be able to note and perhaps learn from them but not be influenced by them in such a way that potentially unhelpful transformations of function (for example, experiential avoidance) result.

The perspective on behavior afforded by self-as-context helps also by affording stability. Self-as-process is characterized by experiential variation. On the plus side, such variability, in contrast with the rigidity of self-as-content mode, can support behavioral flexibility. But, as also suggested, variability per se can be insufficient to provide a guide to living a psychologically fulfilling life over the long term. In contrast, self-as-context, as a consistent locus from which all selfing activity occurs, does facilitate such stability by potentially providing a consistent and unchanging psychological platform from which one can notice and learn from one's experience, including both the variability of self-as-process and the guidance afforded by self content such as values.

Hence healthy or flexible selfing essentially involves consistent and frequent engagement in self-as-process, supported by self-as-context, so as to maximize flexibility with respect to self content while in pursuit of values. Self-as-process, which involves relationally framing present-moment experience, is characterized by variation and thus supports behavioral flexibility. But it requires the perspective taking and stability of self-as-context, in which self-experiences are hierarchically related to the *I*, in order for this potential flexibility to be harnessed in the service of valued living.

Fostering Healthy Selfing in Clients

From a CBS point of view, healthy selfing involves consistent engagement in a combination of selfing-as-process and selfing-as-context, affording maximal behavioral flexibility with respect to the pursuit of values. As described earlier, self-as-process is a key aspect of healthy selfing. It involves the ongoing framing of current experience in all its variation over time, which potentially supports the efficient discovery and pursuit of values as one interacts with one's environment. Crucially, however, the full potential of self-as-process is realizable only via engagement with self-as-context, which facilitates taking perspective on other selfing activity, thereby affording maximal flexibility with respect to learning afforded by that other activity.

If the processes just described are indeed central to healthy selfing, then a key question for the practitioner interested in promoting healthy selfing is how best to foster those processes. In what follows, we present an approach to promoting healthy selfing that draws on key aspects of this analysis. This approach will also draw on an analysis previously developed by Villatte, Villatte, and Hayes (2016), who in addition have presented techniques that can be used in applied settings to establish and strengthen the core processes involved. This approach explains and discusses the training of four processes:

1. *I* as various (the variety of experience)

2. *I* as perspective (stability in a sense of perspective)

3. *I* as container (self-as-context and hierarchical relations)

4. *I* as flexible (able to respond in line with values in action)

Table 7.1 summarizes the four processes suggested for targeting to promote healthy selfing, or what can also be referred to as a *contextual sense of self*. It should be noted that although these processes are presented here in a particular sequence, it is not necessarily the case that this sequence needs to be adopted in addressing them. Similarly, it is not necessarily the case that all four processes need be addressed to the same extent. Furthermore, switching between processes may be deemed helpful in particular circumstances.

In the first process, the practitioner helps the client notice that her experiences vary across time and points of view (*I* as various), which is a key aspect of self-as-process. In the second process, the practitioner helps the client contact the observer perspective that is stable across all experiences (*I* as perspective), which is the central defining element of self-as-context and underlines the importance of the stability of this repertoire. In the third process, the practitioner extends the training of self-as-context, begun in the second process, by placing particular emphasis on the hierarchical dimension of the observing self (*I* as container). This emphasizes the potential for this repertoire to facilitate taking perspective on content. In the fourth process, the practitioner helps the client see that she can, from the stability of this observer perspective, flexibly respond in line with her values (*I* as flexible). Let's take a closer look.

Table 7.1. Selfing Processes Targeted for Change in the Promotion of Healthy Selfing

Target	What the practitioner can say
The variety of experience: *I* as various	How do you feel now?…and now?…and now? Remember different situations and moments of your life. How did you feel then? Is that different from how you feel now?
Stability in a sense of perspective: *I* as perspective	Notice who is noticing thoughts, sensations, and feelings across a variety of experiences in your life (last summer, five years ago, when you were a teenager…). Notice who is noticing the experiences of you today, yesterday, in a year's time….
Self-as-context and hierarchical relations: *I* as container	Your experiences are part of you. You are the container of all your experiences
Able to respond in line with values in action: *I* as flexible	Given your history, it is not surprising that you made these choices. Now, with the knowledge that your experiences are only part of you, what can you do that is in line with what matters to you? Are you able to respond in line with your values?

I *as Various*

The first process is discrimination of the variability of experience. In order to find variability in the process of awareness, the practitioner needs to facilitate the client's noticing fluctuation in her experiences (thoughts, feelings, and sensations) across time. The practitioner can do this in a number of ways, such as by helping the client engage in long-term meditative practice, or by repeatedly directing the client's attention to the present (asking, for example, "How do you feel now…and now…and now?") to help her notice the changes in her experiences, or by getting the client to notice changes in perspective (for example, by recalling different situations and moments of her life and noticing how her experiences vary across these situations and moments). One metaphor that may help in this respect is that of time-lapse photography. When the photographer sets the camera down in one location, this sets the perspective. If, after allowing the camera to take pictures over a particular period, the photographer then reviews the results, he will see how the scenes change over time. For example, he will see that the same spot changes from darkness to light, that things enter the frame and leave, and even that things constantly in the frame change in appearance over time.

When a client comes to therapy and indicates that she is constantly having one particular feeling or thought that seems to subsume all other experiences (for example, *I am disliked by everyone*), helping her find variability through the process of awareness is an important step toward helping her develop a flexible selfing repertoire. As mentioned earlier, regular meditation or mindfulness practice can help a person notice the variability of his or her experiences. In addition, in the therapeutic context the practitioner can point to how experiences vary during the session. For example, if a client says that she has a recurrence of a certain feeling (such as anxiety) or thought (such as *I am stupid*), the practitioner can ask the client, "Is that thought showing up now?…and now?" (the repetition of "now" allows differentiation of different points in time) or "What are you feeling now?…and now?"

Thus, the key aspect of the first process is training the client to notice variance in her experience, both in the short term (from moment to moment, as in a therapeutic session) and over the longer term (over the course of several sessions, the current year, or perhaps her life until now). Clients don't notice that their moment-to-moment experiences (self-as-process), including their thoughts about themselves (self content), vary when they are operating from rigid self content (self-as-content). This also results in weak self-as-process and weakness in clients' tracking of their own experiences. With appropriate prompting from the therapist, however, this variance can become apparent. Here is an example of a client–practitioner role-play that illustrates how the practitioner can help the client notice variability in her experiences:

Client: I am feeling really overwhelmed.

Practitioner: Is that the case right here and now?

Client: That's right. It has been going on all week. It's basically constant.

Practitioner: Right.... Can you tell me what you are you feeling, exactly?

Client: It's hard to say—just edgy, confused, agitated.

Practitioner: Right now, as you're talking, are you feeling edgy and confused?

Client: Yup. Even talking about it makes me agitated.

Practitioner: I see. Can you tell me what the sensation of being agitated feels like? Where do you feel it?

Client: A tightening in my chest.

Practitioner: Is it present now?

Client: Well...actually, it is kind of gone now.

Practitioner: I see. What is there now?

Client: Weird...but the tightness is coming back.

Practitioner: Interesting. This sensation is coming and going?

Client: Yeah. Does that seem strange?

Practitioner: (*smiles*) Is the contraction still there?

Client: Only a little.

Practitioner: It comes and goes in waves?

Client: Yeah, that's it. It comes and goes all the time.

Practitioner: Interesting—so it changes back and forth.

Client: Yeah.

Here, the practitioner helps the client discriminate that her private experiences vary (even during the session) so that she can see that what feels like a constant experience is actually a fluctuating one. This is just one way in which awareness of the variability of experience can be fostered. As well as guiding the client to see that experiences can fluctuate over the relative short term, the practitioner can also guide her to see that her view and experience of herself can vary from day to day across different situations. The practitioner can do this by prompting the client to explore differences in how she sees herself in different circumstances. For example, if a client appears to hold the view *I am unstable*, the practitioner can help her consider a number of alternative scenarios in her day-to-day life when she may not think about herself in this way. For example, the practitioner can ask, "Is this always the case, or are there ever times when you are not unstable?" By prompting the client to consider various different situations in which she may hold alternative views of herself, the practitioner helps the client see that a view that seems to override all others is just one view and that, even though it may have seemed to be something that held consistently when she expressed it in therapy, it probably has varied across time and situations. Here is an example of how the practitioner can help the client notice that her experience varies in terms of the variety of views she holds about herself across different situations in her life:

Client: I wish I didn't seem like an aggressive person. As a woman, it makes me feel wrong and misunderstood.

Practitioner: So what are the parts of you that are misunderstood?

Client: I'm honest, I want to help people, I am direct, and I tell it like it is.

Practitioner: What is it you like about being honest?

Client: That the world is more straightforward.

Practitioner: Are you aggressive with everyone in all contexts?

Client: With my sister I am more open and calm than aggressive and direct. She accepts me for who I am, though, so I don't feel wrong for being myself around her.

Practitioner: Would you say that there is a version of you that is aggressive and direct around people, and a different version of you that is open and honest around your sister?

Client: I suppose I am different around different people, and depending on where I am or who I am with. Actually, maybe when I am aggressive, it is more about feeling misunderstood.

Practitioner: And what about here? What kind of person are you with me?

Client:	I'm not sure. This is different—this is therapy. I am able to be honest around you, not in the same way I am with my sister, and not aggressive, either.
Practitioner:	So would you say that this is another version of you? In some sense there is the version of you that is aggressive and direct with people who make you feel misunderstood, the version of you that is open and calm with your sister, and the version of you here that is open and honest?
Client:	Yeah. I suppose it changes, depending on where I am and who I am speaking to.

In this example the practitioner helps the client to see that her perspective on herself and what kind of person she is varies across different situations in her life. This is another important means by which the practitioner can help the client get a sense of the variability in the process of awareness.

As a further example of an exercise to help induce an experiential sense of the "I as various" process, consider the group-based "that makes me feel" experiential exercise. In this exercise, the group is divided into pairs, and one person in each pair starts by identifying what he is currently feeling, using a sentence that takes the form "I feel x." The other person then responds with how the first person's identification of his feeling makes her feel in turn, saying, "That makes me feel y." The first person then responds to this statement, saying, "That makes me feel z," and so on. The two continue to go back and forth, each in turn identifying how the other person's last utterance makes him or her feel. Consider the following sequence:

Person 1:	I feel anxious.
Person 2:	That makes me feel sad.
Person 1:	That makes me feel remorseful.
Person 2:	That makes me feel uncomfortable.
Person 1:	That makes me feel annoyed.
Person 2:	That makes me feel curious.
Person 1:	That makes me feel calm.

The pairs are asked to continue to do this for one to two minutes. This exercise has a few potential outcomes, including inducing perspective taking on the other person's reactions to one's behavior. The most relevant such outcome for the present purposes, however, is that participants are induced to notice the potential variation in their own emotions (I as various) across time and on the basis of context. As explained earlier, facilitating this sense of the variability of experience is an important step toward broadening a person's sense of self, undermining the rigidity characteristic of self-as-content, and promoting psychological flexibility.

I as Perspective

Teaching the client to notice variability of experience is an important step toward promoting psychological flexibility, but it is just one element of the overall process. Furthermore, although highlighting the variability of experience is an important step forward, contacting nothing but variability can work to disrupt one's sense of self. Culturally, we learn that our self resides in the content of our thoughts, feelings, and so forth. If our experiences always vary, then what is stable across time? In other words, who are we? In a second element of the intervention, a sense of stability is provided by facilitating a sense of the client's consistent perspective on events.

We can find stability in a sense of perspective by noticing that there is a common perspective across experiences and situations—in other words, not just by noticing thoughts, feelings, and sensations but also by noticing who is noticing these experiences. Returning to the metaphor of time-lapse photography, we can say that our perspective is like the camera, which is a constant that takes images across time and events. Although the events it tracks change across time, the camera remains the same, stable and ever present.

For the client in psychotherapy, discriminating the stability of the observer perspective is a critically important complement to noticing the fluctuations or variations in experience across time. The client must be guided to notice that there is a stable locus across time that provides the background for his variable experiences, and from which this variation can be seen. In order to help the client gain this sense of stability while noticing variability, the first thing that the practitioner must do is to help the client identify this sense of perspective (the observer perspective).

The practitioner can promote development of the observer perspective by helping clients notice common perspective taking across activities and points of view. The practitioner needs to guide clients in seeing that although experiences differ across time, place, and situation, the person who notices these experiences is the same. The practitioner should guide clients in noticing *who* is noticing their various experiences, both in the immediate context (thoughts, feelings, and sensations that clients may have during a session) and in the context of activities or events that took place in the past or are taking place over the longer term (earlier today, yesterday, last year, in a year's time). Thus, in helping clients discriminate the observer perspective, the practitioner can start by prompting them to notice the variety of their experience at some level. Then the practitioner can prompt clients to notice the common thread of the perspective that they hold on those events. For example, the practitioner can begin by responding to a client's statement "I am a loser," helping the client notice a variety of alternative views (*I as various*) that he has held about himself across different situations: "How did you think about yourself when you were a college student? And what about when you won the marathon?" The practitioner can then guide the client to discriminate that, across all these various views of himself, there is a stable part that has noticed the variety of these views: "What is the part of you that has noticed all these different views of yourself?" Here is an example of how the practitioner can help the client notice common perspective taking across various experiences (that is, help the client notice that a part of himself notices his experiences):

Client: I lost my job a couple of months ago, and I have been feeling like half a man since. I'm spending most of the day in the house watching TV, and I don't even want to go outside in case the neighbors see me and start wondering why that guy's not at work. Yeah…I am feeling like a loser.

Practitioner: So you are viewing yourself as a loser and as half a man since you lost your job. And what was your view of yourself before you lost your job?

Client: When I was working, I was really hardworking and proud of that, and I was well able to look after myself. I was independent—but that is all gone now.

Practitioner: So before, you viewed yourself as independent and hardworking, and you were proud of that, and now you view yourself as half a man, and you have lost your independence. What if they were to offer you the job back again—how would you view yourself then?

Client: There is no way I would go back to working for them, after what they have done. I would be like a puppet on a string to go back to working for them now.

Practitioner: So that is another view of yourself. If you were to go back, you would view yourself as a puppet? So we see three different views of yourself—independent and hardworking, a loser and half a man, and a puppet. So—different views of yourself.

Client: Yeah.

Practitioner: What is the part of you that is noticing these different views of yourself?

Client: I don't really follow.

Practitioner: There seems to be a part of you that noticed yourself as the hardworking person. And there is a part of you that notices you are half a man, and a part of you that would notice that you are a puppet if you went back. So is there is a part of you that notices all these different views? Let's imagine for a minute that these different views of yourself were to be shown in a film. When a film is playing, it can't notice itself. So who does notice it? What is this aspect of you that sees the variety of views that you hold about your experiences over time? Is a part of you noticing this variety of views? Is that true from your experience?

Client: Right…right. Is it not all just me?

Practitioner: I think there is an interesting variation in the views we have about ourselves across time—for example, your view of yourself if you took the job back, versus how you feel about yourself now, versus how you felt about yourself before you lost the job.

Client: Okay.

Practitioner: So in that sense there seems to be something about you that has changed across time, no?

Client: Yeah.

Practitioner: But across all those changes or views, there is also something about you that is the same.

Client: I kind of get what you're saying. Although my attitude toward myself has changed over time, it's still always me at some level.

Practitioner: Yes, there is a you that is there across all your experiences. It's possible and likely that your view will change again if you get a new job.

Client: Right...right. If I got a new job, I think my self-esteem would go up, and I'd feel myself as a guy who is pulling his weight again.

Practitioner: So if and hopefully when you get a new job, your view of yourself would change again. Your view would be of someone who is confident, with high self-esteem. There are varying, different views you can have of yourself, and who is noticing these different views?

Client: That part of me that has been consistent. The part of me that has been the same through all of these experiences.

Practitioner: You have been you your whole life.

Client: I can get a sense of that now, and I am just wondering what the relevance is.

Practitioner: What is important is that you can see that your views can change, and yet a part of you stays the same. You are not the views. Is that your experience?

Client: I get you. I can get a sense of that. I'm not just the view that I'm half a man.

In this example, the practitioner helps the client notice the variation in his experience (or view of self) across different situations: at the current time, having lost his job; a few months ago, before he lost his job; and at a hypothetical time in the future, when he may get his job back. The practitioner prompts the client to change points of view, and this opens the client up to notice that across these perspectives there is a stable sense of self that is permanent and unchanging—that there is a common perspective across points of view. In other words, experiences are different across time, place, and perspective (today, last year, and so forth), but the noticer is the same.

As another example of the induction of the "I as perspective" process, this time in a group context, consider the "invalidated self" exercise:

> Think of a time when you were in distress, and someone invalidated your pain. As you scroll through the different memories, keep in mind that there is no right or wrong memory. Any time that you felt invalidated can work for this exercise.... When you have settled on a memory, please raise your right index finger.... Bring to mind the colors you could see at that time...the sounds that you could hear at that time.... Contact what you were thinking at that time.... Contact how you felt at that time.... Now gently come back to your breath, here and now.... Notice that you were there then, and you are here now. Now we are going to go to a different memory.... Think of a time when you invalidated someone else's pain when that person was distressed. Any time that you invalidated someone else's pain can work for this exercise.... When you have settled on a memory, please raise your right index finger.... Bring to mind the colors you could see at that time...the sounds that you could hear at that time.... Contact what you were thinking at that time.... Contact what you felt at that time.... Radiate kindness to yourself at that time.... Now gently come back to your breath, here and now.... Notice that you are here now, you were there at that time when you were invalidated, and you were there at that time when you invalidated someone else.... Now imagine yourself going back in time and responding differently to this person.... Gently come back to your breath, here and now.

Once again, the point is to induce those taking part to shift perspective in order to notice the stable unchanging perspective that is always present in all their experiences. In this instance, it is done by bringing to mind different times when the individual was involved in an instance of interpersonal invalidation. Across different instances, the individual has to adopt the perspective both of a person who has been invalidated and of a person who has invalidated another. This kind of shift across these opposing roles may be particularly powerful as a means of highlighting the unity of perspective across differing experiences.

Ideally, by being guided to shift perspectives, individuals will begin to gain a sense of self that is stable across experiences. This perspective is then emphasized further by exercises that focus on building on the sense of perspective and helping the client notice that the stable sense of self is superordinate to all the experiences, feelings, memories, and so forth, that make up the self.

I *as Container*

So far, we have looked at the importance of helping clients to notice the variability in their experiences and developing perspective-taking skills to foster a broad sense of self that is stable across time (the unchanging observer). These are important skills that help promote awareness of key aspects of the self. They also provide key supports for the third element involved in a flexible selfing repertoire, which is a particularly important one.

As we saw earlier, coherence is built into human language and is a critically important aspect of verbal human experience. We have discussed examples of how people can fall into coherence traps, and of how this can prevent them from living in accordance with their values. For example, believing in, and behaving in line with, a thought like *If I go to the party I will make a fool of myself, so I should stay at home*. While this shows the potential problems with coherence, it also suggests how psychologically important and central coherence is. As such, helping clients find coherence in context—coherence in a psychologically healthy and workable sense—is a particularly important part of developing a flexible selfing repertoire. Doing so involves facilitating the development of a more contextual sense of self that brings together the variability of experiences and the stability in the sense of perspective on these experiences into a coherent network based on hierarchical relations.

Viewing the self hierarchically, as a context of all our experiences, allows for a broader symbolic network that integrates both the awareness of experiential processes and the key concept of perspective taking. In other words, I am the container or context for all my experiences. They are all my experiences and thus have contributed to the verbal me, yet I am not identical with those experiences and thus can stand back and take perspective on them. This framing is key to facilitating behavioral flexibility with regard to those experiences, and behavioral flexibility in turn is particularly important for the pursuit of values.

This hierarchical dimension of self is targeted by a number of self-as-context exercises and metaphors in acceptance and commitment therapy, such as the chessboard metaphor (see Hayes et al., 2011, p.231). In this exercise, the practitioner draws a parallel between the person's psychological experience and a game of chess involving a battle between the white pieces (representing "good" or appetitive mental content, such as feelings of joy) and the gray pieces (representing "bad" or aversive mental content, such as feelings of despair). The central insight of this metaphor is that you are not any of the pieces, whether good or bad; instead, you are the chessboard that contains all the pieces. Exercises such as this suggest at one level that there is a distinction between the self and psychological experiences (that is, the chessboard is separate from the pieces). But at a higher and more integrated level, they suggest that there is a hierarchical relation between the self and experiences because just as the chessboard is the context for the game, the self is the context of all our experiences.

The practitioner should continue to promote the key functional aspects of this metaphor, including an awareness of experiences in all their diversity, a sense of distinction from and perspective on those experiences, and a sense of the integration of all these aspects in a hierarchical frame. Table 7.2 illustrates the distinction between relating to the self hierarchically and relating to the self in coordination with one's experiences.

Table 7.2. Coordination Relation Versus Hierarchical Relation to the Self

	Relational frame	
Experience	**Rigid self-labeling (coordination relation)**	**Taking perspective (hierarchical relation)**
Thoughts	I *am* my thoughts.	I *have* and *include* my thoughts.
Sensations	I *am* my sensations.	I *have* and *include* my sensations.
Feelings	I *am* my feelings.	I *have* and *include* my feelings.

Figure 7.1. "I as Container" Exercise*

Therapist speaks to client or group.

In this exercise, you will be invited to track your bodily sensations, emotions, and thoughts as they come and go.

Therapist gives client or group members a diagram of the human body accompanied by a list of adjectives and followed by blank lines for writing.

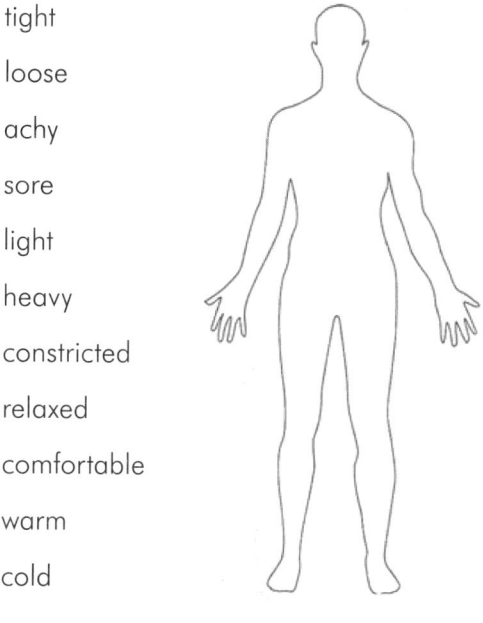

tight
loose
achy
sore
light
heavy
constricted
relaxed
comfortable
warm
cold

_____

_____

Therapist continues speaking.

Look at this diagram of the human body, and at the list of words that describe various sensations that commonly arise in the human body. To do this exercise, take a few moments to contact the present moment via your breath. Then start to notice the different sensations that come up in your body. Perhaps your back aches from lifting too much at work. Or perhaps your stomach is knotted up with nervousness. Just notice how your body feels.

Therapist can give alternative or additional specific cues that speak to what makes sense for the individual client or group he or she is working with.

---

* Adapted from *Acceptance and commitment therapy: The process and practice of mindful change*, by S. C. Hayes, K. D. Strosahl, and K. G. Wilson, 2011 (New York: Guilford Press), p. 236, and from *Get out of your mind and into your life: The new acceptance and commitment therapy*, by S. C. Hayes and S. Smith, 2005 (Oakland: New Harbinger), p. 102. Adapted with permission.

Therapist continues speaking.

As the feelings arise, write an X on the picture. For example, if your shoulder is tight, write an X on the shoulder in the diagram. Take one minute now to notice bodily sensations as they come in and go out of your body now. There is no way of failing this exercise. We're just going to look at whatever you're thinking or feeling, so whatever shows up is fine.

Therapist pauses for one minute.

Therapist continues speaking.

Now come back to noticing your body. Notice how you are sitting in your chair. Notice any bodily sensations that are there. As you notice each sensation, just acknowledge the feeling and identify where in the body it is by writing an X on the picture of the human body.

Therapist pauses.

Therapist continues speaking.

Now notice any emotions you are having, and if you have any, just acknowledge them, and write an O on the body where you feel any emotions.

Therapist pauses.

Therapist continues speaking.

Now get in touch with your thoughts, and write down your current thoughts in a thought bubble next to the diagram of the body.

Therapist pauses.

Therapist continues speaking.

Now I want you to notice that as you noticed these things, a part of you noticed them. You noticed those sensations...those emotions...those thoughts...and that part of you we will call the Observer You. Now I want you to remember something that happened last summer. When you have selected a memory, bring the image of that time to mind. You can close your eyes if it helps you bring the memory to mind. Remember all the things that were happening then. Remember the colors you could see.... Remember the sights... the sounds...your feelings...and as you do that, see if you can notice something that we don't normally consider. You were there then, noticing what you were noticing. You were there then, and you are here now. Just notice the experience of being aware, and check and see if it isn't so that in some deep sense, the you that is here now was there then. The person aware of what you are aware of is here now and was there then. See if you can notice the essential continuity—in some deep sense, at the level of experience, not of belief, you have been you your whole life. Once you have completed the exercise, take a few minutes to jot down on the blank lines some notes about what you experienced.

A number of different techniques can be employed to help foster a hierarchical (observer) sense of self. In order to emphasize the hierarchical dimension of self (self-as-context), the practitioner will deliberately use hierarchical framing. This will assist in helping the client formulate her experience as something she *has* rather than something she *is*. The importance of emphasizing a hierarchical dimension of self rather than just the "*I* as perspective" process lies in the fact that hierarchical relating is more complex and involves containment and not just difference or separation. This more complex relationship arguably coheres better with the psychology of the situation because it acknowledges that an individual's experiences are hers while allowing some separation from those experiences if need be, which facilitates flexibility with regard to those experiences. Here is an example of the use of a hierarchical relation with the client's perspective at the top of the hierarchy and her experiences as dimensions subsumed within that hierarchy:

Client: I can't stand these feeling of jealousy toward my best friend's new relationship. She wants me to go on a double date with her next week, and I am worried the jealousy might show.

Practitioner: It sounds like this friendship means a lot to you.

Client: Yes, it does. I really care about her and want her to be happy, but for some reason I feel jealous. It just doesn't make sense. I am a terrible friend.

Practitioner: That must feel confusing. Let's look at the different emotions, such as jealousy and happiness. And we can add in thoughts, too, like *I am a terrible friend*. Imagine your thoughts and feelings are like pieces on a chessboard. The positive ones are like the white pieces, and the negative ones are the gray pieces.

Client: Okay.

Practitioner: It's like we try to fight off the negative thoughts and feelings with the positive ones. Like playing a game of chess, where we want the white team to win. But when we are playing that game, we think we are the pieces. What if the pieces are just part of us, but we are much more than that?

Client: Like what?

Practitioner: Well, in a game of chess there is more than just the pieces. What else is there?

Client: Well…there is the board, too.

Practitioner: Yes, exactly. You are more than the pieces—you are like the board. All the pieces can be there. You don't need either the white team or the gray team to win. It's as if there is a chessboard that goes out infinitely in all directions. It's covered with both gray pieces and white pieces. They work together in teams, like in chess—the white pieces fight against the gray pieces. You can think of your thoughts, such as *I am a terrible friend*, or feelings, such as jealousy or happiness, and beliefs, such as *I should be happy for my friend*, as these pieces; they come together in teams, too. When we play the game, we select which side we want to win. But there's a problem with trying to win this game, and it's that from this position, parts of yourself are your own enemy. In other words, if you need to be in this war, there is something wrong with you. And when we think of ourselves as the pieces, it can seem like the pieces are as big as ourselves, or even bigger, even though these pieces are simply part of us, of our experience. When you are playing the game, you are trying to knock enough of the pieces off the board so that you will eventually win. The problem is that your experience tells you that the exact opposite happens. So the game goes on. Playing this game can be a confusing and unwinnable way to live.

Client: It is!

Practitioner: So when you are operating from board level rather than at the level of the pieces, is it possible that you could feel jealous and care about her happiness at the same time?

Client: Like both are there, but I am more than them. I don't have to fight away jealousy for happiness to be there.

Practitioner: Yes, you are more than either jealousy or happiness alone—these are just experiences that you have, like parts of you.

> There is also a broader you—the board—that notices both these experiences.

In the preceding example, the practitioner is helping the client derive a hierarchical relation between herself and her experiences. She is not the same as (coordinated with) her experiences. At the same time, though, she is not completely distinct from or separated from them, because they are still *her* experiences. Instead, she has or contains them (hierarchical relation), which means that she can safely acknowledge them while acting independently of them.

It is important not to become overly intellectual in discussions of selfing. In the preceding example, the chessboard metaphor is used to point the client toward what is involved, but the metaphor does not experientially create the distinction between repertoires of selfing. The client might ask, "If that's so, then how can I stay as the board?" It is best not to answer this question directly, because an experiential rather than intellectual sense of self is being developed. The former is new; the latter may just feed into more self content. One way to respond is to say, "It involves learning a new skill, and we'll get to that shortly. But right now let's just notice that it is impossible *not* to struggle with thoughts and feelings if that is who we are." When helping the client get a sense of the "I as container" process, we want to provide her with an experience of her self as the context or container for psychological content. The hierarchical relation "I as container" is critically important in helping her separate herself from her experience and act independently of that experience. As mentioned, a crucial reason why hierarchy is effective in this context is that hierarchy is a relatively complex relation that subsumes a number of other relations, including sameness, distinction, and containment, the particular combination of which, in this context, contributes to a relatively sophisticated understanding of psychological experience. In fact, it may be more accurate to describe hierarchy as a relational repertoire or relational network than to describe it as a relational frame. The key point, however, is that in its coherent subsuming of a number of other relations in this way, hierarchy can create an understanding of the psychological situation that allows a useful transformation of functions—that facilitates, in other words, useful behavioral change.

The integrative (that is, coherence) function of the hierarchical sense of self-as-context is important; the hierarchical sense of self contains the insights of the elements of experiential variability and perspective taking while weaving these elements together in a coherent framework. This facilitates understanding and communication and probably makes therapeutically useful transformations of function more likely. Furthermore, evidence from the empirical lab supports the idea that it is specifically hierarchical relational responding, and not simply particular aspects of the hierarchical repertoire, that facilitates this change (Foody, Barnes-Holmes, Barnes-Holmes, & Luciano, 2013; Gil, Luciano, Ruiz, & Valdivia Salas, 2014). For example, the research by Foody et al. (2013) supports the use of hierarchical relations over distinction relations in developing effective self-as-context interventions. Specifically, these researchers showed that an intervention was more effective in helping people cope with distress when it combined perspective taking with hierarchical relations than when it combined perspective taking with distinction relations. The research participants had to write down a negative self-evaluation (such as "I'm not good enough") and read it aloud. They were then exposed to one of two different self-as-context–type interventions. One intervention induced them to see themselves as distinct from their private content (thoughts, feelings, and bodily sensations), as in the following prompt: "Remember that this is just a thought or just a memory.... You do not need to do anything with it, just observe it. Try to notice that you are here, and the thought that you are contemplating is there, written in front of you. Again, just notice that it is you who are watching that thought." The other intervention induced them to derive a hierarchical relation with their content (to see, that is, that they contained it), as in this prompt: "Now try to imagine yourself as so big that you can have room for all the thoughts that you have had today—for all the sensations, feelings, and memories. Imagine that your thoughts and feelings are like moles or freckles on your body. We all have moles or freckles, and we can all walk wherever we want with them on our bodies." The findings of this research showed that both interventions reduced distress, but that the hierarchy-based intervention was more effective in doing so. This result was important for RFT broadly in that it indicated the utility of analyzing psychological experience in relational framing terms, by showing that different frames can lead to different functional outcomes. It was important in a more specific sense in showing the utility of hierarchical relational framing specifically for inducing psychological flexibility.

An exercise that can be used to foster the "I as container" process is the "observer you" exercise (see Hayes et al., 2011, p. 236). Figure 7.1, an adapted version of this exercise that incorporates parts of an exercise from Hayes and Smith (2005), is a script for the therapist to read to an individual client or to a group. Once the client who is completing the exercise has written notes on what he experienced, the therapist can ask him to notice that he was "there then" and that he is "here now." Then the therapist can ask the client what he noticed during the exercise. For example, did he notice aspects of himself that changed across time? Aspects that stayed the same? Then the therapist can emphasize that there is a part of us all that is stable across time. An exercise such as this promotes a stable sense of self and makes it possible to notice content that is part of the self but does not define the self. This "observer self" can head in the direction of what the client values, regardless of the client's self content. The aspect of healthy selfing that involves taking a direction in line with what matters is the aspect to which we turn next—namely, the "I as flexible" process.

I *as Flexible*

Operating in accordance with the "I as container" process facilitates responding in line with values. Once a client has had exemplars of the "I as various," "I as perspective," and "I as container" processes and is able to respond accordingly, she will have a broader sense of self that is less restricted by either her self content or her current process. As such, she will be able to better notice both the impact of context on her behavior and the impact of her behavior on her situation as she tries to flexibly pursue her values. In what follows, we consider how the practitioner can encourage and support each of these processes so as to facilitate flexible values-oriented action on the part of the client.

NOTICING THE IMPACT OF CONTEXT

The practitioner can help the client become aware of the influence of contextual variables on her actions by making observations and asking questions about a variety of current and past elements that may have contributed to those actions:

- Given your history, it is not surprising that you made these choices.
- Can you think of things that characterized that day that may have led you to act in this way?
- If you were me right now, how would you view this situation?
- Given your history, how could it be any other way?

What follows is an example of how the practitioner can help the client notice the impact of context on her behavior; noticing this can allow the client to see that she need not shoulder full responsibility for her circumstances in ways that are not useful or not helpful in moving her forward:

Client: I didn't succeed in quitting smoking. I didn't stick to the quit date I agreed on last week. I completely forgot about it when the day came. It's typical of me to mess up.

Practitioner: What do you think happened?

Client: I just forgot. I was really busy. I had meetings all day on the day I had set to quit, and I just forgot.

Practitioner: I understand. So when you are really busy, you forget things?

Client: Yes. When I am really busy, I forget to do things—they just slip my mind. And once I failed to quit on my quit date, it seemed pointless—like I realized I will never be strong enough to kick the habit.

Practitioner: What could help you remember things when you are busy?

Client: I don't know.

Practitioner: What *doesn't* help you remember when you are busy?

Client: Not writing my appointments into my diary? That is true. I could write a note in my diary to remind me of my quit date. Actually, I could post a sticky note on the door of my closet so that I see it first thing before I smoke.

Practitioner: And if you see the sticky note, what can you do?

Client: Remember not to smoke. It would still be hard. But, to be honest, smoking is hard, too, because I am sick of being a smoker. It actually embarrasses me going outside. I feel weak.

Practitioner: Does beating yourself up about being weak help you remember things when you are busy?

Client: No, it actually distracts me further.

Practitioner: Yes, I imagine it would.

Client: In a way, I can organize my world to give me a better shot at succeeding when the chips are down. The fact that I haven't been using reminders almost seems odd now.

Therapist: A bit like you weren't really giving yourself a shot to succeed, and then giving yourself a hard time when you didn't succeed!

Client: Yeah! (*laughs*).

In this example, the client first reports that she is a failure or weak for not engaging in values-congruent actions. But after she is prompted to notice the influence of contextual variables on her actions, she is able to see that her behavior was affected by things like being extremely busy and the absence of reminders.

NOTICING THE IMPACT OF BEHAVIOR

The practitioner also needs to help the client discriminate the impact of his actions on the contextual variables: "With this knowledge, what can you do that is in line with what matters to you?" In addition, the practitioner needs to help the client discriminate the impact of his actions more directly: "When you study, how does that impact your grades or your relationship with your parents?" Here is an example in which the practitioner helps the client notice the impact of his behavior and see that he is able to respond in ways that will change the consequences he experiences:

Client: What I would really like would be to have a girlfriend. I think it would really improve my social life and well-being, but it just hasn't worked out, and there is nothing much I can do about it.

Practitioner: What has changed since you started coming to therapy?

Client: If I'm honest with you, nothing much, really.

Practitioner: I remember when you came a few weeks ago—you said there's no way you'd want to date, and no way you'd even consider putting yourself out there.

Client: Yeah. And I think I was right, you know, because I'm pretty much in the same position again.

Practitioner:	Has there been anything that you've tried in order to get into a relationship?
Client:	Well, I signed up for this dating website and arranged a few dates and went on them, but as of now I'm pretty much back to square one. Nothing has come of it.
Practitioner:	What was going on for you right before you signed up for the website? Or right before you went on the dates? What was different then?
Client:	I suppose back then I was really keeping to myself. I was more alienated. It seems like maybe now I'm more active than I was then, but I'm still in the same position. Before, it's like I was standing still, but now I'm on a treadmill. I'm still in the same position.
Practitioner:	On a treadmill, though?
Client:	Yes.
Practitioner:	Is being more active something that matters to you?
Client:	Yeah, yeah. It's important to me to be getting out there and being more outgoing.
Practitioner:	So in some senses, then, being on a treadmill can be a better place to be than standing still? Something that matters to you is changing?
Client:	Yeah. Engaging more in life was a primary motivation for coming here.

This example shows how the practitioner can help direct the client's attention toward the impact of his actions on contextual variables. In this case, the practitioner leads him to see that things have indeed changed in a valued direction since he started therapy, albeit more slowly than he was hoping for. The change in his actions is having the desired consequences, and in that sense his responding is working.

CHAPTER 8

Assessing for Selfing Problems

The aim of this chapter is to consider assessment of selfing problems, using a functional approach. The basic idea of functional assessment is that behavior serves a purpose (a function) in a particular context and that we can usefully understand a person's behavior by considering what contextual variables (antecedent and consequential) are affecting it. Although arguably more complex than many other patterns of behavior, various patterns of selfing can also be approached in this way and, in particular, problematic selfing patterns can be identified with a view to potentially providing effective intervention. The extent to which a clinician or practitioner will focus on assessment and treatment of selfing per se is a matter of clinical goals, which will depend on a client's situation. Typically, selfing work will be only one aspect of a treatment approach. Given the theme of this book, however, we will focus on assessment of selfing issues.

Functional Assessment of Human Behavior

Before considering functional assessment of selfing specifically, we will briefly consider functional assessment of human behavior more broadly. All behavior is affected by context. Take, for example, the contextual variables (antecedents and consequences) affecting an infant's crying. The likelihood of crying may be affected both by the antecedent of food deprivation and by the consequence of receiving food. This is a clear-cut example of how environmental variables can affect behavior. But this is also a particularly simple example, and the main thing that makes it so is that the infant in this example is nonverbal. Once a child starts to develop the capacity for relational framing, things become much more complex.

Consider the behavior of crying on the part of a boy of five. Crying on the part of this child after he has fallen may still be considered a relatively simple operant if, for example, parental sympathy or attention appears to maintain or strengthen this pattern of behavior. But things have the potential to become much more complex as a result of the transformation of function through relational frames. Now the functions of all three aspects of the operant—the antecedent, the behavior, and the consequence (ABC)—can be transformed. For instance, if the child has fallen because he was tripped by his brother, then he may blame his brother and resent him, whereas if he fell without anyone else's involvement, then he may label himself clumsy, particularly if he can recall other cases when he tripped. If the reaction to his fall is sympathy from someone else who happens to be there—for example, a friend—then he may think of this person as kind and caring, whereas if the person doesn't react or perhaps laughs, then he may judge that person as unkind or cruel. This labeling may also change his emotional reaction in the situation, perhaps increasing his affection for the friend in the first case or heightening his feelings of anger in the second. The reactions of others may also transform the functions of the behavior itself. If a parent, for example, tells him that big boys don't cry, then he may experience shame for crying and perhaps make an effort to avoid crying the next time he falls. A similar reaction may be evoked if a friend laughs at him when he has fallen.

As such, the functions both of behavior itself and of the context in which it happens are subject to substantial modification through relational framing. Furthermore, and of particular relevance to the core theme, any such relational framing can also contribute to a child's developing self-concept. In the preceding example, the child's experience may prompt him to perceive himself as clumsy, or perhaps weak or emotional if he derives such a self-evaluation on the basis of the hypothetical parental intervention. The impact of relational framing can be clearly seen in this example, which involves the behavior of someone whose verbal repertoire is still in the early stages of development. In the case of a verbally sophisticated adult with a complex repertoire of selfing, aspects of the behavior and context are probably subject to more complex, nuanced, and (in some respects, at least) far-reaching transformations of functions through relational framing. Thus, functional assessment can be relatively complex for a practitioner dealing with a typical adult client.

Nevertheless, the therapist's job is to provide a functional assessment of such potentially complex behavior. Consider an example in an adult clinical setting. The client, Fred, has a hard time with intimacy. When a relationship gets to a certain point, Fred becomes elusive, stops calling the person he is dating, and looks for a way out. This is behavior that would typically be labeled inappropriate. But it serves its purpose—Fred manages to avoid getting too intimate in a relationship. He may be unaware of how his behavior functions, but it is nevertheless effective in achieving avoidance of intimacy. As mentioned earlier, a key part of functional assessment is identifying the antecedents and consequences of certain types of behavior in a person's life. With a verbally sophisticated individual who has a complex selfing repertoire, however, things are more complex than the simple identification of discrete, temporally proximate antecedents and consequences, as might be possible in the case of the nonverbal infant in the earlier example. Or consider the case of Jim, discussed at the beginning of chapter 7. In the first scenario, Jim's recent job loss has impacted him negatively in a number of different ways with respect to how he views himself and the self-evaluations he has made. These views and evaluations are the results of transformations of function through relational frames. His framing about who he is now that he has lost his job includes verbal antecedents (thoughts of being a loser) and consequences (feeling temporarily safe from evaluation by other people) that maintain such behavior as avoidance (staying inside). Table 8.1 summarizes the ABCs for both Jim and Fred.

Table 8.1. Antecedents, Behaviors, and Consequences for Two Patterns of Avoidance Behavior

Client	Antecedent	Behavior	Consequence
Jim	Job loss, with thoughts of being a loser	Stays home and doesn't go outside	Feels temporarily safe from anticipated judgments by others
Fred	A new relationship that starts to become more serious	Stops calling the person he has been dating	Avoids intimacy

Functional assessment of selfing is not simple, because verbal humans engage in relatively complex languaging that facilitates quite complex, temporally extended patterns of behavior (such as values). Furthermore, selfing behavior includes and is affected by a substantial degree of private behavior, including thoughts, feelings, and emotions, which means that the assessment of private behavior is very important when it comes to assessment of selfing. Private behavior, for the most part, cannot be directly observed by the practitioner, and of course this means less direct influence over behavior than might be desirable in some circumstances. At the same time, private behavior can still be functionally assessed, and the methods used to assess it can provide the basis for prediction and influence. Nevertheless, functional assessment of verbal behavior, such as selfing, can be challenging both because the behavior is complex and because it involves less direct influence than practitioners may sometimes prefer.

Assessment of Selfing

The last several chapters provide a contextual behavioral science (CBS) account of selfing. They identify where and how selfing problems can emerge, and they provide suggestions for remediating selfing problems when they arise. Chapter 7 describes healthy selfing as involving consistent practice of both selfing-as-process and selfing-as-context; facilitating minimal inflexible relational framing with respect to self-as-content; and maximizing values-concordant behavior. In contrast, unhealthy selfing has been described as involving inflexible relational framing with respect to the self, which tends to put one out of contact with one's current experience and to be unhelpful with respect to realizing one's values.

Assessment for selfing issues should examine these four areas:

1. Whether the individual can verbally discriminate his or her own ongoing experiences (self-as-process; see chapters 4 and 5)

2. Whether the individual has a fluent deictic relational responding repertoire (see chapter 4)

3. Whether the individual has any self-as-content issues (see chapter 6)

4. Whether the individual has a contextual sense of self (see chapter 7)

With respect to methods, when selfing problems in a client need to be assessed, the practitioner has three basic resources at his or her disposal:

1. The client may arrive with an existing formal diagnosis. A number of diagnostic criteria for specific categorized disorders (such as personality disorders and depression) are explicitly linked to selfing repertoires (a grandiose sense of self, low self-worth, and so forth). Thus, a client's formal diagnosis can suggest potential selfing problems for which an assessment can be made.

2. Specific measures are available that the practitioner can use to assess the client's selfing.

3. The practitioner can use observations of the client's in-session behavior and self-reports.

We will look at each of these resources in turn.

Diagnostic Considerations

In clinical and primary care settings, many referrals to practitioners come with formal diagnoses before treatment, or practitioners themselves may formally diagnose clients in at least some cases. Categorical diagnosis is not the primary concern of a contextual behavioral practitioner, but diagnostic categories can provide some information about the types of selfing problems for which the practitioner may want to assess. Although CBS is not concerned with categorical diagnoses per se, differential diagnosis can prompt the consideration of one or more selfing problems when the same selfing problems are central to the diagnosis of certain disorders. For example, one of the diagnostic criteria for autism spectrum disorder is social communication deficits (American Psychiatric Association, 2013); deictic relational framing has been demonstrated to be weaker in this population (Rehfeldt et al., 2007), and therefore assessing for fluency in deictic relational responding would be prudent with this group. One characteristic often identified in those diagnosed with narcissistic personality disorder is a grandiose sense of self, which can be viewed from a CBS perspective in terms of inflexible relational framing of the self as positive (Almada, 2016). Depression features low self-worth, which may be conceptualized in terms of inflexible relational framing of the self as negative (Zettle, 2007). Therefore, it can be useful to take a client's preexisting diagnosis into account in assessing for selfing problems. Armed with a CBS-based analysis of the functionally defined processes associated with particular diagnoses, a practitioner may more readily be able to efficaciously identify and treat the problematic issues at hand.

Selfing Assessment Tools

We want to highlight some existing measures available for the assessment of selfing problems. These measures can be used to assess selfing behavior in clients before, during, and after an intervention, to see whether selfing interventions are needed or have been successful:

- The RFT Perspective Taking Protocol (McHugh, Barnes-Holmes, & Barnes-Holmes, 2004)

- The Deictic Relational Task (Vilardaga, Estévez, Levin, & Hayes, 2012)

- The Self-as-Context Scale (Gird, Zettle, Webster, & Hardage-Bundy, 2012)

- The Self Experiences Questionnaire (Yu, McCracken, & Norton, 2016)

- The 3-Dimensional Reno Inventory of Self Perspective (Jeffcoat, 2015)

- The Experience of Self Scale (Kanter, Parker, & Kohlenberg, 2001)

- The Functional Self-Discrimination Measure and Interview (Styles & Atkins, 2018)

Table 8.2 presents a summary of these measures. It should be noted that not all of them are explicitly CBS measures; indeed, they may not have been originally intended for use in a functional assessment per se. But they are useful nevertheless because, interpreted correctly, they constitute potentially important selfing indicators and can provide important information with regard to the selfing issue(s) that a client first brings to therapy.

Table 8.2. Summary of CBS Selfing Measures

Measure and source	Description of measure/aspect of selfing measured	Sample
RFT Perspective Taking Protocol (RFT PT) McHugh, Barnes-Holmes, & Barnes-Holmes (2004)	Measures deictic relation type (*I–you, here–there, now–then*) and level of relational complexity (simple, reversed, double reversed)	Children over three years old and adults Children diagnosed with autistic spectrum conditions Patients with schizophrenia Individuals with anhedonia Individuals diagnosed with Down syndrome
The Deictic Relational Task (DRT) Vilardaga, Estévez, Levin, & Hayes (2012)	Measures deictic relations (as the RFT PT also does), but tests *you–you* relational responding, not *I–you* relational responding	Adults
Self as Context Scale (SACS) Gird, Zettle, Webster, & Hardage-Bundy (2012)	Measures self-as-context	Adults

Measure and source	Description of measure/aspect of selfing measured	Sample
Self Experiences Questionnaire (SEQ) Yu, McCracken, & Norton (2016)	Based on the CBS three selves model; does not reflect all three selfing dimensions (that is, does not measure self-as-process) but does make a clear distinction between a content-based self and a contextual self	Adults with chronic pain
3-Dimensional Reno Inventory of Self Perspective (3D-RISP) Jeffcoat (2015)	Measures fusion with self content, the ability to take a centered self-perspective (self-as-process), and verbal awareness of the transcendent nature of that perspective (self-as-context)	College students Adults Adolescents
The Experience of Self Scale (EOSS) Kanter, Parker, & Kohlenberg (2001)	Functional analytic psychotherapy–based; measures degree of public and private control over the experience of self	Adults College students Individuals with borderline personality disorder
The Functional Self-Discrimination Measure and Interview (FSDM-FSDI) Styles & Atkins (2018)	Qualitative measure; classifies functional units of responses from those interviewed in terms of how they take perspective on their experience and talk about themselves	Adults

Observations and Client Self-Reports

Although the practitioner knows the questions that should be asked, it is the client, drawing on his or her own experience, who provides the answers (Villatte et al., 2016). Through the capacity to derive relations, what happens outside the intervention session can be brought into any session. Assessment that connects the therapeutic process to the client's own experience can be achieved via three sources:

1. Client self-reports

2. Experientially evoked client reports

3. The client–practitioner interaction

Client self-reports involve what the client arrives with in therapy and reports as the issue at hand (for example, "I am very self-critical"). Experientially evoked reports are the result of therapist-led questions or exercises. For example, the therapist can ask a simple question, such as "If I could listen in to your mind when it's beating you up, what are the meanest things I'd hear it saying about you?" The client–practitioner interaction can also provide important information about selfing issues—how the client interacts with the practitioner provides an example of the client's social interactions. As mentioned at the beginning of the chapter, the practitioner wants to assess the client's selfing repertoire in order to select a useful intervention plan.

What to Assess For

We have looked at a number of repertoires that are important for healthy selfing, such as the ability to verbally discriminate ongoing experiences accurately, also referred to as *self-as-process*, *deictic relational framing* (chapter 4), *self-as-content issues* (chapter 6), and a *contextual sense of self* (chapters 5 and 7). A practitioner assessing for selfing problems may wish to consider each of these repertoires.

Verbal Discrimination of Ongoing Experiences: Self-as-Process

Verbal discrimination of ongoing experiences (thoughts, feelings, sensations and so forth), also referred to as *self-as-process*, is critical to our sense of self. The practitioner should assess whether the client is able to discriminate his or her internal experiences and should look to see whether there are any limitations or distortions in this repertoire. For instance, the practitioner can discover weak discrimination of internal experiences if the client struggles to identify what his or her experience is. Here is an example of such a client-therapist exchange:

Therapist: I notice you seem distracted today. What are you feeling at the moment?

Client: Nothing.

Therapist: Do you often feel nothing?

Client: I don't really think about it.

Therapist: When was the last time you remember feeling something?

Client: I was really angry at my brother a couple of weeks ago.

This deficiency may be a result of an undeveloped or only partially developed repertoire (seen in young children or those with developmental delays), of distorted learning of certain internal experiences (for example, perhaps as a child the client was repeatedly told that anxiety is weakness), or of learned avoidance of internal experiences as a coping strategy.

With respect to monitoring improvements in discrimination of ongoing experiences (self-as-process), these can be assessed at each moment in session or via reports about a client's interactions outside the therapy room. In-session client improvements in discrimination of ongoing experiences will be evident when the client is accurately tacting internal experiences that were previously inaccurate or not labeled. For example, initial questions from the practitioner ("What are you feeling now?") may have been met with responses such as "I don't know," "Nothing," or "Bad." As sessions progress and discrimination of ongoing experiences becomes more accurate, the client may start to identify certain feelings and sensations that he or she is experiencing ("My heart is racing, and I am having waves of anxiety"). Another in-session indication is that a client who previously was uncomfortable with experiential exercises (such as mindfulness exercises) that involve slowing down and identifying current experiences demonstrates less resistance to engaging in such exercises. Indicators can also be reported by the client from events outside the therapy room, such as the client's identifying feelings that occurred in relevant situations that the client had not previously identified. For example, a client who previously said that he didn't feel anything in certain key life situations may start to report feelings: "I used to think I never felt anything on first dates, but this week I was on a first date, and I noticed that I felt really embarrassed when I said something stupid." Assessment and monitoring of accurate discrimination of ongoing experiences can be done all through the intervention process. Monitoring for changes in self-discrimination allows the practitioner to determine whether self-discrimination issues persist or whether the treatment plan can move forward.

Deictic Relational Responding Repertoire

Functional assessment of the client's deictic relational responding repertoire involves testing for responding across interpersonal (*I–you*), spatial (*here–there*), and temporal (*now–then*) relational frames. This repertoire is more likely to be underrehearsed than deficient, with the exception of very young or developmentally delayed clients. For such cases, one way the practitioner can assess for this repertoire is to employ the deictic relational protocol developed by McHugh et al. (2004; see table 8.2). Tasks that assess for this can vary according to the age and verbal skill of the individual. In cases in which the repertoire is merely underrehearsed rather than deficient, the practitioner may assess for fluency by asking questions that involve taking the perspective of another: "If you were your father, what would you think?" The practitioner may also assess for transformation of emotional functions via deictic relations (that is, empathy): "If you were your husband, and you just found out about the cheating, how would you feel?"

With certain topics, situations, or people, the client's perspective taking may be poorer than in other contexts, but this need not mean that the client's perspective-taking repertoire itself is deficient; instead, this may be more symptomatic of avoidance (that is, the client's being unwilling to take perspective in those particular contexts). In such cases, derivation and transformation of functions across deictic relations may not occur, perhaps as a result of avoidance of internal experiences. For example, a man who was abandoned by his father as a young child may not want to take the perspective of his father at the time when his father left; in fact, it may feel threatening or invalidating to his own pain. In such cases, if perspective taking would be useful (for example, if in this particular case forgiving his father could help the client move in a valued direction), then willingness to experience internal events, rather than deictic relational fluency, would be the target for intervention. Of course the potential benefit would need to be clear to the client and explicitly linked to the client's goals for therapy.

As for monitoring improvements in deictic relational responding, this repertoire, as mentioned earlier, is more likely to be underrehearsed than deficient. In cases where deictic relational responding has been deficient from the outset (as in developmental delay), monitoring for improvements will involve the practitioner's tracking whether the client is demonstrating a fluent repertoire of deictic relational responding and an ability to respond to questions that involve *I–you*, *here–there*, and *now–then* relation types across varying levels of complexity. The practitioner looking for selfing problems will want to assess whether the repertoire is in place by asking deictic questions: "If I were you, where would I be sitting now?" (Refer to table 4.1 for a series of questions ranging from very basic to more complex.) If the repertoire is present in that context, then its absence in others may indicate avoidance in those other circumstances (for example, around taking the perspective of a person the client has difficulty with). Therefore, monitoring improvements will differ according to the source of the deictic relational failure—that is, monitoring will depend on whether the failure is due to a basic repertoire deficit, is due to underrehearsal (as may occur in cases of social anhedonia, where the individual does not get pleasure from social interaction; see Villatte et al., 2008), or is specific to particular contexts (topics, situations, or individuals). For example, a client may have a proficient deictic relational responding repertoire and respond easily to perspective-taking exercises in the intervention setting or in unpressured situations but cannot take perspective when angry or anxious, and so forth. The practitioner will want to monitor for these context-specific difficulties in perspective taking and for how they are impacting the client's life. From the CBS point of view, perspective-taking skill is foundational to a healthy sense of self, and therefore this must be in place for selfing work to be effective.

Self-as-Content Issues

Assessing for self-as-content issues involves looking at how the client conceptualizes his or her self and determining whether the client's pattern of doing so is benign or may be blocking him or her from living a meaningful life. To that end, focusing on inflexibility with respect to self content is key.

ASSESSING FOR SELF CONTENT ISSUES

Self content includes the labels, evaluations, and descriptions that individuals hold about themselves. As described in chapter 6, how we respond with respect to that content is important. As discussed in that chapter, consistently responding to self content as *here* and *now*, rather than at least sometimes taking perspective on it by responding to it as *there* and *then*, entails strong patterns of transformation of function such that we identify with that content, and this limits our sense of self. This is what is referred to in acceptance and commitment therapy as *fusion*. As previously discussed, several features of verbal behavior (coherence, literality, rule following) and of socioverbal training of children (inappropriate ideals, inaccurate rules, simplistic labels, roles) can contribute to and exacerbate this pattern. The practitioner wants to assess for self content issues in order to determine whether selfing work is needed in the area of broadening the client's sense of selfing beyond self content. For almost all clients, self content issues will be present at least to some degree. There are certain indicators that can help the practitioner identify potential issues with respect to rigid attachment to self content. Some of these are listed in table 8.3.

Clients can see themselves in coordination with labels, roles, evaluations, and descriptions (lecturer, woman, kind, caring, aggressive). In session, the practitioner may assess for rigid attachment to self content. Such an assessment will be based on "I am" statements that the client makes in session: "I am an introvert," "I am annoying," and so forth.

Table 8.3. Examples of What to Assess For with Respect to Rigid Attachment to Self Content

Context for rigid attachment	What to assess for	Example of statement by client
Self-descriptions	"I am" statements	I am kind. I am annoying.
Justifications for self-descriptions	"I am…because" statements	I am a failure because I never got an education. I am boring because I'm an introvert.
Coherence of self stories	Elaborate self stories	I am stupid. I was a high school dropout. I have never held down a job for more than three months. I often don't understand what people are talking about.
Self rules	"If…then" statements	If I am flawed, then I do not deserve love.
Self content	Belief that story about the self is true, and defense of the story as factual	But I am an actual failure—that is plain to see.

In addition, clients often give reasons why particular descriptions may apply to them: "I am boring because I am an introvert, and there is nothing I can do about it." In this example, the client sees being an introvert as the reason why he is boring. This implies that he is stuck. That is, he can't change his being an introvert, and so he is stuck with being boring. In the assessment, the practitioner will also want to access the self rules the client holds and find out how and why the client responds to these self rules. Sometimes self rules are spontaneously expressed by the client during the session: "If I annoy my father, he will cut me out of his will." But if self rules are not spontaneously expressed, then the practitioner can ask questions about the client's specific behavior. For example, imagine a client who freezes and stops talking at certain points in therapy. The therapist may ask, "What were you thinking before you froze and stopped talking?" In this case, the practitioner is helping the client identify an antecedent to the behavior in question. Alternatively, the practitioner may ask the client to state the assumed consequences of his or her behavior: "What would have happened if you had continued talking?"

One final and critically important thing that should be noted is the importance of function as opposed to topography. Ultimately, the therapist is not simply looking for particular types of content per se but for rigid attachment to that content. Identifying patterns of rigid attachment to content (such as descriptions, self stories, rules, reasons, and so on) is the first step in facilitating an alternative and healthier pattern of responding to such content.

MONITORING IMPROVEMENT IN SELF CONTENT ISSUES

To gauge improvements in a client's self content issues, the practitioner should look for patterns in which the client adopts different perspectives, demonstrates curiosity about new ideas, contacts long-term consequences of his behavior that may previously have been overlooked, shows increased accuracy in tracking, or responds on the basis of useful coherence (such as coherence with personal values) rather than on the basis of social approval. The practitioner may assess the extent to which the client can respond flexibly with respect to evaluations, descriptions, and labels that the client holds about himself. The practitioner may also monitor the extent to which the client shows flexibility around self rules that may previously have been limiting. For example, a rule formerly held as important, such as "If I am not rich, my life is a failure," may come to be evaluated in terms of whether it helps the client live a meaningful life rather than in terms of how right or true the rule is. Here is an example of an exchange in which the client starts to take a different perspective:

Client: You know, when I came in here, I believed that because I wasn't rich, I was a failure. Absolutely 100 percent believed that. Over the past few weeks, I have been looking at what my mind says to me, and when it is useful for me. One

Therapist: Did it block you this week?

Client: Yeah. I was with my son for the afternoon on Sunday, and he wanted to play ball with me outside, and I was feeling sorry for myself and like a failure, and I told him to go play with the neighbor kid. Then I realized sending him off and not spending time with him is me being a failure, because I love that kid and want to be a good father.

Monitoring improvements in the client's self content issues will help the practitioner identify whether the client is still rigidly attached to his self content or has flexibility regarding labels, rules, and reasons that he holds about himself that previously kept him stuck in unhealthy patterns of behavior.

A Contextual Sense of Self

Ultimately, the aim of therapeutic intervention should be to establish a repertoire of healthy, flexible selfing. Of course an important aspect of this process is the identification of problematic patterns of selfing, such as we have just discussed. But the flip side to monitoring for problems is looking out for signs of psychological health. In other words, the practitioner will also want to assess for the emergence of a more flexible, contextual sense of self. We have already mentioned several potentially relevant self-report questionnaires designed to measure various aspects of the three selfing repertoires (self-as-process, self-as-content, and self-as-context). In session, the practitioner may also assess for a client's contextual sense of self via the client's in-session responding or on the basis of the client's reports of events outside the therapy room. In assessing for a contextual sense of self, the practitioner should try to determine whether the client has a flexible selfing repertoire in four key areas:

1. Awareness of the variability of his experiences (*I* as various)

2. Stability in a perspective (*I* as perspective)

3. A hierarchical sense of self (*I* as container)

4. Ability to respond in line with his values (*I* as flexible)

Therefore, the practitioner may examine whether the client notices that his experiences vary, can see that he has a common sense of perspective across his experiences ("What part of you is noticing that?"), has a hierarchical sense of perspective on his experiences ("There's a part of you that contains those experiences"), and can respond flexibly in valued directions without interference from his self-concept or self rules. Note, however, that in cases of developmental delay, as in the third case example later in this chapter, the first two repertoires are the main focus for the practitioner.

With respect to monitoring improvements in a contextual sense of self, the practitioner will notice a contextual sense of self developing in a client when the client starts to indicate that she notices the variability of her experiences, can flexibly take perspective, talks in terms of an observer self ("A part of me noticed my thoughts"), notices her self content as content rather than as her core self ("I am having the thought that I am not good enough"), and starts to behave in line with her values rather than being blocked by self content. This shift can occur in session, as when the client says, "I notice that I feel anxiety and want to make an excuse for leaving, and I think that tells me I should stay" or "The thought that I am not good enough is coming to mind when you ask me what I want, and I guess that is just a thought I am having." It may also be seen in reports about experiences outside the therapy room: "Last week I was extremely premenstrual, and the anxious me that shows up was there, seeming like it was speaking the truth. I just noticed my thoughts and how believable they seemed, and how intense the anxiety seemed, and I thought *I am more than this experience, and if I keep reacting to it, I am going to have no friends left* and I decided to go to the party with anxiety along for the ride. Somehow it was there, but there was a larger me that was able to hold it." A contextual sense of self that is moving toward valued life directions is the ultimate goal for selfing work in session. As the client starts to demonstrate a contextual sense of self across sessions, the larger part of the selfing work will be complete, and reminders or top-up experiential exercises can be used to keep that repertoire rehearsed and fluent.

Selfing Problems: Three Case Examples

In this section, we look at selfing issues in the context of three particular case examples. The first is characterized by inflexible framing of negative self content. The second involves inflexible framing of positive self content. The third has to do with a deficiency in deictic relational responding. Although the forms of the self problems in the first two cases differ—they involve issues of primarily positive and negative self-concept, respectively—the functionally defined phenomenon of inflexible responding with respect to self content is similar in both cases. It should be noted that many individuals showing either inflexible responding with respect to self content or deficits in deictic framing may not meet diagnostic criteria for a particular formally defined disorder. Alternatively, people with the same functionally defined behavior may meet criteria for different clinical categories. Furthermore, it is not just clinical psychologists who may have to assess for and intervene with selfing problems such as those described in what follows but also professionals across diverse arenas of application (coaching, sports psychology, educational settings, and so forth). Hence, although functional assessment can overlap with traditional clinical diagnosis, it need not do so, and the cases discussed here are relevant in a much wider way than simply with respect to clinical problems.

Case Example 1. Nessa: Inflexible Relational Framing with Respect to the Self as Negative

Nessa, a forty-five-year-old female, describes her experience as follows:

I'm just…nothing. I'm not even worth my own time or effort. I don't do anything that matters. I am not the mother I would like to be to my children. I am distracted when I am around the kids, and so I cannot engage with them and have fun like mothers should. And things I do try, I always manage to screw up somehow. To the people in my life, if I'm not totally inconsequential, I'm causing unnecessary pain. I can't stand me. I can't imagine how anyone else could. I should just stay away and save everyone the trouble.

Nessa's evaluations of herself as worthless and burdensome limit her engagement in therapy, in her social world, and in her life broadly. Furthermore, in withdrawing, she limits her contact with potential sources of values-based reinforcement (such as a connected relationship with her husband and children), which could improve her experiences of herself, the world, and others and increase variability in her behavior.

A CBS approach would be to help Nessa experience herself as more than just the labels and evaluations that she has for herself. The practitioner would want to help her experience relationships, therapy, and her life broadly as more than just places where she either doesn't matter or causes harm.

CLIENT SELF-REPORTS

Nessa says she's "finally" seeking therapy because she's "sick of feeling so awful all the time." She says it's been five years since she felt something other than "depression and shame." She describes her life in terms of "the real me, before I got depressed" and "this person I've become." She says she doesn't go places or do things because she is "just too ashamed," and that the shame "takes away anything that used to be good" about her life. She says she hates to have her family see her this way.

EXPERIENTIALLY EVOKED CLIENT REPORTS

Nessa completed a written exercise in session that required her to identify her attempts to deal with her feelings of depression. She evaluated each attempt in terms of how effective this response was both in the short term and over the long term. She indicated that one way she tried to deal with feeling low was by avoiding social interactions. She reported that in the short term, this helped her conceal her depression from others, but over the long term it has led to her feeling worse and more ashamed of herself. She also said that she watches daytime TV in her bedroom to distract herself, and this makes her feel like a "worthless person." Finally, she said that coming to therapy was also an attempt to get rid of her low mood, but that so far its short- and long-term benefits were unclear to her.

CLIENT–THERAPIST INTERACTION

While interacting with the therapist, Nessa has been tearful and expressed discomfort around experiential exercises that involved exploring current feelings. Nessa has indicated that looking at her feelings of shame in session will be very painful for her, and she tends to wander off topic when these exercises begin, indicating that the therapist does not understand how difficult it is for her. In session, Nessa is persistently tearful and has trouble following directions and giving contingent responses.

ASSESSING FOR SELFING ISSUES

Ability to Discriminate Experiences and Accurately Label Internal Experiences

From Nessa's self-reports and experientially evoked reports, and from the client–therapist interaction, we can see that Nessa's discrimination of her ongoing experiences is somewhat limited. Nessa has some awareness of her depressed mood in terms of what happens before, what happens after, when it is likely to occur, whether it happens in certain locations, with certain people, and so forth. But she is unaware that attempts to get rid of her internal experiences of depression and shame trigger more depression and shame. These attempts to avoid internal experience also trigger more thoughts of being worthless and of not being the person she once was. She also reports that she has felt "only" depression and shame for the past five years. Here we can see a lack of awareness of the variability of her experience across time. Although much of her time may involve experiences of depression and shame, she will also have had other types of experiences.

Deictic Relational Responding Repertoire

Nessa has a fluent deictic relational responding repertoire, but it is under-rehearsed in some situations, as evidenced by her lack of perspective on her own experiences. One reason for the latter may be her social exclusion over the past five years. Nessa also appears to avoid taking the perspectives of those close to her. This may be due to her avoidance of doing so because she is so ashamed and scared of what they may feel. This may also be occurring with the practitioner as Nessa wanders off topic when present-moment exercises are introduced, since she has indicated that the therapist does not understand how difficult these are for her.

Self-Related Coherence Issues

Looking at Nessa's fluency, flexibility, and self rules, we can see that there is rigidity in the labels, evaluations, and descriptions that she uses about herself (for example, she says that she is not "the real me" and that she is "worthless"). Nessa is caught in a coherence trap, seeing her feelings of shame as the reason she is not going places or doing things: if feelings of shame mean she can't go places or do things, then in order to engage in those activities, she first has to get rid of shame, which she can't do. Here we see an example of inaccurate tracking. That is, Nessa cannot discriminate that she can behave in line with her values even when depression and shame are present. When Nessa says, "I am not the mother I would like to be to my children," we can see inflexible relational framing with respect to a self role and how a mother should be. In addition, she buys into self rules about being "trouble" and therefore says she should "stay away" from everyone ("I should just stay away and save everyone the trouble").

Contextual Sense of Self

Nessa is demonstrating a weak or absent contextual sense of self. First, she is struggling to notice that her experiences vary; she thinks that she is experiencing only depression and shame. Second, her sense of a hierarchical perspective is absent in that she views herself in coordination with particular feelings and labels (such as "worthless"). Third, she blames herself and does not see the possibility of being able to respond in line with her values. Her self-concept is rigid and inflexible, and her behavior is out of contact with her values (such as being a good parent).

CONCEPTUALIZING A POTENTIAL INTERVENTION

One way to conceptualize or plan an intervention for Nessa will be in terms of building a broader, more flexible sense of self. The goal in therapy will be to create a context where she can practice being more flexible in terms of getting out and doing more things, getting in touch with her values, being more present in session and in her life, and experiencing herself as the same person she's always been, with just as many choices.

From Nessa's self-reports and experientially evoked reports, and from the client–therapist interaction, we can see that one useful strategy for intervention will be to work on her awareness of variability in her experiences (that is, *I* as various). Nessa is struggling to notice that her experiences vary. From this point on, the therapist can move toward supporting stability in a sense of perspective (that is, *I* as perspective) rather than a conceptualized self (in Nessa's case, inflexibility in her relational framing). This can be followed by more explicit work to build on this stable sense of self and develop a contextual sense of self (that is, *I* as container), which can afford more flexibility. It will be important throughout this work to help Nessa see that she is able to respond in line with her values (that is, *I* as Flexible). The therapist should enable her to see that she is not to blame for her current situation but is now able to respond in meaningful directions. (See chapter 7 for a detailed account of how to facilitate a contextual sense of self in clients when it is absent or deficient.)

Case Example 2. Geoff: Inflexible Relational Framing with Respect to the Self as Positive

Some individuals struggle with inflexibility regarding primarily negative self content; others struggle with inflexibility regarding positive self content. Inflexible relational framing with respect to positive self content can be as problematic as inflexible relational framing with respect to negative self content, if not more so. Actually, these patterns are closely linked. Functionally, inflexible framing with respect to positive self content is very often tied to avoidance of negative self content. For example, if a person's identity and self-worth are tied to the idea that he is superior to others, then if he is confronted by people who appear superior along some dimension, he may feel the need to belittle or avoid them in order to feel worthwhile. And there can be further problems; for example, a pattern of responses of this kind may have a negative impact on the person's relationships and may result in social isolation or toxic relationship dynamics that only reinforce this behavioral repertoire.

Geoff is a thirty-two-year-old man who recently married a forty-eight-year-old divorcée who has adult children. Geoff's relationship with his wife's grown children is strained, and he has come to therapy in order to sort out the stress caused by their issues with the marriage. He speaks in an exasperated tone of voice throughout the initial therapy session.

CLIENT SELF-REPORTS

Geoff reports that, really, the issue here is not with me. I met a great woman, fell in love, and we got married. Unfortunately, my wife's children are incredibly disrespectful to her. Our relationship is fantastic, but other people seem to have a problem with that. I suspect they are jealous of our situation. They're not willing to allow their mother to just be happy. It has to be on their terms. They're just so selfish. Her son Mark in particular shows no respect and complains that his mother is moving too fast and ignoring their emotional needs. Their father was an alcoholic and left years before we met. They hardly expected their mother to stay alone forever, did they? Did they want her to be miserable? I am a very personable man, but they make it difficult for me. Mark and his wife always end up in fights with his mother when they come to visit. I assume they are miserable in their own marriage, and that is why they start these fights. The whole situation has been causing me tremendous stress. I would never behave so badly toward my parents. And I certainly would never raise children to show such disrespect. I have come here to get some advice on how to make my wife's children see sense.

EXPERIENTIALLY EVOKED CLIENT REPORTS

When Geoff was asked to report on the perspective of his wife's adult children, he struggled to identify what their position or feelings in the situation might be. He talked more about their jealousy of his and his wife's situation than about any feelings they may have toward him. Here is an excerpt from Geoff's dialogue with the therapist:

Therapist: And what do you think Mark was thinking when his mother told him she was going to get married again?

Geoff: No idea. It's hard to tell with Mark. He's very dramatic and theatrical. It's all front. I do suspect he is jealous of our happiness. I know it causes me high levels of stress and upset. My stress levels escalate when I hear they are coming to visit.

Therapist: Is there anything else that he might have been feeling?

Geoff: Not that I know of. And I'm not really sure where you are going with this. How is this going to sort out my problem with them? How do I convince them to behave better? They just don't see my point of view. They're so selfish. How do I make them be less selfish? I hope you know what you are doing here.

CLIENT–THERAPIST INTERACTION

Geoff is defensive around conversations that suggest that there are two sides to the situation or that he may be at fault. He frequently cuts the therapist off and corrects him. He is very persistent in his position that it is others and not himself who are to blame for the current situation. He questions the therapist's credentials and is dismissive when the therapist tries to move him toward taking anyone else's perspective.

ASSESSING FOR SELFING ISSUES

Ability to Discriminate Experiences and Accurately Label Internal Experiences

From Geoff's self-reports and experientially evoked reports, and from the client–therapist interaction, we can see that Geoff has difficulty seeing the perspective of his wife's children or, indeed, the perspective of anyone else who does not share his own perspective. This inability is related to the fact that he has difficulties in discriminating his own behavior; that is, he is willing to see only a perspective that puts him in a positive light, and he has limited ability to discriminate internal experiences of discomfort about himself or his behavior.

Deictic Relational Responding Repertoire

Geoff cannot understand how the relationship between these two adult children and their mother is different from their relationship with him. This failure to take their perspective may be due to a deficit or lack of fluency in *you–you* deictic relational responding. That is, it may be the result of his not having rehearsed taking the perspectives of others when doing so did not involve referencing the self (*I*). The practitioner can test to see whether there is a *you–you* deictic relational responding deficit. One way to do this is first to see if Geoff can take the perspective of the therapist and, ideally, one other person. For example, the therapist can say, "Imagine that my friend lost her job and was feeling really depressed. If I were my friend, what would I be feeling?" Both Geoff's capacity to provide the correct answer to this question and the fluency of his responding should be assessed.

Self-Related Coherence Issues

Looking at Geoff's fluency, flexibility, and self rules, we can see that there is rigidity in the labels, evaluations, and descriptions he holds about himself as right and positive in terms of his part of the interaction. He does not see that his actions may be contributing to the problem. Geoff is inflexible in his relational framing of his wife's children as being solely to blame.

Contextual Sense of Self

Geoff has a limited contextual sense of self as observer. He is rigid in his narrative about being right and sees himself in coordination with his positive self labels. He is unable to take a hierarchical contextual perspective on his experiences because he rigidly defends his positive self-concept.

CONCEPTUALIZING A POTENTIAL INTERVENTION

Looking at Geoff's self-reports and experientially evoked reports, and at details of the client–therapist interaction, we can say that one place for the therapist to start will be working to see that Geoff is able to respond in line with his values (*I* as flexible). It will be important to emphasize that this will not involve having Geoff blame himself; that is, blame does not need to be allocated to others or to the self. It will be useful instead to teach Geoff to respond in more valued and more workable ways, irrespective of whether that alters his self-concept of being in the right. In cases like this, when the client is resistant to taking any responsibility for the situation, a useful first step is to reframe the therapy agenda as effective influencing of others:

Therapist: So if our work here could be about learning to influence these difficult people in your life more effectively, would that be useful?

Client: Yes, that would be very helpful.

Therapist: So can we have a look at what you've tried saying and doing so far that hasn't worked to influence them the way you want?

This form of exchange is in line with what Geoff has come to therapy for, and he buys into the idea that he and the therapist are on the same page and that the therapist can help him move through important steps for building a healthy sense of self. Once the value of being in therapy is set for Geoff, the therapist can move on to assessing whether Geoff's deictic relational responding repertoire is deficient, underrehearsed, or just lacking in this particular context with his wife's adult children. If the repertoire is deficient or underrehearsed, then the therapist can expose Geoff to training exercises to develop the repertoire. (See chapter 4 for examples of exercises to help with the development of deictic relational responding in individuals in whom it is underrehearsed or deficient.) From here, the therapist can work on Geoff's understanding that his experiences vary (I as various). This may involve exercises that involve Geoff's contacting the present moment and noticing that his thoughts and feelings vary across time. Next may come work to support Geoff's gaining stability in a sense of perspective and broadening his "I am right" narrative (I as perspective). This work can be followed by work on building a contextual sense of self (I as container). (Again, see chapter 7 for how to roll out an intervention to promote a broader contextual sense of self.)

When an individual comes to therapy to solve a problem that he thinks is caused solely by others, it is important for the clinician to emphasize the need for work that will "responsibilize" the client. To that end, the clinician needs to do two things:

1. Identify what the client wants in terms of specific goals and overarching values

2. Help the client focus on his own behavior instead of waiting for someone else's behavior to change

If the practitioner does not start there, then any work on the "I as various" process or the "I as perspective" process will not be effective, because the client will not want to do it. Usually in these cases the practitioner will start with goals before moving on to values. This work may begin with questions like "What do you want others to say or do differently?" and "So would you say that our aim is to look at how you can influence their behavior flexibly?" At that point, the practitioner can segue into values with statements like "You can influence them in ways that make you look bad and worsen your relationship—aggression, criticism, lies, intimidation, and blame—or you can influence them in ways that make you look good and improve your relationship with them."

Case Example 3. Owen: Developmental Delay in Perspective Taking

Owen is a seven-year-old child diagnosed on the autism spectrum. He was taken to an educational psychologist for assessment and for development of a program of intervention that can help him socialize and play with other children. At school, Owen typically plays on his own during recess. He loves Thomas the Tank Engine, a fictional steam locomotive, and he constantly wants to talk about Thomas, but his classmates aren't interested. Owen can't understand why his classmates won't play games based on Thomas when he wants them to. He typically doesn't initiate conversations with others except when he wants to talk about Thomas, is hungry, wants screen time, or wants certain snacks.

CLIENT SELF-REPORTS

Owen mentions playing alone and not having friends at school. He says this makes him sad. He has not initiated any conversations with the practitioner and has responded to most questions with one-word answers.

EXPERIENTIALLY EVOKED CLIENT REPORTS

The therapist assessed Owen with the RFT Perspective Taking Protocol (McHugh et al., 2004). Owen's responses on the protocol indicated that he could respond accurately to simple *I–you*, *here–there*, and *now–then* deictic tasks, but not to tasks that required reversed and double reversed relational responding (of the type "If here were there" and "If I were you and now were then," respectively). This finding suggests that Owen has a limited deictic relational repertoire. Therefore, training in deictic relations is needed, particularly reversed and double reversed *I–you*, *here–there*, and *now–then* relations. Owen became distressed and confused when he was asked how he was feeling.

CLIENT–THERAPIST INTERACTION

Owen's eye contact was poor. His social communication was limited. He seemed uninterested in interacting with the practitioner and wanted only to talk about Thomas the Tank Engine. When he was asked deictic questions ("What are you wearing today?" "What am I holding now?"), he either refused to respond or responded inaccurately.

ASSESSING FOR SELFING ISSUES

Ability to Discriminate Experiences and Accurately Label Internal Experiences

Owen had weak discrimination of his ongoing experiences, and he became distressed and confused when he was asked about how he was feeling. Owen needs to be prompted to emote self experience and to tact his preferences and needs.

Deictic Relational Responding Repertoire

As mentioned earlier, Owen was assessed with the RFT Perspective Taking Protocol (McHugh et al., 2004). He was found to have very weak responding across all deictic relational tasks except simple *I–you*, *here–there*, and *now–then* tasks.

Self-Related Coherence Issues

Because of Owen's limited deictic relational responding repertoire, his self-concept is relatively limited.

Contextual Sense of Self

Owen has no contextual sense of self as observer. He lacks the basic deictic and hierarchical relational skills.

CONCEPTUALIZING A POTENTIAL INTERVENTION

Owen has a weak repertoire of deictic relational responding. He also has had limited exposure to interactions that involve learning to discriminate his own internal experiences. In order to facilitate the development of Owen's basic deictic relational responding repertoire, multiple-exemplar training in deictic relational responding tasks involving *I–you*, *here–there*, and *now–then* trials, starting with simple *now–then* trials and moving on to reversed and double reversed *I–you*, *here–there*, and *now–then* trials, will be required. This training should be accompanied by explicit discrimination training to aid Owen in tacting of his own and others' emotional experiences.

Signs That Self Work Is Needed

Table 8.4 reprises the list of self issues that we saw in table I.1, along with that table's list of typical statements expressing each of the issues, but table 8.4 also includes suggestions for where the practitioner might begin a selfing intervention in each instance. The table shows what may work across many contexts, and it shows potential starting points, but of course it is impossible to determine the function of any given behavior without knowing the context in which it occurs. From the perspective of contextual behavioral science, healthy selfing involves flexibility in all the selfing repertoires suggested in the table: deictic relational responding, self-as-process, *I* as various, *I* as perspective, *I* as container, and *I* as flexible. If you are unsure about any of the suggested interventions, see chapter 4 (deictic relational training and rehearsal; self-as-process and self-discrimination training) and chapter 7 (*I* as various, *I* as perspective, *I* as container, and *I* as flexible) for additional details.

Table 8.4. Signs That Self Work Is Needed, with Suggested Starting Points for Selfing Interventions

Issue	Example of statement by client	Where to begin selfing intervention
Lack of clarity about values	I don't really know what I care about.	Self-as-process
Self-righteousness	I'm more honest than you—I'd never lie like that.	*I* as perspective
Operating on autopilot	Sorry, I missed that—I'm up to my neck in it.	Self-as-process
Feeling of threat from internal experiences	I can't stand these feelings.	*I* as various
Lack of perspective	I don't care how he feels—he brought it on himself!	Deictic relational training/rehearsal
Hyperattentiveness to views of others	Have I offended you? Are you upset with me?	Self-as-process
Lack of connectedness to others	I don't fit in—I'm different.	*I* as container
Personal rigidity	But this is just who I am.	*I* as various
Sense of emptiness	I feel empty—there is nothing to me.	*I* as perspective
Painful self-judgments	I should have said something—I'm so weak!	*I* as flexible

Afterword

Many of the challenges that arise in applied psychological settings, especially clinical settings, have to do with the self. Therefore, it is important for practitioners to have a useful, scientifically valid account of the self and of self-related issues.

Our aim in this book has been to describe the self from the pragmatic, scientific perspective of contextual behavioral science (CBS). We began with an introduction to contextual behavioral science's basic philosophy (functional contextualism) and psychological science (behavior analysis). From this perspective, all behavior can be seen as contextually situated, potentially guidable action.

But our capacity for symbolic language is what truly makes human beings different and enables us to acquire self-knowledge and awareness beyond that of any other species. Relational frame theory (RFT) explains language as the learned repertoire of relational framing. Once we acquire this hugely generative and transformative repertoire, we see and respond to the world in ways that no nonverbal creature can do. And one of the most powerful and experientially profound aspects of our acquiring this repertoire is that we also acquire a repertoire of selfing. In this book's eight chapters, we described the acquisition of selfing, from its origins in infancy to its full emergence in adulthood as the separable selfing dimensions of content, process, and context.

At the heart of the CBS/RFT approach is the question of how selfing problems characterized by rigid attachment to self content can be remediated through consistent practice of selfing in the current moment (selfing-as-process), in tandem with an appreciation of self as the psychological container of one's experiences (selfing-as-context). On the basis of that approach, we examined how psychological suffering can arise and how it can be addressed, outlining a framework for assessing and remediating clients' selfing problems. We believe that the book offers a tremendously practical, useful step toward understanding the self from a pragmatic point of view, and we hope that our descriptions of the CBS/RFT approach are clear and useful.

References

Allyon, T., & Azrin, N. H. (1964). Reinforcement and instructions with mental patients. *Journal of the Experimental Analysis of Behavior, 7,* 327–331.

Almada, P. (2016). *Examining the role of deictics, empathic concern, and experiential avoidance in prosocial and coercive behavior: Contributions from relational frame theory.* (Unpublished doctoral dissertation). University of Wollongong.

American Psychiatric Association. (2013). *Diagnostic and statistical manual of mental disorders* (5th ed.). Washington, DC: American Psychiatric Association.

Baer, D., M., Peterson, R. F., & Sherman, J. A. (1967). The development of imitation by reinforcing behavioral similarity to a model. *Journal of the Experimental Analysis Behavior, 10,* 405–416.

Barnes-Holmes, D., & Barnes-Holmes, Y. (2000). Explaining complex behavior: Two perspectives on the concept of generalized operant classes. *Psychological Record, 50,* 251–265.

Barnes-Holmes, D., Barnes-Holmes, Y., Hussey, I., & Luciano, C. (2016). Relational frame theory: Finding its historical and intellectual roots and reflecting upon its future development: An introduction to Part II. In R. D. Zettle, S. C. Hayes, D. Barnes-Holmes, & A. Biglan (Eds.), *The Wiley handbook of contextual behavioral science* (pp. 117–128). Chichester, West Sussex, England: Wiley-Blackwell.

Barnes-Holmes, D., Barnes-Holmes, Y., Luciano, C., & McEnteggart, C. (2017). From the IRAP and REC model to a multi-dimensional multi-level framework for analyzing the dynamics of arbitrarily applicable relational responding. *Journal of Contextual Behavioral Science, 6,* 434–445.

Barnes-Holmes, D., Hayes, S. C., & Dymond, S. (2001). Self and self-directed rules. In S. C. Hayes, D. Barnes-Holmes, & B. Roche (Eds.), *Relational frame theory: A post-Skinnerian account of human language and cognition* (pp. 119–140). New York: Kluwer Academic Press/Plenum Press.

Barnes-Holmes, D., O'Hora, D., Roche, B., Hayes, S. C., Bissett, R. T., & Lyddy, F. (2001). Understanding and verbal regulation. In S. C. Hayes, D. Barnes-Holmes, & B. Roche (Eds.), *Relational frame theory: A post-Skinnerian account of human language and cognition* (pp. 103–118). New York: Kluwer Academic Press/Plenum Press.

Barnes-Holmes, Y. (2001). *Analysing relational frames: Studying language and cognition in young children.* (Unpublished doctoral dissertation). National University of Ireland.

Baron, A., Kaufman, K., & Stauber, K. (1969). Effects of instructions and reinforcement-feedback on human operant behavior maintained by fixed-interval reinforcement. *Journal of the Experimental Analysis of Behavior, 12,* 701–712.

Biglan, A., & Hayes, S. C. (1996). Should the behavioral sciences become more pragmatic? The case for functional contextualism in research on human behavior. *Applied and Preventive Psychology: Current Scientific Perspectives, 5,* 47–57.

Davlin, N., L., Rehfeldt, R. A., & Lovett, S. (2011). A relational frame theory approach to understanding perspective-taking using children's stories in typically developing children. *European Journal of Behavior Analysis, 12,* 403–430.

Dennett, D. (1991). *Consciousness explained.* Boston: Back Bay Books.

Dougher, M. J., Augustson, E. M., Markham, M. R., Greenway, D. E., & Wulfert, E. (1994).The transfer of respondent eliciting and extinction functions through stimulus equivalence classes. *Journal of the Experimental Analysis of Behavior, 62,* 331–351.

Dougher, M. J., Hamilton, D. A., Fink, B., & Harrington, J. (2007). Transformation of the discriminative and eliciting functions of generalized relational stimuli. *Journal of the Experimental Analysis of Behavior, 88,* 179–197.

Downs, A., & Smith, T. (2004). Emotional understanding, cooperation, and social behavior in high-functioning children with autism. *Journal of Autism Developmental Disorders, 34,* 625–635.

Durand, V. M. (1993). Functional communication training using assistive devices: Effects on challenging behavior and affect. *Augmentative and Alternative Communication, 9,* 168–176.

Dymond, S., & Barnes, D. (1994). A transfer of self-discrimination response functions through equivalence relations. *Journal of the Experimental Analysis of Behavior, 62,* 251–267.

Dymond, S., & Barnes, D. (1995). A transformation of self-discrimination response functions in accordance with the arbitrarily applicable relations of sameness, more than, and less than. *Journal of the Experimental Analysis of Behavior, 64,* 163–184.

Dymond, S., & Barnes, D. (1996). A transformation of self-discrimination response functions in accordance with the arbitrarily applicable relations of sameness and opposition. *Psychological Record, 46,* 271–300.

Dymond, S., & Rehfeldt, R. (2000). Understanding complex behavior: The transformation of stimulus functions. *Behavior Analyst, 23,* 239–254.

Dymond, S., May, R. J., Munnelly, A., & Hoon, A. E. (2010). Evaluating the evidence base for relational frame theory: A citation analysis. *Behavior Analyst, 33,* 97–117.

Farb, N. A. S., Segal, Z. V., Mayberg, H., Bean, J., McKeon, D., Fatima, Z., & Anderson, A. K. (2007). Attending to the present: Mindfulness meditation reveals distinct neural modes of self-reference. *Social Cognitive and Affective Neuroscience, 2,* 313–322.

Foody, M., Barnes-Holmes, Y., & Barnes-Holmes, D. (2012). The role of self in acceptance and commitment therapy. In L. McHugh & I. Stewart (Eds.), *The self and perspective taking: Contributions and applications from modern behavioral science* (pp. 125–142). Oakland, CA: New Harbinger.

Foody, M., Barnes-Holmes, Y., Barnes-Holmes, D., & Luciano, C. (2013). An empirical investigation of hierarchical versus distinction relations in a self-based ACT exercise. *International Journal of Psychology and Psychological Therapy, 13,* 373–388.

Freeman, H. (2014, April 29). So "debonair" George has been "tamed," while "tragic" Jen was "saved"—no surprise there. *The Guardian,* https://www.theguardian.com/commentisfree/2014/apr/29/george-clooney-amal-alamuddin-jennifer-aniston-engagement.

Gallagher, S. (2000). Philosophical conceptions of the self: Implications for cognitive science. *Trends in Cognitive Sciences, 4*, 14–21.

Gallup, G. G. Jr. (1977). Self-recognition in primates: A comparative approach to the bidirectional properties of consciousness. *American Psychologist, 32*, 329–338.

Gil, E., Luciano, C., Ruiz, F., & Valdivia Salas, S. (2014). A further experimental step in the analysis of hierarchical responding. *International Journal of Psychology and Psychological Therapy, 14*, 137–153.

Gird, S., Zettle, R. D., Webster, B. K., & Hardage-Bundy, A. (2012, July). *Developing a quantitative measure of self-as-context: Preliminary findings.* Presentation at the annual conference of the Association for Contextual Behavioral Science, Washington, DC. Retrieved from https://contextualscience.org/files/MeasureSACGrid_.pdf

Giurfa, M., Zhang, S., Jenett, A., Menzel, R., & Srinivasan, M. (2001). The concepts of "sameness" and "difference" in an insect. *Nature, 410*, 930–933.

Gordon, T., & Borushok, J. (2017). *The ACT approach: A comprehensive guide for acceptance and commitment therapy.* Eau Claire, WI: PESI.

Harris, P., Johnson, C. N., Hutton, D., Andrews, G., & Cooke, T. (1989). Young children's theory of mind and emotion. *Cognition and Emotion, 3*, 379–400.

Hayes, S. C. (1984). Making sense of spirituality. *Behaviorism, 12*, 99–110.

Hayes, S. C. (1993). Analytic goals and the varieties of scientific contextualism. In S. C. Hayes, L. J. Hayes, H. W. Reese, & T. R. Sarbin (Eds.), *Varieties of scientific contextualism* (pp. 11–27). Reno, NV: Context Press.

Hayes, S. C. (1995). Knowing selves. *Behavior Therapist, 18*, 94–96.

Hayes, S. C. (2004). Taxonomy as a contextualist views it. *Journal of Clinical Psychology, 60*, 1231–1235.

Hayes, S. C. (2011). Discussion on the Association for Contextual Behavioral Science listserv.

Hayes, S. C., Barnes-Holmes, D., & Roche, B. (Eds.). (2001). *Relational frame theory: A post-Skinnerian account of human language and cognition.* New York: Kluwer Academic Press/Plenum Press.

Hayes, S. C., Barnes-Holmes, D., & Wilson, K. G. (2012). Contextual behavioral science: Creating a science more adequate to the challenge of the human condition. *Journal of Contextual Behavioral Science, 1,* 1–16.

Hayes, S. C., Brownstein, A. J., Haas, J. R., & Greenway, D. E. (1986). Instructions, multiple schedules, and extinction: Distinguishing rule-governed from scheduled-controlled behavior. *Journal of the Experimental Analysis of Behavior, 46,* 137–147.

Hayes, S. C., Fox, E., Gifford, E. V., Wilson, K. G., Barnes-Holmes, D., & Healy, O. (2001). Derived relational responding as learned behavior. In S. C. Hayes, D. Barnes-Holmes, & B. Roche (Eds.), *Relational frame theory: A post-Skinnerian account of human language and cognition* (pp. 21–50). New York: Kluwer Academic Press/Plenum Press.

Hayes, S. C., & Gifford, E. V. (1997). The trouble with language: Experiential avoidance, rules, and the nature of verbal events. *Psychological Science, 8,* 170–173.

Hayes, S. C., Hayes, L. J., & Reese, H. W. (1988). Finding the philosophical core: A review of Stephen C. Pepper's *World Hypotheses: A Study in Evidence. Journal of the Experimental Analysis of Behavior, 50,* 97–111.

Hayes, S. C., & Smith, S. (2005). *Get out of your mind and into your life: The new acceptance and commitment therapy.* Oakland, CA: New Harbinger.

Hayes, S. C., Strosahl, K. D., & Wilson, K. G. (2011). *Acceptance and commitment therapy: The process and practice of mindful change.* New York: Guilford Press.

Hayes, S. C., & Wilson, K. G. (1993). Some applied implications of a contemporary behavior-analytic account of verbal events. *Behavior Analyst, 16,* 283–301.

Hayes, S. C., Zettle, R. D., & Rosenfarb, I. (1989). Rule following. In S. C. Hayes (Ed.), *Rule-governed behavior: Cognition, contingencies, and instructional control* (pp. 191–220). New York: Plenum.

Heagle, A. I., & Rehfeldt, R. A. (2006). Teaching perspective-taking skills to typically developing children through derived relational responding. *Journal of Early and Intensive Behavior Intervention, 3,* 1–34.

Hooper, N., Erdogan, A., Keen, G., Lawton, K., & McHugh, L. (2015). Perspective taking reduces the fundamental attribution error. *Journal of Contextual Behavioral Science, 4,* 69–72.

Hooper, N., Saunders, J., & McHugh, L. (2010). The derived generalization of thought suppression. *Learning and Behavior, 38*, 160–168.

Hughes, S., & Barnes-Holmes, D. (2016). Relational frame theory: The basic account. In R. D. Zettle, S. C. Hayes, D. Barnes-Holmes, & A. Biglan (Eds.), *The Wiley handbook of contextual behavioral science* (pp. 129–178). Chichester, West Sussex, England: Wiley-Blackwell.

Jackson, M. L., Mendoza, D. R., & Adams, A. N. (2014). Teaching a deictic relational repertoire to children with autism. *Psychological Record, 64*, 791–802.

James, W. (1981). *The principles of psychology.* Cambridge, MA: Harvard University Press.

Jeffcoat, T. R. (2015). *Development of the Reno Inventory of Self-Perspective (RISP): Measuring self in the ACT model.* (Unpublished doctoral thesis). University of Nevada, Reno.

Kanter, J. W., Parker, C. R., & Kohlenberg, R. J. (2001). Finding the self: A behavioral measure and its clinical implications. *Psychotherapy, 38*, 198–211.

Kaufman, A., Baron, A., & Kopp, R. E. (1966). Some effects of instructions on human operant behavior. *Psychonomic Monograph Supplements, 1*, 243–250. Goleta, CA: Psychonomic Press.

Lattal, K. A. (1975). Reinforcement contingencies as discriminative stimuli. *Journal of the Experimental Analysis of Behavior, 23*, 241–246.

LeBlanc, L. A., Coates, A. M., Daneshvar, S., Charlop-Christy, M. H., Morris, C., & Lancaster, B. M. (2003). Using video modeling and reinforcement to teach perspective-taking skills to children with autism. *Journal of Applied Behavior Analysis, 36*, 253–257.

Lovett, S., & Rehfeldt, R. A. (2014). An evaluation of multiple-exemplar instruction to teach perspective-taking skills to adolescents with Asperger syndrome. *Behavioral Development Bulletin, 19*, 22–36.

Maslow, A. H. (1964). *Religions, values, and peak experiences.* Columbus: Ohio State University Press.

Matthews, B. A., Shimoff, E., Catania, A. C., & Sagvolden, T. (1977). Uninstructed human responding: Sensitivity to ratio and interval contingencies. *Journal of the Experimental Analysis of Behavior, 27*, 453–467.

McAuliffe, D., Hughes, S., & Barnes-Holmes, D. (2014). The dark-side of rule-governed behavior: An experimental analysis of problematic rule-following in an adolescent population with depressive symptomatology. *Behavior Modification, 38,* 587–613.

McHugh, L., Barnes-Holmes, D., & Barnes-Holmes, Y. (2004). A relational frame account of the development of complex cognitive phenomena: Perspective-taking, false belief understanding, and deception. *International Journal of Psychology and Psychological Therapy, 4,* 303–324.

McHugh, L., Bobarnac, A., & Reed, P. (2011). Brief report: Teaching situation-based emotions to children with autistic spectrum disorder. *Journal of Autism and Developmental Disorders, 41,* 1423–1428.

McHugh, L., & Stewart, I. (Eds). (2012). *The self and perspective taking: Contributions and applications from modern behavioral science.* Oakland, CA: New Harbinger.

Michael, J. (2007). Motivating operations. In J. O. Cooper, T. E. Heron, & W. L. Heward (Eds.), *Applied behavior analysis.* 2nd ed. Upper Saddle River, NJ: Prentice Hall.

Miller, J., Fletcher, K., & Kabat-Zinn, J. (1995). Three-year follow-up and clinical implications of a mindfulness-based stress reduction intervention in the treatment of anxiety disorders. *General Hospital Psychiatry, 17,* 192–200.

Monestès, J. L. (2016). A functional place for language in evolution: The contribution of contextual behavioral science to the study of human evolution. In R. D. Zettle, S. C. Hayes, D. Barnes-Holmes, & A. Biglan (Eds.), *The Wiley handbook of contextual behavioral science* (pp. 100–114). Chichester, West Sussex, England: Wiley-Blackwell.

Monestès, J. L., Villatte, M., Stewart, I., & Loas, G. (2014). Rule-based insensitivity and delusion maintenance in schizophrenia. *Psychological Record, 64,* 329–338.

Montoya-Rodríguez, M. M., McHugh, L., & Molina, F. J. (2017). Teaching perspective-taking skills to an adult with Down syndrome: A case study. *Journal of Contextual Behavioral Science, 6,* 293–297.

Montoya-Rodríguez, M. M., Molina, F. J., & McHugh, L. (2017). A review of relational frame theory research into deictic relational responding. *Psychological Record, 67,* 569–579.

O'Connor, M., Farrell, L., Munnelly, A., & McHugh, L. (2017). Citation analysis of relational frame theory: 2009–2016. *Journal of Contextual Behavioral Science, 6,* 152–158.

O'Neill, J. (2012). *Training deictic relational responding in people with schizophrenia.* (Doctoral dissertation). University of South Florida. Retrieved from http://scholarcommons.usf.edu/etd/4188.

O'Neill, J., & Weil, T. M. (2014). Training deictic relational responding in people diagnosed with schizophrenia. *Psychological Record, 64,* 301–310.

Page S., & Neuringer, A. (1985). Variability is an operant. *Journal of Experimental Psychology: Animal Behavior Processes, 11,* 429–452.

Pepper, S. C. (1942). *World hypotheses: A study in evidence.* Berkeley: University of California Press.

Pliskoff, S., & Goldiamond, I. (1966). Some discriminative properties of fixed ratio performance in the pigeon. *Journal of the Experimental Analysis of Behavior, 9,* 1–9.

Pryor, K., Haag, R., & O'Reilly, J. (1969). The creative porpoise: Training for novel behavior. *Journal of the Experimental Analysis of Behavior, 12,* 653–661.

Rehfeldt, R.A., & Barnes-Holmes, Y. (Eds.) (2009). *Derived relational responding: Applications for learners with autism and other developmental disabilities: A progressive guide to change.* Oakland, CA: New Harbinger.

Rehfeldt, R. A., Dillen, J. E., Ziomek, M. M., & Kowalchuk, R. K. (2007). Assessing relational learning deficits in perspective-taking in children with high-functioning autism spectrum disorder. *Psychological Record, 57,* 23–47.

Rogers, C. (1961). *On becoming a person: A therapist's view of psychotherapy.* London: Constable.

Shimoff, E., Catania, C., & Matthews, B. A. (1981). Uninstructed human responding: Sensitivity of low-rate performance to schedule contingencies. *Journal of the Experimental Analysis of Behavior, 36,* 207–220.

Skinner, B. F. (1945). The operational analysis of psychological terms. *Psychological Review, 52,* 270–277.

Skinner, B. F. (1974). *About behaviorism.* London: Penguin.

Stewart, I. (2016). The fruits of a functional approach for psychological science. *International Journal of Psychology, 51,* 15–27.

Stewart, I., & Barnes-Holmes, D. (2004) Relational frame theory and analogical reasoning: Empirical investigations. *International Journal of Psychology and Psychological Therapy, 4,* 241–262.

Stewart, I., Hooper, N., Walsh, P., O'Keefe, R., Joyce, R., & McHugh, L. (2015). Transformation of thought suppression functions via same and opposite relations. *Psychological Record, 65,* 375–399.

Styles, R. G., & Atkins, P. W. B. (2018). *The Functional Self-Discrimination Measure & Interview: A measure of verbal behaviour that predicts wellbeing.* Leanpub, https://leanpub.com/FSDM_I.

Teper, R., Segal, Z., & Inzlicht, M. (2013). Inside the mindful mind: How mindfulness enhances emotion regulation through improvements in executive control. *Current Directions in Psychological Science, 22,* 449–454.

Törneke, N. (2010). *Learning RFT: An introduction to relational frame theory and its clinical applications.* Oakland, CA: New Harbinger.

Vilardaga, R. (2009). A relational frame theory account of empathy. *International Journal of Behavioral Consultation and Therapy, 5,* 178–184.

Vilardaga, R., Estévez, A., Levin, M. E., & Hayes, S. C. (2012). Deictic relational responding, empathy, and experiential avoidance as predictors of social anhedonia: Further contributions from relational frame theory. *Psychological Record, 62,* 409–432.

Vilardaga, R., & Hayes, S. C. (2011). A contextual behavioral approach to pathological altruism. In B. Oakley, A. Knafo, G. Madhavan, & D. S. Wilson (Eds.), *Pathological altruism* (pp. 31–48). New York: Oxford University Press.

Vilardaga, R., Waltz, T., Levin, M., Hayes, S. C., Stromberg, C., & Amador, K. (2009, July). Deictic relational framing and connectedness among college students: A small analog study. Presentation at the Third World Conference on ACT, RFT, and Contextual Behavioral Science, Enschede, The Netherlands.

Villatte, M. (2016, November). *A manifesto for clinical RFT.* Keynote address at the 10th conference of the Association of Contextual Behavioral Science, Australia and New Zealand chapter (ANZ ACBS), Melbourne.

Villatte, M., Monestès, J. L., McHugh, L., Freiza i Baqué, E., & Loas, G. (2008). Assessing deictic relational responding in social anhedonia: A functional approach to the development of theory of mind impairments. *International Journal of Behavioral Consultation and Therapy, 4*, 360–373.

Villatte, M., Villatte, J., & Hayes, S. C. (2016). *Mastering the clinical conversation: Language as intervention.* New York: Guilford Press.

Wegner, D. M. (1994). Ironic processes of mental control. *Psychological Review, 101*, 34–52.

Weil, T., Hayes, S., & Capurro, P. (2011). Establishing a deictic relational repertoire in young children. *Psychological Record, 61*, 371–390.

Weiner, H. (1970). Human behavioral persistence. *Psychological Record, 20*, 445–456.

Wilber, K. (1997). An integral theory of consciousness. *Journal of Consciousness Studies, 4*, 71–92.

Wilson, D. S., Hayes, S. C., Biglan, A., & Embry, D. D. (2014). Evolving the future: Toward a science of intentional change. *Behavioral and Brain Sciences, 37*, 395–416.

Wilson, K. G., & Blackledge, J. T. (2000). Recent developments in the behavioral analysis of language: Making sense of clinical phenomena. In M. Dougher (Ed.), *Clinical behavior analysis* (pp. 27–46). Reno, NV: Context Press.

Wulfert, E., Greenway, D. E., Farkas, P., Hayes, S. C., & Dougher, M. J. (1994). Correlation between self-reported rigidity and rule-governed insensitivity to operant contingencies. *Journal of Applied Behavior Analysis, 27*, 659–671.

Yu, L., McCracken, L. M., & Norton, S. (2016). The Self Experiences Questionnaire (SEQ): Preliminary analyses for a measure of self in people with chronic pain. *Journal of Contextual Behavioral Science, 5*, 127–133.

Zettle, R. D. (2007). *ACT for depression: A clinician's guide to using acceptance and commitment therapy in treating depression.* Oakland, CA: New Harbinger.

Zettle, R. D., & Hayes, S. C. (1982). Rule-governed behavior: A potential theoretical framework for cognitive behavior therapy. In P. C. Kendall (Ed.), *Advances in cognitive behavioral research and therapy* (pp. 73–118). New York: Academic Press.

Zettle, R. D., Hayes, S., C., Barnes-Holmes, D., & Biglan, A. (Eds.). (2016). *The Wiley handbook of contextual behavioral science.* Chichester, West Sussex, England: Wiley-Blackwell.

Louise McHugh, PhD, is associate professor of psychology at University College, Dublin; a peer-reviewed acceptance and commitment therapy (ACT) trainer; fellow of the Association for Contextual Behavioral Science; and coeditor of *The Self and Perspective Taking*.

Ian Stewart, PhD, is a faculty member in the school of psychology at the National University of Ireland, Galway. He is coauthor of *The Art and Science of Valuing in Psychotherapy* and *ACT and RFT in Relationships*, and coeditor of *The Self and Perspective Taking*.

Priscilla Almada, PhD, is a contextual behavioral scientist/practitioner based in Sydney, Australia. She is founder and director of On Becoming Us, an independent, research-based initiative for developing and pursuing prosocial leadership and communities. To further explore or support this work, visit: onbecomingus.com or drpriscillaalmada.com.

Foreword writer **Steven C. Hayes, PhD**, is foundation professor in the department of psychology at the University of Nevada, Reno, and cofounder of ACT.

Index

A

ABC contingency, 16, 20, 25, 167
abolishing operations, 25
about this book, 4–5
abstraction, 83
acceptance and commitment therapy (ACT), 102, 109–110, 154
act-in-context, 12, 15, 20
alexithymia, 88
Almada, Priscilla, 5
analogy relations, 37
analytic reflexivity, 18
Aniston, Jennifer, 132
antecedents, 8, 13–14, 16, 20, 25
appetitive stimulus, 8, 24
arbitrarily applicable relational responding, 33–36. *See also* relational framing
arbitrarily applicable sameness, 36
Asperger's syndrome, 84
assessment, 165–181; of human behavior, 165–168; measures available for, 170–172; observations and self-reports for, 173, 183, 186–187; of selfing issues, 168–181, 184–185, 187–188, 191
at-home practice, 94
augmenting, 55–57
authoritarian caregivers, 85, 87
autistic spectrum disorder (ASD), 84, 92, 98, 169, 190
autopilot, operating on, 2, 193
aversive stimulus, 8, 24
avoidance, 24, 91–92, 114, 140, 167

B

Barnes-Holmes, Dermot, 68
behavior, 8; context related to, 165–166; functional assessment of, 165–168; influence over, 13–14, 15; noticing impact of, 163–164; rule-governed, 53, 55, 56; self-regulation of, 73; in three-term contingency, 16, 20, 21; topography of, 12
behavior analysis, 20–29; behaviorism distinguished from, 17; contextualist interpretation of, 19; key technical terms in, 8–9; operant learning and, 16, 20–29; radical behaviorism and, 16, 19
behavioral influence, 13–14, 15
behavioral psychology, 11
behavior-behavior explanation, 17
behaviorism: behavior analysis vs., 17; methodological, 17; radical, 16–19
bidirectional relating, 38–39, 45, 46–47
blind men parable, 7

body image issues, 93, 94

C

case examples of selfing problems, 181–192; developmental delay in perspective taking, 190–192; inflexible framing of negative self content, 182–185; inflexible framing of positive self content, 186–190
catastrophizing, 43
categorical diagnosis, 169
CBS/RFT approach, 2–3, 4, 195–196. *See also* contextual behavioral science; relational frame theory
chessboard metaphor, 154, 159
child neglect/abuse, 114
class-based concepts, 26–29
classical conditioning, 22
client–therapist interaction, 173, 183, 187, 191
client self-reports, 173, 183, 186, 190
Clooney, George, 132
cognition-behavior explanation, 17
cognitive behavioral therapy (CBT), 3
cognitive developmental approach, 3
cognitive fusion, 109, 119, 126, 177
cognitive psychology, 11, 68, 102, 118
coherence, 48–51, 58; advantages of, 49–50; dark side of, 50–51, 122–125; literality related to, 126–127; self-as-content and, 108–109, 122–125, 140; self-as-context and, 117, 153; self-as-process and, 112; self-related issues with, 184–185, 188, 191
combinatorial entailment, 40–41, 58

comparison relations, 37, 39–40, 41, 43
compassion-focused therapy, 102
complexity, 57–58; self-as-content and, 108; self-as-context and, 117; self-as-process and, 112
conceptualized self, 106–111, 118, 139
conditioned reinforcers, 22
conditioned response, 22
conditioned stimulus, 22
connectedness, lack of, 2, 193
consciousness, viii, 64
consequences, 8, 13–14, 16, 20, 22–25
content. *See* self content
context, 8; behavior affected by, 165–166; coherence in, 123, 124; events in, 12; linguistic, 125; noticing impact of, 161–163
contexts of literality, 125
contextual behavioral psychology, 10, 15–29; behavior analysis and, 16, 19, 20–29; radical behaviorism and, 16–19
contextual behavioral science (CBS), 2; approach to the self, 2–4, 7, 61; behavior analysis and, 19, 195; functional contextualism and, 15, 195; psychological application of, 15–29; selfing concept in, 136
contextual control, 43–44
contextual cues, 34, 35, 36, 37, 44
contextual sense of self, 142, 153, 180–181, 185, 188, 191
contextualism, 11, 12–13, 15, 19, 20–21. *See also* functional contextualism

210

coordination relations, 37, 39, 53, 154
corrective feedback, 92
correlational analysis, 15
covert activity, 17, 63

D

deictic relational framing, 79, 82–84, 97
deictic relational responding, 77, 97–103; acquisition of, 97–98; assessment of, 175–177, 184, 188, 191; examples of exercises involving, 102–103; levels of complexity in, 99, 100; prerequisite skills for, 99; training protocol for, 99–103
Deictic Relational Task (DRT), 170, 171
deictic relations, 37, 54
delayed gratification, 73
deliberate avoidance, 140
depression, 169
depth criterion, 14
derivation, 57; self-as-content and, 108; self-as-context and, 117; self-as-process and, 111–112
derived extinction, 74–75
descriptive contextualism, 15
diagnostic considerations, 169–170
dialectical behavior therapy (DBT), 102
differential diagnosis, 169
discrete-trial formats, 99
discrimination, 27; of ongoing experiences, 174–175, 184, 187–188, 191; of private experiences, 81. *See also* self-discrimination

discriminative stimulus, 8, 25
distinction relations, 37, 160
distortion, deliberate, 89–91
double reversed relational response, 99, 100
Down syndrome, 98
Dymond, Simon, 68

E

echoic responding, 38
emotion-focused therapy, 103
emotions: absence of talk about, 88–89; avoidance of unwanted, 91–92; deliberate distortion of, 89–91; discriminating and labeling, 94, 95–97; exercise for promoting contact with, 95–97; self-as-context and, 117; teaching the tacting of, 92–97
empathy, 98
empirical self, 118
emptiness, sense of, 2, 193
environmental variables, 13–14, 16
escape response, 24
establishing operations, 25
event-in-context, 12
executive functioning, 118
Experience of Self Scale (EOSS), 170, 172
experiential avoidance, 46, 114
experiential self, 118
experiential variation, 141
experientially evoked client reports, 173, 183, 187, 190–191
extinction, 8, 23–24, 74–75

F

flexibility: healthy selfing and, 136–164; language use and, 126; relational framing and, 58, 59; self-as-content and, 108, 109, 138; self-as-context and, 117; self-as-process and, 112, 140
formative augmenting, 55
formism, 12
framing: hierarchical, 116, 153, 157; metaphorical, 116. *See also* relational framing
function, 8
functional analysis, 28
functional assessment: of human behavior, 165–168; of selfing issues, 168–181. *See also* assessment
functional class concepts, 26–29
functional contextualism, 10, 13–15; criteria supporting, 14; emphasis on function in, 28; operant concept in, 20–21; radical behaviorism and, 16–19; shared goals of, 13–14, 15
Functional Self-Discrimination Measure and Interview (FSDM-FSDI), 170, 172
fundamental attribution error, 98, 103
fusion, cognitive, 109, 119, 126, 177

G

generalization, 9, 27
generalized conditional discrimination learning, 38
generalized operants, 28–29
generalized relational responding, 29
generativity, 47–48

H

Hayes, Steven C., ix, 115
healthy selfing, viii, 135–164; fostering in clients, 141–164; "I as container" process in, 142, 143, 153–161; "I as flexible" process in, 142, 143, 161–164; "I as perspective" process in, 142, 143, 148–153; "I as various" process in, 142, 143–148; self-as-context in, 140–141; self-as-process in, 137–141
here–there deictic frame, 82, 83, 97, 99, 100, 101
hierarchical framing, 116, 153, 157, 160
hierarchical relations, 37, 153, 157, 159–160
hierarchical sense of self, 153–154, 157, 159, 180
higher-order operants, 28
humanist tradition, 3
humanistic psychology, 118, 119
hyperattentiveness, 2, 193

I

"I as container" process, 142, 143, 153–161
"I as flexible" process, 142, 143, 161–164
"I as perspective" process, 142, 143, 148–153
"I as various" process, 142, 143–148
I–here–now perspective, 114

I–you deictic frame, 82, 83, 97, 99, 100, 101
idealized roles, 132–133
ideals, inappropriate, 129–130
if-then frame, 72–73
imitation, 28–29
Implicit Relational Assessment Procedure, 58
impulsivity, 123–124, 125
inaccurate rules, viii, 130
inappropriate ideals, 129–130
incoherence, 106, 108
incongruence, 118
inflexibility, 109, 110, 138
influence over behavior, 13–14, 15
internal experiences: feeling of threat from, 2, 193. *See also* tacting internal experiences
interpersonal dimension, 78
interventions, conceptualizing, 185, 188–190, 192
"invalidated self" exercise, 152

J

James, William, 3
joint attention, 38, 99

K

knowing self, 111–114, 118

L

labeling private experiences, 80–82; integrating discrimination with, 94, 95–97; teaching to individuals, 92–97. *See also* tacting internal experiences
labels, simplistic, 130–131
language: bidirectional relating and, 38–39; coherence and, 122–125; flexibility in use of, 126; importance of human, 32; key features of, 44–57; literality and, 125–127; rule following and, 127–129; self content and, 122–129
language explosion, 48
learning: operant, 9, 10, 16, 20–29; respondent, 9
literality, 125–127

M

manipulable variables, 3, 13, 14, 17, 20
match-to-sample task, 34–36
McHugh, Louise, 5
mechanistic worldview, 11, 12, 13
Mendeleyev, Dmitry, 31
mentalistic explanation, 17
metacognition, 118
metaphorical extension, 67
metaphorical framing, 116
methodological behaviorism, 17
mindfulness meditation, 119
mislabeling private experiences, 81
motivating operation, 9, 25
motivative augmenting, 55–56
multidimensional multilevel (MDML) framework, 57; self-as-content and, 107–108; self-as-context and, 116–117; self-as-process and, 111–112
multiple-exemplar training, 98
mutual entailment, 40, 41, 58

N

narcissistic personality disorder, 169
narrative self, 118
negative reinforcement, 24
negative self content, 109, 124, 126, 140, 182–185
neurocognitive approach, 3
neuroscientific evidence, 118
nonarbitrary relational responding, 33, 34–36
nonverbal self-awareness, 73, 115
now–then deictic frame, 82, 83, 98, 99, 100, 101

O

observations, therapist, 173
observer perspective, 137, 142, 148–149
"observer you" exercise, 160–161
observing self, 114–117, 157, 161, 181
operant, 10, 16, 20–21, 28–29, 33
operant learning, 9, 20–29; antecedents in, 25; behavior in, 21; class concepts and, 26–29; consequences in, 22–25; language and, 33
operant psychology, 16, 62
opposition relations, 37
organicism, 12
overarching operants, 28
overt activity, 17, 63

P

pain, psychological, 117
pathological altruism, 98
Pavlovian conditioning, 22
peak experience, 119
periodic table, 31
perspective taking, 77, 82, 97–98, 103; developmental delay in, 190–192; functional assessment of, 175–177; "I as perspective" process and, 142, 148–153, 180; self-as-context and, 115, 116, 117, 118–119, 140–141, 142; sign indicating lack of, 2, 193
pliance: definition of, 55, 86; problematic dominance of, 85–88; rule following and, 55, 85, 86–87
positive psychology, 3, 102
positive reinforcement, 24
positive self content, 124, 186–190
pragmatism, 11
precision criterion, 14
prediction, 13, 14, 15
predictive verification, 11, 12
primary punishers, 23
primary reinforcers, 22, 23
private behavior, 17, 64, 168
problem solving, 49
psychoanalysis, 3
psychodynamic approach, 3, 68
psychological pain, 117
punishers, 23
punishment, 9, 20, 23, 24–25

Q

qualitative difference, 66
quantitative difference, 66

R

radical behaviorism: behavior analysis and, 16, 19; functional contextualism and, 16–19

reference, 45–47
reinforcement, 9, 20, 22–23, 24, 65
reinforcement schedules, 65
reinforcer sampling, 56
reinforcers, 22–23
relation types, 37
relational frame theory (RFT), 2, 10, 31–60, 195; approach to the self in, 61, 66–75; basic concepts of, 33–44; functional analysis of rules in, 53–54; key features of language and, 44–57; MDML framework used in, 57–60; selfing-as-context in, 137; values conceptualized in, 110
relational frames, 33, 37
relational framing, 33–60; coherence and, 48–51; combinatorial entailment and, 40–41; deictic, 79, 82–84, 97; developmental origins of, 38–40; explanation of, 33–37; generativity and, 47–48; impact assessment of, 166; key features of language and, 44–57; MDML framework and, 57–60; mutual entailment and, 40; negative self content example of, 182–185; positive self content example of, 186–190; properties of, 40–44; reference and, 45–47; rule following and, 51–57; self-as-context and, 116; selfing processes and, 68–69; transformation of functions and, 42–44
relational network, 48, 54, 55, 56, 59, 67, 106
relational responding: arbitrarily applicable, 33–36; deictic, 97–103;

generalized, 29; nonarbitrary, 33, 34–36
relational responses, 59
respondent learning/conditioning, 9, 22, 23
responding to one's own responding, 62–66, 70
response differentiation, 27
response frequency, 24
response induction, 26
reversed relational response, 99, 100
RFT Perspective Taking Protocol (RFT PT), 170, 171, 190
rigidity, personal, viii, 2, 193
Rogers, Carl, 129
role assignments, viii, 132–133
root metaphor, 10–11, 12, 15
Rosenfield, Steve, 130–131
rule following, 51–57; advantages of, 52; dark side of, 52–53, 127–129; functional analysis of, 53–54; functional categories of, 54–57; pliance- vs. tracking-type, 55, 86; self content and, 127–129
rule-based insensitivity, 52, 53, 86
rule-governed behavior, 53, 55, 56, 86
rules: definition of, 52; inaccurate, viii, 130; self-directed, 113, 179; stereotypical, 127

S

schemas, self, 118
schizophrenia, 98
scientific worldviews, 10–11, 15
scope criterion, 14
secondary punishers, 23
secondary reinforcers, 22, 23

self: common issues related to, 2; conceptualized, 106–111, 118; contextual sense of, 142, 180–181, 185, 188, 191; hierarchical sense of, 153–154, 157, 159; knowing, 111–114, 118; nonhuman model of, 65–66; observing, 114–117, 157, 161, 181; operant conceptualization of, 62; relational frame theory and, 61–75; transcendent, 115; unusual approach to, 64–65; verbal, 66–68, 115

self content, 121–133; assessing for issues with, 177–179; coherence and, 122–125, 140; flexibility and, 109; healthy selfing and, 138–139; inaccurate rules and, 130; inappropriate ideals and, 129–130; inflexible relational framing of, 182–190; literality and, 125–127; monitoring improvements with, 179–180; role assignments and, 132–133; rule following and, 127–129; simplistic labels and, 130–131; socioverbal community issues and, 129–133; sticky content as, 140; values as type of, 110

Self Experiences Questionnaire (SEQ), 170, 172

self-actualization, 119

self-as-content, 106–111, 121; assessing for issues related to, 177–179; psychological approaches and, 118; self-as-process vs., 118, 138, 141

self-as-context, 106, 114–117; hierarchical self sense and, 137, 154, 157, 159; interventions for cultivating, 154, 160; perspective taking and, 115, 116, 117, 118–119, 140–141, 142

Self-as-Context Scale (SACS), 170, 171

self-as-process, 106, 111–114, 137–141; flexibility enabled through, 109; functional assessment of, 174–175; self-as-content vs., 118, 138, 141; traditions emphasizing, 118; variability of experience and, 140, 141, 142

self-awareness, viii, 64, 65, 66, 73, 75

self-concept, vii, viii, 106, 108, 118

self-descriptions, vii–viii, 72, 75, 120

self-directed rules, 113, 179

self-discrimination: labeling integrated with, 94, 95–97; self-as-context and, 115; self-as-process and, 174–175; training others in, 63–64, 93–97; verbal vs. nonverbal, 72–75

selfing: healthy or flexible, viii, 135–164; relational framing and, 68–69; skills foundational to, 79

selfing problems, 165–193, 195–196; assessment of, 168–181, 184–185, 187–188, 191; case examples of, 181–192; four areas to examine for, 168; signs that work is needed on, 192–193

selfing repertoires, 77–103, 105–120; alternative approaches to, 117–120; deictic relational responding, 97–103; optimal environment for acquiring, 78–79; processes involved in acquiring, 77–78;

self-as-content, 106–111; self-as-context, 114–117; self-as-process, 109, 111–114; tacting of internal experiences, 80–82, 85–97
self-judgments, 2, 193
self-knowledge, 62, 63, 72, 114
self-reference, 118
self-regulation, 73
self-reports, 173, 183, 186, 190
self-righteousness, 2, 193
self-transcendence, 119
sense making, 49
sensory experiences: exercise for promoting contact with, 95–97; self-discrimination of, 93–95
shaping, 9, 27
simple relational response, 99, 100
simplistic labels, 130–131
situation-based emotions, 92
Skinner, B. F., 16–18, 19, 62, 63, 64
social anhedonia, 98
social anxiety, 94
social judgments, 103
socioverbal community issues, 129–133; assigned roles, 132–133; inaccurate rules, 130; inappropriate ideals, 129–130; simplistic labels, 130–131
spatial dimension, 78
spatiotemporal frames, 82
Stepford Wives, The (film), 132
stereotypical roles, 132, 133
Stewart, Ian, 5
sticky content, 140
stimulus equivalence, 69
subclinical narcissism, 98
subject-object distinction, 3

suffering: human language related to, 32; verbal self-knowledge and, 73–74
symbolic language, 32, 195

T

tacting internal experiences, 85–97; explanation of, 80–82; foundational selfing skills and, 79; problems related to inaccurate, 85–92; teaching or training others in, 92–97; verbally advanced individuals and, 93–97
task self-efficacy, 17–18
teaching/training: deictic relational responding, 99–103; tacting of internal experiences, 92–97
temporal dimension, 78
temporality relations, 37, 53
"that makes me feel" exercise, 147–148
therapeutic relationship, 118
thoughts: fusion with, 109, 126; language as basis of, 32
3-Dimensional Reno Inventory of Self Perspective (3D-RISP), 170, 172
three-term contingency, 16, 20, 25
time-lapse photography metaphor, 144, 148
topography, 12, 28, 29
tracking, 55, 86
transcendent self, 115
transcendental experiences, 115, 119
transformation of functions, 42–44, 47, 48, 54, 125, 126
transpersonal psychology, 119
truth criteria, 10–11, 12, 15

U

unconditioned stimulus, 22
unidirectional conditioning, 45

V

values: "I as flexible" process and, 142, 161–164, 180; lack of clarity about, 2, 193; motivative augmenting and, 56–57; self-as-content and, 109–111; self-as-process and, 113
variability of experience: "I as various" process and, 142, 143–148, 180; self-as-process and, 140, 141
variables: contextual, 161; environmental, 13–14; manipulable, 3, 13, 14, 17, 20
verbal discrimination, 174–175
verbal extinction, 74
verbal self, 66–68, 115
verbal self-knowledge, 72–73

W

Watson, John, 11
What I Be Project, 130–131
worldviews, 10; contextualist, 11–12; functional contextualist, 13–15; mechanistic, 11, 12, 13; root metaphor of, 10–11, 12, 15; truth criterion of, 10–11, 12, 15

MORE BOOKS from
NEW HARBINGER PUBLICATIONS

EVOLUTION & CONTEXTUAL BEHAVIORAL SCIENCE

An Integrated Framework for Understanding, Predicting & Influencing Human Behavior

978-1626259133 / US $39.95

CONTEXT PRESS
An Imprint of New Harbinger Publications

CONTEXTUAL SCHEMA THERAPY

An Integrative Approach to Personality Disorders, Emotional Dysregulation & Interpersonal Functioning

978-1684030958 / US $49.95

CONTEXT PRESS
An Imprint of New Harbinger Publications

THE BIG BOOK OF ACT METAPHORS

A Practitioner's Guide to Experiential Exercises & Metaphors in Acceptance & Commitment Therapy

978-1608825295 / US $49.95

GET OUT OF YOUR MIND & INTO YOUR LIFE

The New Acceptance & Commitment Therapy

978-1-57224-425-2 / US $21.95

GETTING UNSTUCK IN ACT

A Clinician's Guide to Overcoming Common Obstacles in Acceptance & Commitment Therapy

978-1608828050 / US $29.95

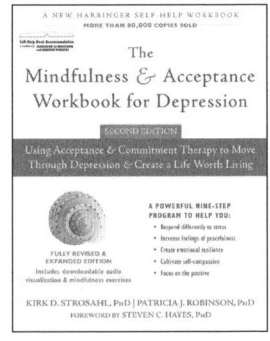

THE MINDFULNESS & ACCEPTANCE WORKBOOK FOR DEPRESSION, SECOND EDITION

Using Acceptance & Commitment Therapy to Move Through Depression & Create a Life Worth Living

978-1626258457 / US $24.95

newharbingerpublications
1-800-748-6273 / newharbinger.com

Follow Us

(VISA, MC, AMEX / prices subject to change without notice)

QUICK TIPS for THERAPISTS
Fast and free solutions to common client situations mental health professionals encounter every day

Written by leading clinicians, Quick Tips for Therapists are short e-mails, sent twice a month, to help enhance your client sessions. **Visit newharbinger.com/quicktips to sign up today!**

Sign up for our Book Alerts at **newharbinger.com/bookalerts**